GIRL MEETS GOD

Praise for *Girl Meets God*

"[A] memoir, literary and spiritual, sharing Anne Lamott's self-deprecating intensity and Stephen J. Dubner's passion for authenticity . . . She reveals herself through abundant, concrete and often funny descriptions of her life, inner and outer. Winner's record of her own experience so far is a page-turning debut by a young writer worth watching."

—*Publishers Weekly* (starred review)

"Her narrative's real strength . . . is its addictive readability combined with the author's deep knowledge of, delight in, and nuanced discussion of both Christian and Jewish teachings. . . . Intriguing, absorbing, puzzling, surprisingly sexy, and very smart."
—*Kirkus Reviews* (starred review)

"A humorous, sexually frank portrait of a deeply engaged faith shopper, 'stumbling her way towards God.' Winner offers a rare perspective, connecting Christian and Jewish traditions in unexpected ways." —*Library Journal*

"She is very much what a reader wishes a memoirist to be: insightful, wry, probing. . . . It is hard not to be caught up in Winner's soul struggles."
—*Booklist*

"Eye-opening . . . vivid." —*Winston-Salem Journal*

"Unusually challenging and satisfying. In a day when so much popular religion gives the impression that there are no mysteries still hidden, no problems unsolved, no questions unanswered and no distant horizons that still summon us to a magnificent, never-ending pilgrimage, this book is a refreshing invitation to plumb our own spiritual depths." —*The Roanoke Times*

"Imagine C. S. Lewis raised on a diet of Flannery O'Connor, Michael Stipe, and the Talmud, and you get some sense of the wild ride that awaits in this astonishing memoir. Keep your nostalgia—give me Lauren Winner."
—CHARLES MARSH, author of *The Last Days*

"Lauren Winner tells the story of her spiritual pilgrimage with modesty and charm. She describes her path so appealingly that many readers will ask, 'How can I meet this guy, too?'" —FREDERICA MATHEWES-GREEN, NPR commentator and author of *Facing East*

"Lauren Winner soulfully, thoughtfully, and authoritatively expresses the spiritual essences of Judaism. Through her embodied life experiences and her study, Winner witnesses what Jews and Christians seeking God in their lives can teach each other. . . . This utterly juicy account, told from a perspective knee-deep in both traditions, does redemptive work."
—VANESSA L. OCHS, Ida and Nathan Kolodiz Director of Jewish Studies, University of Virginia, and author of *Words on Fire*

GIRL MEETS GOD

A Memoir

by

LAUREN F. WINNER

RANDOM HOUSE TRADE PAPERBACKS
NEW YORK

Author's Note

In order to protect the privacy of friends and family, occasional details—names, professions, chronology, and so forth—have been changed. The character of Benjamin is a composite of two people, as is the character of Father Peter.

Library of Congress Cataloging-in-Publication Data

Winner, Lauren F.
Girl meets God: a memoir / Lauren F. Winner.
p. cm.
Originally published: Chapel Hill, N.C.: Algonquin Books of Chapel Hill, 2002. With new reader's guide.
Includes bibliographical references
ISBN 978-0-8129-7080-7 (pbk.)
1. Winner, Lauren F. 2. Christian converts from Judaism—United States—Biography.
I. Title

BV2623.W56A3 2004   248.2'46'092—dc22   2003058704
[B]

Printed in the United States of America

www.randomhousereaderscircle.com

19 18 17 16 15 14 13 12 11

To

Jo Bailey Wells

who has been both Paul and Apollos (I Corinthians 3:6)

and

in memory of

Iola Jimeson Cogdill (1909–1994)

Contents

Sukkot

Oxford, Mississippi

Back when Mississippi was dry, Ole Miss students and any other Oxford residents who wanted a drink would drive to Memphis, just across the state line, stock up on beer and whiskey, and haul it back in the trunks of their cars. Memphis was also where you went if you needed fancier clothes than you could find at Neilson's department store, or if you just started feeling itchy and trapped in the small hot downtown and wanted to go out dancing. You didn't need to leave Oxford to find a cherry Coke, which you could share with two straws at the Gathright-Reed drugstore, and you didn't need to leave Oxford to go to church. There are plenty of churches in Oxford: Baptist, Methodist, Pentecostal, Episcopal, all kinds.

Before I arrived this week for a Southern history conference, I'd been to Oxford and Memphis exactly once each, on separate trips. I was a bridesmaid at my friend Tova's wedding in Memphis, at the Peabody, the famous hotel where ducks swim in an indoor fountain and where they say the Delta starts.

I don't remember Oxford nearly as well—it had been the stop in between Nashville and Hattiesburg on a rather frantic research trip for my master's thesis, a blur of archives and oral history interviews. I hadn't gotten to do any traditional Oxford activities, like go to a tail-gating party before a football game or recite an ode to Faulkner.

My trip to Oxford this time might not be any more relaxed. I'm here giving a paper at a conference on the Civil Rights movement, and my schedule will be full just sitting in the auditorium and listen-ing to historians talk. But the conference ends on Friday and I'm stay-ing over till Sunday morning so my plan is to try to do one traditional Oxford thing on Saturday. It hasn't occurred to me that I'll spend Saturday doing the most traditional Oxford thing there is, which is going to Memphis.

The conference, all in all, is stressful. Stressful because I feel very much the youthful, inept doctoral candidate reading a paper in front of all these famous historians, including my thesis advisor and other people whose books line my shelves. Stressful because my dress is ever-so-slightly too tight, and I'd managed to leave New York with-out a single pair of stockings. And stressful because one of the other people speaking at this conference is my erstwhile beau. This confer-ence is small, only a dozen or so people participating; I'll never be able to avoid him.

His name is Steven; like me, he's a history grad student. We tried a transatlantic relationship, Steven in Arkansas (where he's getting his doctorate), me in England (where I was finishing my master's de-gree). But I freaked out for reasons I still don't entirely understand and broke up with him in May. I last saw him six weeks ago, early August, one very tense afternoon in Virginia. He was there working with papers at Alderman Library, and he stopped by my mother's house the day I was packing to move to New York. I was tired and distracted and we argued and he said I yelled at him the way you yell at someone you love and I denied it and he left. Later, my friend Hannah looked at me pointedly (it was over the phone, but I could feel her looking pointed) and said, "That was very unwise. You shouldn't have agreed to meet with him." "Well," I said. That was all I said. I couldn't think of anything else to say.

Two months later, I call Hannah from the airport, this time on my way to Mississippi. "Have a good conference," she says, "call us when you get there." Then she adds, "Don't let Steven get you alone like you did in Virginia."

Steven ignores me at first, won't even make eye contact or say hello, but the second night of the conference we all attend a reception at the Episcopal church, and he's half drunk on red wine by the time I get there. It's the only time I've ever seen him even approximate drunkenness. He had this delinquent youth in Boston, smoked pot every day from the age of twelve, passed out on the pavement from angel dust, crashed his mother's car after downing too much bourbon, and shoplifted antiques and canned goods. Once, a friend of his had been entrusted with several hundred dollars, to buy provisions for a church youth group trip. He and Steven spent all the money on drugs and then stole $400 worth of groceries: hams, gallons of milk, bags of apples. The chronology has always been a little fuzzy—I'm not sure when exactly he stopped breaking the law, but I think during college. And since then Steve's walked the straight and narrow, the extremely straight and narrow. Doesn't smoke. Doesn't chase skirts. Doesn't drink much. Swims every day. Eats wheat germ in his oatmeal at breakfast.

But there he is, standing on the patio of St. Peter's Episcopal, putting away red wine and getting slightly glassy-eyed, which I know only because he decides finally to make eye contact with me. The eyes are enough of an invitation. I walk over to him and we talk about this and that, how smart his paper had been, whether he plans to ignore me for the rest of our professional lives. When everyone else goes inside for dinner, we stay outside and talk, and finally we duck out of the back of the church and find a restaurant, where I drink a gimlet and eat the best chicken I've had in months. Then we go to Faulkner's grave, an exciting and authentic Oxford activity, and Steven, who knows these things, says that when you visit Faulkner's grave you have to drink bourbon in his honor. So we find a little liquor store, and buy a tiny bottle of Maker's Mark, like the kind they give you on airplanes, and go and sit by his tombstone, and I shiver slightly in the September air, thinking about how Willie Morris had died over the summer, and how my friend Pete, who was in Jackson then, had drunk a bottle of George Dickel in Willie Morris's honor and then gone to Choctaw Books and bought *The Courting of Marcus Dupree*. I think about how Faulkner is buried here right next to his wife, even though they had the most miserable marriage. And I think about how much Steven loves me, and I try to remember why I had broken up with him in the first place. This may have been precisely what Hannah was worried about.

"What are you doing on Saturday?" I ask. I vaguely recall that months before, Steve had said he might go to Hattiesburg to do research, and if that is still his plan, I might tag along. I could always use another day in the Hattiesburg archives, and it would be better than sitting around in Oxford car-less and alone, especially now that I've already done the Faulkner thing.

"I'm planning on going to Memphis," he says.

"Oh yeah, what for?"

"There's this church there that I went to when I was up in Memphis in August. I thought I'd go back."

"But Steve, tomorrow is Saturday. One goes to church on Sunday."

He clears his throat and coughs. "This is a Messianic Jewish church. Synagogue. They meet on Saturdays, you know."

I do know. I am a Jew, after all. I've devoted more Saturdays than I could count to worshipping in synagogues of one stripe or another. That wedding in Memphis had been full of Orthodox Jews, kosher-keeping, Sabbath-resting Orthodox Jews in modest clothes singing Hebrew songs and dancing whirling, ecstatic, sex-segregated dances; the wedding was on a Sunday, and I spent the morning before chanting familiar prayers in the women's section of Memphis's Orthodox shul.

That was before I gave in to Jesus, admitted I'd been fighting with him all these years the way you fight with someone you love, prayed the Sinner's Prayer and got baptized. I knew all about Jewish services on Saturdays. It is one of the things you know when you are part of the olive tree onto which all the other Christians have been grafted.

EVANGELICAL FRIENDS OF mine are always trying to trim the corners and smooth the rough edges of what they call My Witness in order to shove it into a tidy, born-again conversion narrative. They want an exact date, even an hour, and I never know what to tell them. The datable conversion story has a venerable history. Paul, the most famous Jew to embrace Jesus, established the prototype of the dramatic, datable rebirth. He was walking on the road to Damascus, Luke tells us, off to persecute the zealous disciples of the newly dead carpenter when Jesus appeared to him, and Paul became his follower instead of his foe. Centuries later, John Wesley, the founder of Methodism, was atttending a meeting in Aldersgate Street; listening to Luther's Preface to the Epistle to the Romans, his heart was "strangely warmed." At that instant, Wesley later wrote in his journal, he felt that he "did trust in Christ alone for salvation; and an assurance was given me that He had taken away my sins, even mine, and saved me from the law of sin and death." Less notable personages have dramatic conversion stories, too. My high school physics teacher sat in her kitchen reading the Gospel of Mark one day when, in an instant, she knew that Jesus was God and had died for her sins. My friend Tim dedicated his life to

Christ when he was four at a mission's conference at Bibletown, in Boca Raton, Florida. He had seen a puppet show about Jesus knocking on your heart. So he opened it and asked Him to come in.

My story doesn't fit very well with this conversion archetype. A literature scholar would say there are too many "ruptures" in the "narrative." But she might also say that ruptures are the most interesting part of any text, that in the ruptures we learn something new.

I had no epiphanic on-the-road-to-Damascus experience. I can't tell my friends that I became a Christian January 8, 1993, or on my twentieth birthday. What I can tell them is that I grew up Jewish. I can tell them about the time I dreamed of Jesus rescuing me from a kidnapping; I can tell them I woke up certain, as certain as I have ever been about anything, that the dream was from God and the dream was about Jesus, about how He was real and true and sure. I can tell them about reading *At Home in Mitford*, a charming if somewhat saccharine novel about an Episcopal priest in North Carolina, a novel that left me wanting something Christians seemed to have. I can tell them about my baptism.

A few years after the dream and a year before the baptism, I sat, drinking cider that scalded my tongue, with a Presbyterian minister I had known since my first week as an undergraduate at Columbia. "Pastor Mike," I said, "I think I am beginning to believe in Jesus."

Pastor Mike sipped his cider in silence. Finally he said, "You know, Lauren, you can't just divorce Judaism."

I felt like I'd been socked in the stomach. Pastor Mike urged me to talk to the campus rabbi, and then he said, "I had no idea when you told me you wanted to get together that you wanted to talk about Christianity. I thought maybe you were going to come out to me as a lesbian." Which, on a campus obsessed with identity politics, might have been more congenial than a Jewish student prattling on about Jesus.

Some weeks later, I walked into the bookstore at Union Theological Seminary and bought a Book of Common Prayer, which felt like the boldest, most daring-do thing I'd ever done. The next day I gave away all my Jewish prayer books. I left them anonymously on the steps of a nearby shul, the way an unmarried mother might have left her baby on the steps of an orphanage in some earlier era.

I haven't spoken to Pastor Mike since that morning. It's been three years. I tried to write him a letter once or twice, to say, *You knocked the wind out of me with that divorce line you cavalierly tossed out over your crumb cake*. But the letter didn't gel. I got through, *Dear Pastor Mike, Remember last time we spoke, at the Hungarian Pastry Shop*, and that was as far as I got.

Pastor Mike's metaphor, I learned, was useful: trading my Hebrew prayer book for an Episcopal Book of Common Prayer felt exactly like filing for divorce. That was the only word I could come up with. The more Christian I became, the more I needed to have nothing to do with Judaism. Every new Christian habit, purchase, or prayer was accompanied by the unlearning of a Jewish habit, the cessation of a Jewish prayer. I donated my Havdalah set and one of my *tallisim* to a synagogue. I gorged on lobster and got drunk on the driest, most expensive bottles of Amarone I could find. I sold crates of sixteenth-century Jewish poetry and Hebrew commentaries on the Torah to a bookstore in Chapel Hill. I got an email from my friend Leah, then a Jewish Studies major at Duke. "I was just at a used bookstore on Franklin Street, and I picked up a *Mikraot G'dolot* for incredibly cheap. 'Lauren Winner' was scribbled in the cover—that wouldn't be you, by any chance?" She didn't ask why I was selling off my library.

The only Jewish habit I couldn't set aside was baking challah, which I kept up every Friday, two misshapen braided loaves, made with whole wheat flour, the recipe my friend Simone taught me. We had spent a long afternoon a few weeks before my Bat Mitzvah baking challah in her kitchen. That challah got me into college: my entrance essay was about baking bread as a feminist experience, about women passing down secrets from one generation to the next, in the kitchen. Pretty sophisticated, I thought, when I wrote it at fifteen. Six cups of flour, four beaten eggs, a packet of yeast dissolved in a dish of warm water, a dollop of honey, some butter, poppy seeds for the top if you want them, or raisins for the inside at Rosh Hashanah, to remind you that the New Year is sweet. Mix it all together, save for some of the egg to glaze with later. Knead it and let it rise in a warm place in a well-oiled bowl and punch it down after it doubles in size. Divide the dough into snakes and braid. The braid will always look better raw, more precise and perfect than after the bread bakes.

Divorce doesn't come easy. I am as bound to Judaism as my parents are to one another. They're not married anymore, but they have daughters, so they still see each other sometimes, at weddings and college graduations, and sometimes they talk on the phone, about going in together on an expensive birthday present for me or my sister.

I gave away all my Jewish books and let go of all my Jewish ways, but I realized, as I spent time with other Christians, that Judaism shaped how I saw Christianity. It shaped the way I read the Bible, the way I thought about Jesus, the way I understood what He meant when He talked about the yoke of the law. I found my heart sometimes singing Jewish songs. I thought I had given away all my Jewish things, but I found that I hadn't. I'd just given away some books and mezuzot and candlesticks. I hadn't given up the shape in which I saw the world, or the words I knew for God, and those shapes and words were mostly Jewish.

SHORTLY AFTER BUYING that Book of Common Prayer, I moved to England, to study for a master's degree in history at Clare College, Cambridge. Cambridge is where I was baptized and confirmed, where I first received communion, where I learned Christian liturgy and hymnody. Cambridge is where I learned to say simple phrases like "I'm a Christian" and "I'm off to church."

When, two years later, I moved back to New York to begin doctoral work, I had to learn something else: how to be a Christian in a neighborhood where everyone knew me as an Orthodox Jew. I didn't know how to tell Jewish friends that I had become a Christian, didn't know how to explain to old professors why I now could attend classes during Rosh Hashana and Yom Kippur, didn't even know what to say to my accommodating Catholic acquaintance who, delighted that I was back in New York, had made dinner reservations for us at a kosher dairy restaurant on the East Side.

Just after Labor Day, barely three weeks after I'd moved back to New York, I traveled to Baltimore to meet with a couple, Jews turned Episcopalians. We sat rather awkwardly in the kitchen of their refurbished Victorian, drinking coffee and making small talk. They were not sure why I had come, and I could not explain. Finally I blurted out, "I tuck my cross underneath my blouse every time I see someone in a yarmulke. On Friday night, I actually ducked behind a fruit cart because I saw an old friend from college—it was clear she was coming from Shabbat services, and it was equally clear that I was headed to a local Italian restaurant where I would do forbidden things like spend money on Shabbat and eat forbidden food like shrimp scampi and prosciutto."

"Oh," said the wife. "Now I see. You've come to see us because you're trying to figure out how to put your life back together."

On the train back from Baltimore to New York, I made up my mind to do several things: buy a Hebrew siddur; call up my friend Tova, whom I had avoided since joining the church; and visit a Messianic Jewish synagogue.

Messianic Jewish synagogues are the spiritual homes to congregations of Jews who have become Christian, but who retain some Jewish practices. They worship on Saturdays, they sometimes pray in Hebrew, they observe some of the Jewish holidays. Their men wear prayer shawls and yarmulkes. Their women dress modestly and sometimes cover their hair.

I have always hated Messianic Jews. They have always made me want to run screaming in the other direction. This hatred is not a very Christian way to feel, but I feel it anyway. They have always freaked me out, they unnerve me, they give me the willies. I want to shake them and say "Make a choice! Pick a religion!" But on the train back from Baltimore I was pierced by a sudden sympathy. Making this choice is not so simple after all. Relinquishing all your Judaism at the foot of the Cross isn't easy. Maybe the Messianic Jews knew something that I did not know.

So it seemed providential when, sitting there by Faulkner's grave, Steven—who is no more Jewish than Quentin Compson—said he planned to spend Saturday morning at Brit Hadasha, home to Memphis's Messianic Jews.

Tova, it turns out, is in Memphis the same weekend, the weekend of my history conference. She's visiting her family for Sukkot, the Feast of Tabernacles. On the drive from Oxford I fantasize about running into her. I know I won't, I know she's tucked away in her parents' house and at her shul, miles from Brit Hadasha, eating a feast her mother prepared in her family's sukkah and singing my favorite Shabbat songs.

Sukkot is one of the things I gave up because of Jesus. I gave up Purim, which I love, and kashrut, which I love, and dipping challah into honey on New Year's, which I love. All because I was courted by a very determined carpenter from Nazareth. People ask me if I miss

Judaism. Yes, of course, I miss it. I miss Purim, and challah, and the way kashrut sanctifies every bit of food you put in your mouth. And I especially miss sitting in a sukkah.

God tells us how to celebrate Sukkot in Exodus 23, Leviticus 23, and Deuteronomy 16. First, we learn that we are to "celebrate a festival" for God when we "gather in [our] crops from the field." Then, we learn that the Feast of Tabernacles takes place on the fifteenth day of the seventh month, Tishri, for seven days. During that time, "all native-born Israelites are to live in booths so your descendants will know that I had the Israelites live in booths when I brought them out of Egypt." And the Bible commands us to Sukkot joy—"Be joyful at your Feast—you, your sons and daughters, your menservants and maidservants, and the Levites, the aliens, the fatherless and the widows who live in your town."

On Sukkot, Jewish families each build a hut, a sukkah, to remind themselves of the sukkot the Jews inhabited while they camped in the desert for forty years. We don't really know what those first desert huts looked like. Rabbi Akiva, a Talmudic sage, says that the original sukkot were flimsy, ramshackle, twigs and bark and cactus needles, but another rabbi, Eliezar, says the sukkot were far grander—they were "clouds of glory" that accompanied the Jews all through their desert wanderings, protecting them from night animals and helping them not lose their way. Today, the sukkah you would build might be an eight-foot cube, made from plywood held together with nails and twine. You cover the roof with greenery (the covering is called a *schach,* and it should be translucent enough to let in starlight) and invite neighborhood children to hang drawings on the walls. You eat all your meals in the sukkah, and drink all your drinks, and sometimes even sleep there. I miss Sukkot because it is while sitting in the sukkah that you learn lessons about dependence on God, that even the walls of your brick house are flimsy. The trick is to grab hold of those sukkah lessons and remember them once you've taken apart your shaky hut and resumed eating your meals in the spacious kitchen of your four-walled split-level.

During the service at Brit Hadasha, I imagine dropping by Tova's house afterward, plopping down in her family's sukkah and joining them for lunch. I imagine lingering over a lacy tablecloth out there in the sukkah, talking about holiday things and peering at the clouds and the sky through the *schach*, through the branches and leaves up above.

In the end, of course, Steven and I don't go sukkah-crashing. We go downtown to eat pulled pork barbecue instead.

BRIT HADASHA IS OFF OF I-240, and the building is non-descript. If you didn't know the name means "New Covenant," you might easily mistake it for a Reform synagogue. Steven and I sit in his green two-door for a few minutes, watching the parking lot fill up with the usual assortment of minivans and SUVs, battered Hondas and old Volvos. I watch carfuls of smiling women and children parade into the sanctuary and wonder what I'm doing here. Couldn't I have done this anonymously in New York? Did I really think it was a great idea to spend Saturday at a house of worship with my ex-boyfriend? My hands shake, and I contemplate staying in the car and reading a novel for two hours while he goes in and prays.

Steven interrupts my reverie. "I like it here because these people are pariahs," he says. "They don't fit in anywhere—not with Jews, not with Christians. Being a Christian means being a pariah, Lauren, it means not fitting in anywhere in this world. Your Episcopalians are no pariahs."

When we walk in, a middle-aged woman with short gray hair and dangly earrings greets us. "Good Shabbess. Welcome to Brit Hadasha. Is this your first visit?" Steven gives a complicated answer about how he had been here on Rosh Hashanah, but it is my first time. "And

where are you from?" Before he could give another complicated explanation, I say, "Arkansas," which is where Steven lives, take my New
Visitor card, and go find a seat.

A man clad in a *tallis*, a prayer shawl, stands at a podium in the
front of the room, and a small choir clusters to his right, leading the
congregation through songs that are printed on a transparency and
displayed on a large screen. In the corner of the room, a circle of
women are dancing, some variation on the hora. I am prepared for
that. I've read a recent ethnography of a Messianic Jewish congregation, and the author explains that dancing is an important element of
Messianic worship services. I feel an unexpected pull to join them.
The dances are similar to those at Tova's wedding. I have not yet
found a group of Anglicans who love Jewish folk dancing.

The service consists mostly of songs, with a little spontaneous
prayer thrown in. No one mentions Sukkot. The fact that it is Sukkot
doesn't seem to be part of the service at all. *Why bother playing at Judaism*, I wonder, annoyed, *if you don't move by the rhythms of the Jewish
calendar?* I have been trying, since I got baptized, to learn to live according to the seasons of Advent and Lent, but so far my body still
thinks in terms of Jewish holidays.

The absence of Sukkot is just one of many things that irritates me
about the service. The pink satin yarmulkes, straight out of a Reform
synagogue in the 1980s, irritate me. The gold-and-magenta banners
proclaiming YESHUA irritate me. And the music irritates me. Rather
than sing the haunting melodies available to anyone who is casually
acquainted with the centuries-old Jewish cantorial tradition, the folks
at Brit Hadasha seem content with songs that sound as though they
had been lifted from the praise music guide at any nondenomina-
tional evangelical church, only Brit Hadasha's songs have a little
Hebrew thrown in.

This is how I feel all morning: that Brit Hadasha's Judaism is just raisins added to a cake—you notice them, but they don't really change the cake. The structure of the service bears no relation to the Jewish liturgy, and I can't tell if my fellow worshippers think that being Jewish leads them to understand Jesus any differently from the Presbyterians down the street. Add Hebrew and Stir. I am bored and show off, screwing my eyes shut when I sing the Hebrew songs so that Steven, and everyone else, will know I that I don't need to read the transliterations flashed up on the screen in front of us.

Occasionally I offer up a silent prayer that the Holy Spirit will work overtime on my heart and help me stop being judgmental long enough to recognize that these people are worshipping the Risen Lord, but I don't really want God to answer this prayer.

SUKKOT COMES AT THE END of the season of repentance, two weeks after Rosh Hashanah, the Jewish New Year, and Yom Kippur, the Day of Atonement. As part of the work of repentance, Jews say special penitentiary prayers called *slichot*. The *slichot* start at midnight the Saturday before Rosh Hashanah, because the rabbis knew that the heavens are most open to prayers at midnight. Among the *slichot* prayers is one you will say again on Rosh Hashanah, and on all the days between Rosh Hashanah and Yom Kippur, and again on Yom Kippur, when God is making His final judgments about who will live and who will die, whom He will forgive and whom He will punish: *Adonai, Adonai, el rachum v'chanun, erech apayim, vrav chesed v'emet, notzer chesed lalafim, nosey avon vafesha v'chatahah v'nakeh.* "The Lord, the Lord, of compassion, Who offers grace and is slow to anger, Who is full of lovingkindness and trustworthiness, Who assures love for a thousand generations, Who forgives iniquity, transgression, and misdeed, and Who grants pardon." It is a list, culled from the thirty-fourth chapter of Exodus, of God's thirteen merciful attributes, attributes that, according to the rabbis, shine most brightly during the season of repentance.

The prayer, a reminder to God not of our merit but of his capacity to overlook our sin, is sung to a particularly haunting melody, my favorite from the entire cantorial literature. It is minor, and repetitive, and dirge-like, and some people say that Jews wailed its tune as they walked to the gas chambers in Treblinka and Sobibor.

At Brit Hadasha, we sing a mostly-English-but-laced-with-Hebrew song also based on that *slichot* prayer, but this tune is zippy, full of rhyme and vim and pep. In the middle of the song I slip out of the sanctuary and make my way, through the circle of dancing women, to the ladies' room, where I stare in the mirror and think. I wish for this service to be organic and seamless, but the seams show everywhere. Whatever part of me had come to Brit Hadasha hoping also to find the key to marrying Judaism with the cross is disappointed. I am not going to find any answers in a church that thinks clapping and tambourining its way through *Adonai, el rachum v'chanun* is a good idea. "This must be why I hate them," I say out loud to the mirror. "I must hate them because I want them to give me a formula for how to be a Christian Jew and I know their formula will never be my formula." After I've spent more time than is respectable in the bathroom, I return to my seat next to Steven, settling in for more praise music, a Torah reading, and the homily. Across the aisle, a red-headed little girl in a white straw hat smiles at me and dances a little dance.

The rabbi is in the middle of a sermon series on the Book of Joshua. "Well, that's refreshing," I whisper. "A whole sermon series on something from the Old Testament. You would never hear that in a regular church." Steven shushes me before I can climb onto one of my favorite soapboxes, the Christians-think-the-Bible-starts-with-Matthew soapbox.

This week's sermon is on chapter 7. In chapter 7, Achan, from the tribe of Judah, steals some silver and gold and a beautiful robe; Joshua takes Achan to a valley and he is stoned to death. Ever after, the Book of Joshua tells us, that valley is known as the Valley of Achor, which means "trouble."

The rabbi proceeds to read this chapter just like rabbis read in the Talmud, the fifth-century compilation of Jewish oral tradition. "Where else is the Valley of Achor mentioned in the Bible?" he asks. This was a favorite rabbinic strategy—if a word appears only two or three times in the Bible, then God is telling us that when we come across one mention, we should think of the other passages that use the same word. This, for example, is how the rabbis figured out what activities were forbidden on the Sabbath. There are two words in Hebrew for "work," *avodah* and *melacha*. In the Torah, we find *avodah* a lot, but God used *melacha* only twice—in the list of the thirty-nine activities that went into building the tabernacle, and in the verses, like Exodus 31:15, that forbid working on the Sabbath: "For six days, work is to be done, but the seventh day is a Sabbath of rest, holy to the Lord." The rabbis reasoned that He used *melacha* in those two places so that we would make a connection: the tabernacle activities must be the activities that are forbidden on the Shabbat.

Achor shows up in Joshua, and then again Hosea 2:15, where God promises to turn the Valley of Achor into a door of hope. "And what does God mean," the rabbi at Brit Hadasha now asks, "when He speaks of transforming this valley of Achor, this Valley of Trouble, into a door of hope? He tells us in John 10:9, when Jesus declares, 'I am the door. Whoever enters through me will be saved.' The door promised in Hosea, a promise that in turn looked back to Joshua, was Jesus, the only door that could undo the trouble of Achor."

His reading is dazzling. I am dazzled. I have not heard anyone read Scripture in this particular rabbinic way since I became a Christian. The rabbi has done just what the rabbis of the Talmud did when they squeezed out the Sabbath prohibitions from the word *melacha*. *There is something Jewish about this place,* I think, *the most important Jewish thing of all. They read like Jews.*

The rabbi's marriage of the Old Testament with the New is so striking that I hardly notice what comes next—an altar call. "If anyone here does not know the Lord," the rabbi says, "I invite you to come forward. I invite you to come up here and pray with me to ask our Savior into your life." We might have been at a Billy Graham crusade. During the altar call Steven weeps, hunched over in his chair, crying like he's just been told the saddest news in the world—when, in fact, he's been told something very wonderful, which is that Jesus died to purge his sins. He weeps, and I sit next to him with my hand on the small of his back and my cheek pressed into his shoulder blade; I am both praying for the Spirit to set up shop in his heart, and wondering at all the work the Spirit had already done.

The couple behind us hollers out loud, peppering the rabbi's words with *amens* like a pair of black Baptists. No one answers the altar call, which doesn't surprise me but is nonetheless a little sad, an unanswered altar call being kind of like an uneaten piece of pie.

THERE IS NO WEEPING on the drive back to Mississippi. We listen, predictably, to Patsy Cline, and Steven drives too fast, and we get pulled over by a cop who looks like he stepped out of a made-for-TV-movie. When the cop has driven off and Steven has tossed the ticket in the backseat, he turns to me and says, "I bet you think cops are your friends, right? You don't get nervous when they pull you over." You would think he was a black high-schooler in the dark of a Los Angeles night, but he's just pulling rank, sage Boston bad boy to the sheltered Southern judge's daughter.

I laugh, and kiss his neck, and for the rest of the drive, Steven keeps to seventy, which gets us to Oxford soon enough. The afternoon is an ice-tea afternoon, under two sprawling trees on campus, and that evening we hope for a rainstorm to run in (but no rainstorm comes) and we hold hands and maybe we pray a little, too.

The next morning he gets up at five to drive me back to Memphis, to the airport, and I go back to New York and he goes back to Arkansas. He tells me I'll forget the weekend as soon as I'm home, that it had been a weekend of borrowed time, a surreal four days when we lounged around a surreal little town and that I would go back to my life and conveniently forget.

I believe him. He knows me pretty well, and he is pretty convincing. I imagine that as my plane hovers over Queens, it will all vanish. It doesn't, though. It doesn't vanish, and I come home and call him and tell him so, and I marvel over all the things that can make us cry: leaving; Jesus; and too much whiskey. He asks me if I think we should try again, "to try to build an us," he says, and I say that yes, I think we should try, and we smile, he in Arkansas and I in New York, and we hang up, and I stretch and drink a glass of water and then take a shower that is long.

SIMCHAT TORAH, THE HOLIDAY that immediately follows Sukkot, is the day Jews set aside to celebrate reading. Every week, in synagogue, Jews read a few chapters of the Torah, just enough so that one hears the entire *chumash,* the entire Five Books of Moses, in a year. On Simchat Torah—literally, "joy of the Torah"—a cantor reads the last *parsha,* the last portion, the final two chapters of Deuteronomy, and the community starts all over again, paging back to the beginning, back before Moses and back before slavery, back before Abraham and Noah and Adam even, back to the creation of the world. Jewish holidays begin at night, and when I step out of the shower and wrap up in a big pink towel, it is getting dark. It is getting to be Simchat Torah.

I have things to do: unpacking, laundry, homework. There are books I need from the library, and I told my father I would call him when I got back to New York, and I have no milk for breakfast. But instead of doing homework or laundry or milk, I find a long purple dress in my closet and somewhere a pair of tights and a wooden barrette from the basket on my sink, and I put those things on, and I go out into the world, down the block past the library and then to shul, for Simchat Torah. To a shul where I sometimes worshipped in college, when I was still an Orthodox Jew, a shul where they know Hebrew and know melodies and know nothing about Jesus.

Simchat Torah is one of the few times you will find men and women mingled together in an Orthodox synagogue. After *maariv,* the evening prayers, the women come down from their balcony, and all the Torah scrolls are taken out of the ark, and everyone dances them around, scroll by scroll, person by person, making what in Hebrew is called *hakafot,* circlings or rings, dancing around the synagogue in a circle that mirrors the circle danced through the Torah each year. As you dance, you pray, *Ana Adonai, hoshia na.* "Oh Lord, save us." The congregation makes seven *hakafot,* seven different circular parades, carrying our scrolling, circular book around and around the shul. The *hakafot* can last hours, on and on.

When I get to shul, *maariv* is over, and men and women are already thronged together in the sanctuary, kissing Torah scrolls and pelting those who carry them with wishes: "Long life!" we sing to the men holding Torahs. And the prayer threads through all of it. *Ana Adonai hoshia na.* "Save us, save us, save us."

After the *hakafot* will come a reading from the Torah, the verses about Moses' death. Tonight the reading will be about his death, and tomorrow morning the Torah will start over, "In the beginning, God created the heavens and the earth."

But I will leave before the Torah reading. I stay for just an hour of *hakafot.* I dance, and I feel the way I felt about Steven when we were sitting there at Faulkner's graveside: I think about how much love there is here, and I wonder why I left in the first place. I watch the crowd's delight, the joy that comes from a year of reading Torah, and while I watch, I calculate another lectionary in my head. In church, we are working our way through the Gospel of Mark, and this week we are starting the tenth chapter, where Jesus, speaking to the Pharisees, recasts the mosaic laws about divorce; I remember that in two months, Advent will start, and the beginning of Advent is when the church has its own Simchat Torah—the beginning of Advent is when the church finishes one yearly cycle of Scripture readings and begins again. As we make our *hakafot* around the synagogue, I sing the prayers, I sing, *Ana Adonai hoshia na, ana Adonai hatzlicha na.* I pray with my hands open, I pray that the Lord our God will save us. And I watch the Torah scrolls dance by, and I know that I have already been saved.

Advent

Morning Prayer: John 8

For a brief spell, things with Steve are alluring and good. We send frantic emails and talk on the phone too much and he ignores his friends' advice to be wary of the bitch who had dumped him out of the blue a few months before.

I daydream all sorts of unwieldy Arkansas fantasies. My fantasies are mostly about watching him sleep and finding a church with both incense and pariahs, about carving out a life in Arkansas amid all the chicken plants and political scandals, about converting that side room he never really uses into a place where I could have a desk and a bookshelf and yellow curtains on all the windows. I find myself wanting to know about the terrain, about the soil and the plants, so I begin reading books by Sue Hubbell, who ran a honey farm in the Ozarks for twenty years. I order guides from the Ozark Society Foundation about Arkansas trees and Arkansas shrubs and Arkansas vines. I start by learning to tell conifers from deciduous, easy enough once I learn that conifer is just a long way of saying pine tree. Wild Sweet Williams dance in my head, and I imagine spending endless Arkansas hours watching local coral snakes molt or local May Apples unfold their umbrella leaves. It feels like we have been in love a long,

long time, and also like it is brand-spanking new, and will stay just that new forever.

The only other person I have fallen in love with that way is Jesus, and I hope that goes more smoothly. I hope I remember, when I'm bored with Him, and antsy, and sick of brushing my teeth next to the same god every morning, I hope I remember not to leave Him. I am not so worried that He will leave me. The Bible, after all, is full of stories about God sticking with His bride, no matter how stiff-necked and prideful and unfaithful she may be.

Things with Steven feel brand-spanking new, but they're not, they are the same as before, only more fraught, and we fight and scream and make each other miserable. We fight about the weather, the best way to write history, my tone of voice, how to decorate a living room. We know we cannot do the thing we want to do, which is make a life together.

HANNAH AND I MET in a bookstore right after I graduated from college, the summer before I moved to England. She was moving to France. We were in the *W* section of the novels. I reached for *The House of Mirth*. I loved her glasses, pointy and rhinestoned, and told her so. Recently, at a flea market, I found my own pair of rhinestoned, pointy, Martha Mitchell glasses, and when Hannah and I are together people laugh and point and say, "Twins!" When she lived in Paris and I lived in Cambridge, we used to meet in London for weekends. She brought French chocolate and we sat in pubs and teashops for hours. We darted in and out of churches and bookshops and walked through parks. When her husband finished his degree, they moved to New York, the same month I started back at Columbia. Hannah and Jim live in Brooklyn. Sometimes I visit and long for a neighborhood with trees and brownstones, and I wish I never had to return to Morningside Heights. Once a month she meets me for morning prayer. We say the morning office and read the daily readings. We drink caramel lattés at Starbucks afterward as people admire our matching glasses.

Today is the Wednesday of the second week of Advent. The Gospel reading, which Hannah reads, comes from the eighth chapter of John: the scribes and the Pharisees come again to test Jesus, to try to figure out who He really is and to trip Him up, to trick Him into saying something treasonous. They drag an adulterous woman before Him, and demand to know what He thinks should be done. "In the law," they say, "Moses commanded us to stone such women. Now what do you say?" At first Jesus does not say anything. Instead, He does something strange and childlike. "Jesus bent down and started to write on the ground with his finger." The Pharisees pester Him and finally He says, "Let you who is without sin cast the first stone."

The epistle reading today is from the fifth chapter of Paul's first letter to the Thessalonians. Paul tells them that when Jesus returns, he will come like a thief in the night. "But you, beloved," he writes, "are not in darkness, for that day to surprise you like a thief; for you are all children of light and children of the day; we are not of the night or of darkness." I have been reading Paul almost every day for three years now, and it still stuns me that I am one of the beloved children of light.

THEY HAVE BEEN MARRIED for four years, Hannah and Jim, and Hannah takes the day's reading, about the adulterous woman, to tell me, caramel steam floating up from her paper cup, that she thinks she is maybe starting to have an affair. Or maybe not. But maybe.

STEVEN AND I MAKE one last effort to salvage what we can. I fly to Arkansas, and on the plane I think about Hannah and what she has told me. I wonder how I can help her, what I am supposed to do. But I also wonder what I am supposed to take from this. *Don't marry the wrong man?* Then I wonder if that has anything to do with it. Her husband, the kind of man he is or how he is in bed or whether he picks the right birthday presents, does that have anything to do with this affair she might have?

Our sorting isn't successful. Steven forgets to pick me up at the airport. I spend three days sobbing. He builds a bookshelf and we play chess every night, the queens and pawns bearing the brunt of our barely sublimated anger. I lose every time. I come back to New York and in a stroke of great cowardice, we break up over the phone.

All Angels'

Finding a church in New York takes awhile. The church I eventually settle into lives in a small, plain building on 80th Street, between Broadway and West End Avenue. All Angels' Episcopal Church, as in the line of instruction from Psalm 148: "Praise him, all his angels, praise him, all his heavenly hosts."

It is the church all my friends in England told me to join when they learned I was moving back to New York. This is its reputation, as it came down to me: vibrant, interracial, youngish, and evangelical. Every interesting evangelical Episcopalian who ever lived in New York seems to have passed through All Angels'. It is Madeleine L'Engle's church, although we have no elevator, and the sanctuary is on the second floor, so she hasn't come around much since she broke her hip.

I sat anonymously through a service here, at All Angels', on my very first Sunday back in New York. During the announcements, after we pass the peace, they ask first-time visitors to stand up and introduce themselves, but I was too shy. I stayed put in my seat. I didn't go back for a long time. All Angels' was in the middle of a tedious search for a new rector, and I figured that since there are over three dozen Episcopal churches in Manhattan, there was no compelling reason to join one without a priest. So I church-hopped, sometimes visiting as many as three churches on a single Sunday. I manufactured good reasons never to return to any of them, but the real reason was probably that it was easier to stay anonymous and aloof than to do the hard, intimate work of actually becoming part of a church.

By the time I return to All Angels', two things have changed. They have called a rector, whom I take to immediately, a sharp and careful man from India named Milind Sojwal; and the very anonymity that made church-hopping appealing has begun to wear me down. I am tired of looking for a church, tired of having my spiritual community be just a patched-together group of Christian friends scattered across the four corners of the earth, folks I can call at any hour but never pray with face to face or eat cheese straws with during coffee hour. I am tired of not being expected anywhere on Sunday morning. I so need a church that it takes just the gentlest push to fall, as though exhausted onto the downiest of feather beds, into All Angels'. When I meet a chaplain at Columbia who happens to worship at All Angels', he says *come check it out,* I do, and I stay.

──────⊗──────

IN THE 1880s, in the South, you said, *Build me a house of worship,* and what came out was a church, even if you were looking, originally, for a synagogue. To see it from the outside, you'd think Congregation Beth Israel, in Charlottesville, was one of the old Episcopal churches, maybe Presbyterian. It is brick, and stained glass, and almost cruciform, and tiny fleur-de-lis, graceful almost-crosses, are sprinkled all across the roof. That was the place I spent my growing up. Some people think about their childhood and what they remember is the rambling, falling-apart old farmhouse where their grandparents lived; or the summer cottage their family always rented for July trips to the beach; or maybe they remember the blacktop basketball court where they perfected their dribble and their jump shot. The place I always go to, when I go to my childhood, is that brick, church-shaped synagogue at the corner of Jefferson and Third.

In the years since I left Charlottesville, they've had a huge fund-raising campaign and built an addition, all glass and light, more Sunday school classrooms, a larger social hall. I see it all the time when I go back to visit my mother, who lives in a town house only two blocks from the synagogue. When I visit, I walk past Congregation Beth Israel every morning, on my way to the downtown mall, where I sit at The Mudhouse and drink coffee and wait for the day to begin. I am always nervous that I will see someone from shul, someone I used to teach with in Hebrew School or worship with on Saturday mornings, someone I haven't seen in years and years.

There is only one woman from Congregation Beth Israel whom I still know. Randi lives in Ohio now, married with a baby and a decent university post and a three-bedroom house. She is my best conversation partner and the person best able to make me laugh.

I have a picture from Purim, 1992. Purim is the holiday that celebrates Esther and Mordecai's saving the Jews of Persia from death and destruction at the hand of wicked Haman. It is Jewish carnival, all full of drunkenness and revelry and inversion. When the Book of Esther is read aloud in synagogue, you boo and stomp and sound noise-makers whenever you get to the name of Haman, you stomp and scream in order to fulfill the command *yomah shmo* (to wipe out his name), and you are enjoined to get so drunk that you finally cannot tell the difference between his name and the name of Ahashverush, the king who eventually stays Haman's hand, sending him to the very gallows Haman had built to hang the Jews.

Also, you dress up in costume; the costumes are another sign of the upside-down-ness, of the farce, of Purim. In the photograph, I am standing in the sanctuary of the synagogue with my arms around Randi.

Randi wears a funny hat, taller than a three-tier cake and glittery gold. I had donned my mother's academic robes and mortarboard. I was dressed up as Hillary Clinton, giving her famous Wellesley commencement address. (Yes, I know. Most teenagers dressing up for Purim take their costume cues from the Bible or else from MTV— your average fifteen-year-old couldn't even conceive of such a ridiculously self-serious costume as Hillary in academic regalia, but there you have it, that's who I was, and the folks at Congregation Beth Israel accepted me anyway.)

In the picture, behind Randi and me, you can see everyone else I loved: Fran, a homeopath and musician with three kids and a glowing smile, Fran dressed as an angel, with gauzy, sparkly wings reaching around her back; her best friend, Simone, turned away from the camera with her red-headed daughter on her hip; sixty-year-old Allie standing off to the side, sporting flamboyant millinery like Randi; and Chava, transformed into a sleek black cat, her long black tail swishing. At fifteen, I was having the usual adolescent troubles with my mother, and I liked the phrase, then in vogue, that your family is a circle of friends who love you. Should anyone ever ask me for a family picture, that is the picture I will show them. We are all there, decked out in finery and celebrating. My mother gave me a lot of valuable things—her cheekbones and her big eyes, and her work ethic and her drive and her temper, her fortitude and her will. The Jews at Congregation Beth Israel gave me most everything else.

After my parents divorced and my sister started college, my mother and I moved from Asheville, North Carolina, to Charlottesville, Virginia, and she enrolled me in Sunday school at Congregation Beth Israel. Each year saw me spending more and more time at the synagogue: Saturday morning services, where I often read from the Torah or offered the *drash*, the homily; the Jewish meditation group; the Sunday school, where I taught a different grade each year. Gradually,

I traded in lacrosse practice and ballet lessons and field hockey sticks, awkward dates at the movie theater and Friday night football games and many other normal teenage activities for more hours, more afternoons and weekends, at the synagogue.

I'm sure a therapist would say I was appointing all those forty-year-old women with whom I hung out to be substitute mothers, that I was looking for a home to stand in for the one my divorced parents broke. Maybe that is true, maybe I was there looking for those things, but I was also there learning the most basic, most rudimentary, most important truths I know, like how to pray and how to study the Bible and how to build a religious community and see God dwelling among us, how to read Hebrew and how to kiss the Torah when the *gabbai* carries it by your pew in the middle of Shabbat morning services, and also how to bake challah and how to clean a classroom when the eighteen second-graders you were in charge of threw finger paint and honey everywhere, and your oh-so-creative Rosh Hashanah craft project turned into something more like a Pollock canvas; how to fast when God has commanded you to and how to feed the poor and how to build a sukkah. When I hear Anglicans talk about *spiritual formation,* I remember the finger paint and the honey and the fasting lessons, and then I am happy that I was formed at Congregation Beth Israel.

I have other pictures, from just over a year after that Purim service, pictures of the going-away party that friends from Congregation Beth Israel threw for me at someone's pool. I am wearing a green-and-white-striped swimsuit and my hair is wet and I pose, in one picture after another, with people I haven't seen since: with Fran and Simone and Allie and Chava; with Sarah, who was a retired attorney and a devout feminist, recently moved to Charlottesville from New York; with Patty, a divorcée from Alabama, back in grad school and creating a second life; with Abe, an incense-burning, vegan, needy sort of man, recently returned to Judaism from years and years out at Yogaville; with Sharon, a faintly uptight philosophy professor who had converted to Judaism decades ago when she married but was now, finally, making it on her own. When they sent me on my way, off to New York for college, I was supposed to come back. One of the presents I received that night was a copy of Ursula K. LeGuin's novel *Always Coming Home*. Allie, the sixty-year-old woman with the funny Purim hat, gave it to me, which was appropriate — it tells the story of a crone, a wise old woman, a grandmother, and that, I think, is what Allie was becoming in the years that I knew her, a wise old mentor woman, and that gift, that novel, was part of her mentoring. I unwrapped the book and Allie read me a poem from it. The poem instructed me to be both careful and fearless, to eat new foods and swim in new rivers. "Return with us, return to us, / be always coming home."

Karen, who was a potter, gave me a present that night, too: two heavy green goblets she had made at her potter's wheel. Other almost-college-freshmen would have taken them for tools of aphrodesia, to be tucked away and brought out with a bottle of champagne when entertaining a man one wanted to impress, or seduce. But I knew they were goblets for Friday night, that they were kiddush cups. I was supposed to use them forever, on a table laden with challot and Sabbath candles, I was supposed to spend a lifetime making kiddush, and I was supposed to come home, and I did neither.

It is Advent, the weeks before Christmas, which means we are waiting for Jesus. It is the season of expectation, of being primed and pumped, the season during which you are supposed to cultivate longing for Him, the type of longing you feel when your beloved has been out of town for three weeks but you know he is coming home tonight. At All Angels' we read the Gospel of Luke, and we say special collects, special short prayers, that remind Jesus to come.

Christmastime may be the hardest season for churches. We are inured not only to the Christmas story itself, but also to our pastors' annual rants against consumerism. Every creative attempt to make the season meaningful, to steal it back inside the church, away from the shopping malls and cheesy radio stations, has been tried, and most of those creative attempts have proved wanting. Perhaps the problem is that we don't know what the meaning of this holiday, of Jesus' pushing into the world, is. If we did, we wouldn't have to worry about consumerism; if we knew what the Incarnation meant, we'd be so preoccupied with awe that we wouldn't notice all the shopping.

All Angels' is the second church I have joined. The first was in England, and it took some finding too, although it needn't have. I moved to England with horror stories in my ears about Oxbridge Christianity, that the college chapels were staffed by gray-haired ministers who believed nothing and kept up the rituals not because they were true, but because they were tradition, no more real or eternal than tea and crumpets. So when I arrived at Cambridge, I avoided my college chapel, and spent several months dipping in and out of the dozens of other churches on Cambridge corners. Finally, one Sunday in November, I gave up. I'd tried ten other churches in Cambridge. May as well try the college chapel.

Morning worship, attended by just a faithful few, was held in the antechamber, on benches in a circle. The college chaplain, Jo Bailey Wells, was a tall, elegant woman who looked a little like a young Mary Poppins. I was wearing a fuzzy brown sweater the color of mushrooms. I edged onto a bench and knew right then that I would make my home at the Clare College chapel for the next two years.

Jo Bailey Wells has an Advent rule. She doesn't go to Christmas parties held before Christmas. She says Advent is about anticipation, not about celebrating weeks before His birth. The waiting, she says, is meant to be a little anxious. I picture Jane Austen heroines. They never are quite sure if their intended will come. We Christians can be sure, we can rest easy in the promises of Scripture. But we are meant to feel a touch of that anxious, handkerchief-wringing expectation all the same.

The calendar tells us that this all culminates on December 25, but really the whole season slouches toward Easter. Jesus becomes incarnate now, in that manger in Bethlehem, but if His incarnateness is meant to make Him more relatable to us, if we are meant to have better access to God because our God has a body like we have, if we relate to Him better because He knows what it is like to weep and throw up and be tempted and suffer, then the Incarnation that starts on Christmas isn't finished until Good Friday. And the miracles that start in the strange, inexplicable Virgin Birth aren't finished until the Resurrection. As Reverend Barbara Cawthorne Crafton wrote of the Virgin Birth, "Hard as it is to swallow, it is nothing compared with what we'll have to deal with come Easter morning, a few short months from now. Look on it as a little something by way of a warm-up." Even his birthplace takes us to the Last Supper: Jesus, the Bread of Life, is born in Bethlehem, *bet lechem*, "house of bread," and at the Last Supper He will break bread for us, and then on the cross He will break His body. Nothing in Scripture, even the names of birthplace towns, is coincidence.

I like edging into Advent here at All Angels'. I like that this is where I will spend Christmas Eve. I like saying the Advent collects in these pews. It feels like a church perched in the middle of changes, of unfolding, and it is a good place to learn to wait.

It takes a long time to learn a church, and I have not learned All Angels' yet. There are still many people's names I don't know, although I now nod and bustle and chat when I walk into services, no longer scrutinizing the program and the hymnal because I don't have anyone to talk to. I don't yet know the rhythms of this church, all its stories or ghosts rattling around in the attic. I don't know what all the tensions are, who all the factions are, how they shift and who sides with whom over what. A vestryman died this year, a pillar of the church, and everyone was sad, shaken. That is how I knew I was still new: I knew the man's name, but couldn't have picked him out of a crowd.

There is another Jewish woman in this church, Esther, a blonde, middle-aged woman with crinkly eyes and a voice like Maria Callas. I love to sit next to her, to listen to her dark soprano working its way around the hymns. She is a lay eucharistic minister, one of the parishioners who dons a white alb on Sunday mornings and serves the communion wine to the rest of us. "The blood of our Lord Jesus Christ," she says, raising the silver chalice to our lips. Receiving from her is my favorite part of Sunday services. She always says her line with such joy, like it is the greatest thing in the world, which, of course, it is.

Conversion Stories

No one in my family—not my Reform Jewish father, nor my lapsed Southern Baptist mother, nor my older sister Leanne—talked about God. Leanne and I knew we were Jewish; that was part of the bargain my parents struck as the first intermarriage in either of their families, that the kids would be Jewish. No one noticed that according to Jewish law, according to Orthodox or Conservative Jews, Leanne and I were as Jewish as Betsy Ross, Judaism being passed to children by their mother. But still, Leanne and I would have checked off Jewish on a list: Southern, Jewish, Tar Heels, Democrats. That checklist translated into a menorah next to our Christmas tree, and we got to skip school on Rosh Hashanah and Yom Kippur. We went to Sunday school at the temple in Asheville. We had a Passover seder every year.

In addition to the Passover seder and the Christmas tree, I had my own religious rituals. I made up a prayer, and said it every night in bed, after the lights were out, never deviating from the text I'd set: first one section of "thank yous," and then a section of "what I'm going to try to do better," followed by a list of things I wanted. And no matter how much I wished to skip ahead to section three, I always forced myself to get through the gratitudes and the repentances first.

My mother continued my Jewish education after my parents divorced. Sometimes I have wondered why. She says that when she and my father got married, she promised him to raise us Jewish; never mind that she wasn't Jewish; never mind that he hadn't kept his promises to her. Upon moving to Charlottesville, my mother and I met with the local rabbi. I spent afternoons with a Hebrew tutor named Rita. I joined a Jewish meditation group. I went to a used bookstore on the downtown mall and bartered for *The Jewish Catalogue* and a couple of books about the Sabbath. I read and read and read. The Christmas wish-lists I presented to my mother each year were nothing but titles of books to be ordered from a well-stocked Jewish bookstore in Maryland.

I read books about Jewish history, Jewish ritual, Jewish law. I pored over old copies of *Lilith*, the Jewish feminist quarterly named for the feisty, headstrong woman to whom, according to Jewish tradition, Adam was married before Eve; with Fran and Simone and other women in my Congregation Beth Israel meditation group, I studied *Miriam's Well*, a book of newly created Jewish rituals for women. I read books of American Jewish history, about the Jewish communities in South Carolina and Rhode Island that dated back to the colonial era, and about the waves of Russian Jewish immigrants who came through Ellis Island in the late nineteenth century. I sat in the Jefferson-Madison regional library, just a block from the synagogue, and read and reread the handful of Judaism books on the shelves—a faded compendium of Jewish holidays, filled with grainy photographs of women with coiffed hair, standing, smiling, next to elaborately braided challah loaves and glowing Sabbath candles; a short guide to Purim; and Anita Diamant's book on Jewish weddings. This last book was the least relevant of all, but I read it over and over, wanting to memorize every detail of Jewish life, even details, like wedding *chuppahs* and glasses broken under grooms' feet, that didn't immediately apply to my teenage self.

But mostly I read about Orthodox Judaism. Lis Harris's loving portrait of a Hasidic family in Brooklyn was published when I was in eighth grade, and I read it about once a month. I read every novel Chaim Potok had written, and I imagined one day having a daughter and naming her Davita, after Potok's one female protagonist. From the bookstore in Maryland, I procured a copy of *Sefer HaChinuch,* a thirteenth-century guide to the mitzvot, the 613 commandments set out in Torah.

The reading bled into my schoolwork, and my teachers indulged me. I did a project in Social Studies on Zionism and the creation of the state of Israel. When assigned an essay about what I did over my summer vacation, I wrote about ordering Bat Mitzvah invitations. In eighth-grade English, we had to read a book each month, any book we wanted, and write a book report. We were to write the reports on a special worksheet that had slots for title, author, plot summary, and evaluation; all of the worksheets were filed into a big three-ring binder, and by the end of the year, the class had compiled reports on over a hundred books. One month, I read the Book of Deuteronomy. "This book is a little slow," I wrote. "It is basically a rehash of laws that were discussed in earlier books of the Bible." In the blank for the author's name, I wrote, "God."

I spent the summers away from Charlottesville. One summer, I attended an academic camp on a college campus in Pennsylvania where I took a creative writing course. There I met a boy, Benjamin, who was Orthodox; he and I were two of the maybe half-dozen kids who turned up for the Friday night Jewish service (another six or so trundled off to church Sunday morning while the other campers played volleyball and tie-dyed T-shirts). After the service, Benjamin walked me back to my dorm, and I left the books I had been carrying—*Jewish Meditation* by Aryeh Kaplan and Kaplan's translation of the Torah—in his backpack. "Don't you want your books back?" he asked.

"Oh, no," I told him coquettishly, "I'm leaving them with you on purpose. So you'll have to find me in the morning and return them."

He did that, found me after breakfast and gave me my books, and we spent Shabbat morning sitting on a bench talking about the novels we loved and what we thought about God. The next day he found me again, and wooed me with his guitar playing, and we got into a fierce argument about what had caused the Civil War, and we spent the rest of the summer in each other's company, taking long walks and sometimes just sitting next to each other reading.

Benjamin was from Washington, D.C., not too far from Charlottesville, and after camp was over and we were back into the rhythms of our school years, I began spending occasional weekends and holidays with his family. When I think back to those visits, what impresses me is his mother. I think I wrote her off then as a parochial, dull secretary, with a Brooklyn accent as thick as her waistline. Now I realize that she was generous and kind, or maybe a little foolish, or maybe just a hip hands-off parent. What must she have thought about this young, unfamiliar girl coming from Virginia to visit her eldest son? Most mothers in her position would have been made nervous by our friendship, by the hundreds of letters we wrote and the phone bills we ran up all through high school. And maybe she was nervous, I don't know. But maybe she also saw that I was stumbling my way toward God.

When I visited his family, Benjamin bunked down in a younger brother's bedroom, and I slept in his room. He always snuck in late at night and we would lie in bed kissing. Maybe kissing him, in that Washington town house with brothers and parents sleeping down the hall should have felt thrilling, or dangerous. I suppose his parents could have walked in on us at any moment, and freaked out, ordered

Benjamin back to his brother's room and me back to Charlottesville. But it didn't feel thrilling or illicit or rebellious; it felt domestic. I had kissed boys before, kisses grabbed in Charlottesville bedrooms when someone's parents were out for the evening, but no one other than my mother ever saw me in a Lanz flannel nightgown.

My generation didn't have my parents' language. We didn't go steady or get pinned, but even if we had known those words, I don't think Benjamin and I would have used them. We had high-pitched conversations about *the state of things* often enough, but we never would have said we were dating. He never would have called me his girlfriend. Still, we both imagined getting married. My own day-dreams were part *The Chosen* and part *Anne of Green Gables*. We would be like Gilbert and Annie, only we would be religious Jews. In one of the daydreams, Benjamin and I grew up to be teachers, teaching at some Jewish high school in New York or D.C., he would teach history and I would teach Bible and sometimes we would send love notes back and forth between our classrooms, carried by a teacher's pet who could be trusted not to read them, or, at least, not to tell.

I spent another high school summer in New York, taking classes at the Drisha Institute for Jewish Education, one of the few places in America where women studied Talmud. I lived with an Orthodox family that summer, Liz and Arthur Goodman and their five children. By the door sat a hatbox full of black berets and magenta caps; Liz donned one every time she left the house. Arthur rose early every morning to lay tefillin, little black leather boxes containing pieces of parchment inscribed with passages from Torah, and recite the morning prayers. That summer I took to wearing only ankle-length skirts, like most Orthodox women, and shirts with enough sleeve to cover at least my shoulder. My nose rings, a hoop and a stud, created a bit of a stir, but one of my Talmud teachers pointed out that Rachel, too, had been bedecked with a *nezem,* a nose ring. I observed the Sabbath laws, learned the lengthy Hebrew Grace After Meals, ate only kosher food. And all day, at Drisha, I studied the Talmud. All the other girls in the program were from Orthodox families, they went to Orthodox schools, they'd grown up on Hebrew and they could find their way around rabbinic texts the way most high school girls can find their way around a shopping mall. They were kind to me. They helped me figure out how to use Aramaic-English dictionaries. They loaned me long skirts and explained how you could tell which brands of yogurt were kosher. I made friends. I studied. I looked forward to going to class every morning, I looked forward to the fresh blonde wood of the classrooms, I even looked forward to breaking my teeth over the Aramaic, to the mind-numbing frustration of foreign words in foreign languages printed on the foreign pages of foreign books.

GRADUALLY, THE SUMMERS away and the weekends in Washington added up to my wanting to live an Orthodox life. No other way to parse Judaism made much sense. If the Torah was true, than we should spend all our time reading it, and all our life living by it. I remember asking Lisa, a woman from Congregation Beth Israel for whom I baby-sat, how it was that she observed the Sabbath laws, but not the dietary laws. All the laws came from the same book; why did she feel bound by one clump and not the other? She said something about tradition. "If you think people should keep Shabbat because of the authority of the Talmud," Lisa said, "then I'm just inconsistent. But I don't observe the Sabbath because I feel bound by Jewish law. I do it because I want to participate in Judaism, and this is one way I can do it that's meaningful for me. I don't find keeping kosher especially meaningful."

I have grown to love theology, but I have always had a pretty theologically unsophisticated mind. Lisa's thinking about law as meaningful, and not as binding, didn't make much sense to me. Either these laws were true or they were not true. Either God revealed all this stuff to Moses on Mount Sinai or He didn't. If He did, then we're bound by it, all of it, every last word, every syllable, every letter. Or else God had nothing to do with it, maybe there was no God, Moses was a megalomaniac or the product of a good fiction writer's imagination. Either there was no Judaism or there was Orthodox Judaism.

Living an Orthodox life would require certain changes — not least that, according to Jewish law, I wasn't Jewish. Reform rabbis, in a 1983 report called "The Status of Children of Mixed Marriages," expanded the definition of a Jew to include those, like me, born to Jewish fathers and non-Jewish mothers, but Conservative and Orthodox Jews stick with the old teaching: Judaism passes through the blood of the mother.

I had been contemplating conversion to Judaism since eighth grade. At Congregation Beth Israel, Rabbi Dan called me into his office and explained that Reform Jews would consider me Jewish, but Conservative Jews and Orthodox Jews would want a formal conversion: study with a rabbi, then immersion in the *mikvah,* the ritual bath. Congregation Beth Israel was a Reform synagogue, so I was okay for now. But Rabbi Dan wanted me to think about converting. What if, he asked, I ever wanted to move to Israel? If I didn't have an Orthodox conversion, I wouldn't be able to gain citizenship under the Law of Return. Or what if I wanted to marry a man who was more observant? A Conservative or Orthodox rabbi would ask for proof that I was Jewish according to halacha, according to Jewish law, before marrying me. Or what if I wanted to become more observant myself?

At first I was insulted. What did he mean, I wasn't really Jewish? It was fodder for my adolescent angst. I struck up a correspondence with our one Orthodox relative, my father's first-cousin, Jane. Was this really true, I asked her, what my rabbi said? Where did these rules about matrilineal descent come from? I wrote to her on yellow legal pads, late into the night. I even rhymed, in order to add to the melodrama of the situation: "So, nu, who is a Jew?" Jane wrote back calmly and sympathetically. She didn't laugh at my theatrics, or suggest I stick to rhymeless prose. She said, gently, that halacha was clear. Because my mother wasn't Jewish, I wasn't Jewish.

By the end of high school, the answer to Rabbi Dan's question seemed obvious. Of course I would convert. I would formally convert to Judaism and change my life and be an Orthodox Jew.

THAT WAS HOW I picked Columbia for college—not because it had a pretty campus or a good lacrosse team or a favorable male-to-female ratio, but because it had hundreds of Orthodox Jews. I delved into Orthodoxy from my first week there. I began attending Orthodox services every day; rose at 6:00 A.M. to study a treatise on *hilchot Shabbat*, the Sabbath laws; worked part-time at a kosher deli; declared to my parents that I couldn't eat off their plates when I came home; was elected the Religious Life Coordinator of Columbia's Jewish Student Union; took up the ritual washing of hands Jews practice first thing every morning; learned the prayer said after going to the bathroom (which thanks God for creating us exactly as we are, with no orifices too few and no orifices too many); made sure to put on my right shoe before my left shoe every morning, in accordance with the Talmud's instructions; virtuously visited the sick at a nearby hospital on Saturday afternoons; and began working with a rabbi to convert.

A conversion requires a *bet din*, a court of three rabbis, and I knew exactly three Orthodox rabbis: an instructor at the Drisha Institute, Rabbi S.; Rabbi W., a congregational rabbi on the West Side of Manhattan, who was friendly with the family I had lived with during my Drisha summer; and Rabbi M., a rabbi in Boston, who had run the program in Israel I had attended just before starting college. Of these three, I was closest to Rabbi M., the rabbi in Boston, but he was too

far away to oversee my conversion closely. Rabbi W. agreed to serve as
av bet din, the head (or literally "father") of the rabbinic triumvirate,
and we met in his office at the West Side synagogue twice a month,
for meetings that were half tutorial, half quiz. He asked me all sorts of
questions about Jewish law, and I stumbled through answers. I found
these conversations both intimidating and thrilling. I felt like I was
participating in remedial versions of the capacious, undulating arguments about Talmud that Danny, the Hasidic boy in *The Chosen,* had
every Shabbat afternoon with his father. Rabbi W. asked me about
tzedakah, charity: how much was I obligated to give? I knew the answer to that was ten percent. "Even if your only source of income, as
it were, is a monthly allowance from your parents?" asked Rabbi W.
Yes. "And tell me about the laws of *muktze,*" he said, the laws that gov-
ern what you can and cannot carry on Shabbat. I was stumped. I didn't
know about *hilchot muktze.* The next week I ranged around the Columbia *beit midrash,* reading everything I could find on the laws of *muktze.*

I called Rabbi M. in Boston every few weeks. Even though he lived
in another state, Rabbi M. was, unquestionably, my rabbi. He was my
mentor and authority in all things religious. He was the man I asked
if I had legal questions (could I drink coffee in a non-kosher restaurant?), and he was the one to whom I turned for spiritual advice. If he
had moved to some faraway kingdom, I would have made pilgrim-
ages to see him there. When I attended his occasional lectures in
Boston, I took notes, and I kept them in a special, sparkly notebook in
my desk.

There was a precise moment he became my rabbi, and I remember it the way some people remember getting engaged. We were on a
bus headed toward Jerusalem, on one of the last days of the summer
program, and I was talking to him about moving to New York, about
starting Columbia, about converting. I was worried I would feel adrift,
that I would need guidance and not know where to find it. "There's

me," said Rabbi M. "I could give you some guidance." And that was that. Later he told me he'd been waiting all summer for me to start this conversation.

Rabbi M. was a *baal teshuva*, a "master of repentance," someone who had not been raised as an observant Jew but had become Orthodox. He was smart, and a little awkward, and he loved high school and college students, and he had a charming French wife and a beautiful daughter, then about seven, named Rayzl. He loved Rayzl above all else. He doted on her. He was one of those dads who even tried to learn to fix his daughter's hair. (He was hopeless. Rayzl always had bumps when Rabbi M. fixed her hair.)

And he loved me. He loved me and he understood me. He could often anticipate what I was going to say before I said it. Over the years that I knew Rabbi M., I came to see that we were a lot alike, that we had the same strengths and weaknesses, that he saw in me something of himself. That sort of self-seeing almost always makes for intensity. I see it now in the history department at Columbia. The teachers here are kind, and magnanimous, and devoted to their students, but sometimes you see a special kind of devotion, a sort of selecting out, and you know that what the professor sees in that student is something of himself. He sees himself again, anew, at some younger, fresher age. I see it myself, in the students who are assigned to my discussion sections. I have liked most all my students—but sometimes there's a special student who loves history and finds subtle questions fascinating, a student who doesn't know the first thing about antebellum Southern planters and then reads *Roll, Jordan, Roll* or *Within the Plantation Household* and finds himself obsessed with cotton and overseers and hoopskirts and slavery; those students remind me of how I was just a few years ago, and I love them for it.

So I called Rabbi M. every few weeks, and I asked him what, precisely, was going to happen on the day of my conversion. Rabbi M.

would come in from Boston, I knew that much, and the three rabbis and I would meet at the *mikvah*, and then what? I knew there would be something of a *bechina*, an exam, before the actual conversion itself. A convert friend of mine from Kansas had told me horror stories about her *bechina*. She said the rabbis had questioned her for two hours, about the most minute aspects of halacha, of Jewish law. I was worried, I told Rabbi M., that I didn't know enough to pass. He always told me not to worry, that I knew plenty, and that he and the other two rabbis didn't want to waste all morning giving me some ridiculous quiz. "We don't expect you to know every jot and tittle of halacha," said Rabbi M. "We just want you to know enough to have a fighting chance of being a decent Jew."

"I'm only going to ask you one question," said Rabbi M. "I'll ask you if you've read the *Ani Ma'amin*, and if you can sign on to it." The *Ani Ma'amin* is, literally, "I believe," just like the Latin verb *credo*, from which our term *creed* comes. It was written by Moses Maimonides, the Rambam, in the twelfth century. The *Ani Ma'amin* is about a page long; it lays out thirteen principles of faith, and Jews typically recite it at the conclusion of morning prayers. "*Ani ma'amin b'emunah shlema*," each of the thirteen lines begins: "I believe with complete faith." I believe with complete faith that the Creator, blessed be His name, creates and guides all Creatures; I believe with complete faith that the Creator, blessed be His name, is unique; that He is not physical; that He is the very first and the very last; that the words of the prophets are true and that the Torah we have was the same one He gave to Moses, and that the Messiah, though he may tarry, will come, and that there will, one day, be a *techiyat hametim*, a resurrection of the dead.

People often say that Christianity is a religion of belief, whereas Judaism is a religion of action, that Jews worry about what you do, not what you believe. That digest of the two faiths has persisted for a long time because there is just enough truth in it. Judaism does care, passionately, about what you do, about what you eat and when you work and how you spend your money and whether or not you gossip and what fabric you use to make your clothes. But Judaism is also a religion of belief. Jews care, passionately, about belief. *Ani ma'amin b'emunah shlema.*

IN THE TORAH, in the middle of a run of short books by obscure prophets, is the prophesy of Obadiah. Obadiah, the Talmud tells us, was an Edomite who converted to Judaism. In the Middle Ages, male converts often took Obadiah as their new name, and Maimonides once wrote a famous letter to an "Obadiah the Convert." This Obadiah had written to Maimonides to ask whether he should recite the prayer, "Our God and God of Our Fathers," since his fathers were not, in fact, children of the Abrahamic covenant. Maimonides told him, "Of course you should pray 'Our God and God of Our Fathers' for in no respect is there a difference between us and you. Do not think ill of your origin. If we trace our descent from Abraham, Isaac and Jacob, your descent is from him by whose word the world was created."

ONE MORNING IN DECEMBER, I got on the subway and rode to 79th Street, and then walked one block to the *mikvah*. The ritual bath is so essential to Jewish communities that Jews are enjoined to build a *mikvah* even before they build a synagogue. Men sometimes take a dip—before Yom Kippur, for example, when they want to purify themselves—but it is rare to glimpse a man at the *mikvah*, whose primary visitors are married women halfway through their menstrual cycle. While she's having her period, and for seven days thereafter, a Jewish woman can't have sex with her husband. And the rabbis, recognizing how very tempted one could be after even just a kiss, employed a common rabbinic strategy: they built fences. To ensure that a man does not have sex with his wife while she's bleeding, the rabbis added: *Don't touch your wife at all. Don't kiss her, don't hold her hand, don't put your arm around her at the movies, don't brush up against her wrist when she comes home with too many bags of groceries and you are taking some of them from her, don't help her zip her dress and accidentally run your fingers along the back of her neck. Don't pass a plate to her at dinner. Don't sleep in the same bed,* which usually means, *have two twin beds that you shove together and cover with one king-sized sheet during the weeks when you can touch, kiss, prod. But during the other weeks, make them up as twin beds. Practice your hospital corners. Don't kick your sheets off in the night and roll too far to the left.*

Then, when a woman's period has ended and seven days have elapsed, she goes to the *mikvah* in the evening. There, an attendant will lead her to a bathroom, where she will undress and remove her wig, all her jewelry, any Band-Aids she might have wrapped around a cut on her finger or her calf. She will shower. She will peel off her nail polish, and she will floss, because the water from the *mikvah* must touch every part of her body; the smallest speck of spinach stuck in her teeth would interfere. Sometimes even scabs are questionable.

The other purpose of *mikvah*s, in addition to purifying women after their periods, is to make converts. Male converts also have to be circumcised, but women have only to immerse in a *mikvah* in front of a *bet din,* and then they are Jewish.

I arrived at 78th Street and was greeted by the *mikvah* lady, the attendant, who, true to stereotype, had an Eastern European accent and a poorly made wig; it would be her job to make sure that I was naked and clean before I went into the *mikvah,* and to see that I immersed myself completely. The *bet din* was already there, and, as Rabbi M. had promised, the *bechina* was a formality. Rabbi W. asked me about the laws of *tzedakah,* which he already knew I knew; Rabbi S. declined to ask me anything at all; and Rabbi M. said, "So, Lauren, have you read the *Ani Ma'amin?*" I nodded. "And do you believe it all?" "Yes," I said. "I believe it all."

Then the *mikvah* lady whisked me off to a bathroom, where I undressed, washed, scrubbed, and donned a paper robe. When a man is converting, the rabbis just stand there and witness it, but the laws of modesty prevent male rabbis from watching a naked woman swimming around in a *mikvah*. This presents something of a logistical challenge. So, when I entered the *mikvah* room, the rabbis all turned their backs, and then, robe on, I plunged into the water. The rabbis heard the splash, and then they filed out of the room. I disrobed, and the *mikvah* lady supervised my three immersions, making sure every hair on my head was saturated and that my toes and fingers weren't clenched together when I dunked down. And then I was a Jew. Somehow the *mikvah* affected a blood transfusion. The rabbis teach that every Jew past and present witnessed the revelation of the Torah on Mount Sinai. Converts, they say, witnessed it, too, but then our *neshamot*, our souls, accidentally got born into non-Jewish bodies. Stepping out of the *mikvah*, that all changed. My body had become right. My *neshama* could rest comfortably. I was a Jew.

⤫

THE VERY FIRST THING I liked about Christianity, long before it ever occurred to me to go to church or say the creed or call myself a Christian, was the Incarnation, the idea that God lowered himself and became a man so that we could relate to Him better. In Christianity, God got to be both a distant and transcendent Father god, and a present and immanent Son god who walked among us. Christians, unlike Jews, spent their time talking to a God who knew from experience what it was like to get hungry, to go swimming, to miss a best friend.

The Incarnation appealed to the literature buff in me. Embodiment was the novelistic culmination of anthropomorphism, of assigning God human characteristics. All through the Torah, God is pictured as having hands, a face. The rabbis say, *Of course God doesn't really have hands, but the Torah uses the language of faces and hands and eyes so that we will have an easier time wrapping our minds around this infinite, handless God.* That is what you say if you are a rabbi. But if you are a good novelist, you actually give Him hands and eyes by the end of the book, and that is what the Bible does. It says, in Deuteronomy, that God brought us out of Egypt with a mighty hand and an out-stretched arm; and then it gives Him an arm in the Gospel of Matthew.

I was impressed in a literary way with this idea of Incarnation. But I wasn't persuaded by it. The rabbis had very clear expectations of what the Messiah would do. He would bring world peace, and he would rebuild the Temple, and he would gather the Jews back into Is-rael, and he would do it all at once, none of this not completing his as-signed tasks and having to come back to earth a second time. Jesus hadn't done those things; ergo, he wasn't the Messiah. It was a good story, this story the Christians had dreamed up, but I was sure that it wasn't, finally, true. It was a good story the way *The Great Gatsby* is a good story. Beautifully written, clever, insightful, but not something to shape your life around. Not something to pray to.

Still, something doesn't have to be true to be interesting, and all through my first years of college, Christianity interested me. I took a New Testament class my first semester; my final exam was about six days after I went to the *mikvah*. I wrote a paper about the Great Awakening for my Colonial American history course. I read contem-porary Southern fiction, and noted that every character in every novel by Lee Smith or Clyde Edgerton or Eudora Welty was Protestant, that they took for granted a vocabulary that included words like *grace* and *saved* and *sin*. I took Southern history classes, and wrote paper after paper about Protestant Christianity. I spent a lot of time wondering how to be both Jewish and Southern. Lots of things were Southern: big hair, social graces, college football, Jack Daniel's, but also Christ. Most of my Jewish friends wanted to move to Israel, but I wanted, eventually, to return to North Carolina or Virginia. I thought a lot about why my sister had not been invited to debut with the Rhododendron Court. It was a slap in her face, and a surprising one: my father represented Asheville in the North Carolina senate, my mother had been president of the Junior League and Buncombe County Woman of the Year. All the right people attended their dinner parties. Some people said she wasn't invited because we were Jewish.

I tried to write a novel about Southern Judaism. The narrator was a young woman who had moved to Israel and learned Hebrew and become an expert bargainer at the *shuk*, but who eventually had to leave her husband and move back to North Carolina because she could not bear to be away from the mountains of Buncombe County another hour. It was a little melodramatic. The protagonist spent a lot of time sick to her stomach. For pages and pages I couldn't make her do anything except throw up bile. I took this as a bad sign and put down the novel.

When I wasn't trying my hand at roman à clef, I hung out at The Cloisters, a museum uptown that displayed wall after wall of dark, wacky, medieval Christian art. I took my textbooks there, and sat in the courtyard and read. I wandered the rooms. I loved the room with the Unicorn tapestries; the tapestries told the story of a hunt for the mythical unicorn, his eventual capture, how the hunters killed him, how, in the last tapestry, he was suddenly miraculously alive again. He was an allegory for Christ. I bought pictures of the final tapestry, where the great horned creature sat surrounded by a circular fence. His white sides were dotted with pink stains. I always thought it was stigmata blood, but recently I read that it was just juice dripped down from the pomegranate tree up above.

My favorite spot at The Cloisters was a room downstairs called the Treasury. In glass cases were small fragile reliquaries and icons and prayer books. In one case was a tiny psalter and Book of Hours that had belonged to the Duchess of Normandy, all tempera and ink and gold leaf on vellum. It lay open to a picture of Christ's arrest. I could barely read the Latin. Sometimes I would stand in front of that psalter for an hour. I wanted to hold it in my hand.

My boyfriend in college was Dov, an Orthodox Jew from Westchester County whom I had met through Rabbi M. Dov thought all this was weird. He watched me watch the Book of Hours, and he watched me write endless papers about religious revivals in the South. He saw that I was reading a book about Southern fiction called, after Flannery O'Connor's memorable phrase, *The Christ-Haunted Landscape,* and he worried. He said, "Lauren, if a Jewish person converted to Catholicism, wouldn't you think it was strange if she then majored in Jewish Studies at college, spent afternoons at the Jewish museum, and read *My Name Is Asher Lev* once a week?"

I lectured him about identity. I explained that his hypothetical Jewish-Catholic made perfect sense, she was probably trying to synthesize all the parts of her being into one seamless whole.

"But Lauren," Dov said, "you didn't grow up going to The Cloisters or reading sermons by Jonathan Edwards! This has nothing to do with marrying together disparate parts of your identity."

"Well, look," I said, "a girl can have an intellectual interest or two, can't she? I'm just interested in this stuff. I'm interested in Southern history. You don't have to go reducing my entire intellectual life to thinly veiled autobiography." Dov wasn't convinced. "You read Arabic," I said. Dov was a Near Eastern Studies major at Harvard. "You spend all your time studying Persian and writing papers about medieval Arabic philosophers and poets," I said, "and I don't worry that you are about to convert to Islam."

"Lauren," Dov said. "It's not the same. It really isn't the same. You chose to be Jewish, ostensibly because you love Judaism so much. Yet you can't be bothered to squeeze one little Hebrew class in between all your courses on the New Testament and the history of North Carolina?"

At the time, I thought Dov was overreacting. Now I think he could see something I could not see. He could see Jesus slowly goading me toward Him.

IN THE MIDDLE of my sophomore year of college, I dreamed about mermaids. In the dream, my friend Michelle and I and a group of women I didn't know were kidnapped by a band of mermaids. They took us underwater, and, though we didn't sprout tails or grow fins, we could function just fine on the bottom of the sea. We could breathe and walk around and talk. Life as a captive to the mermaids wasn't actually so bad. Our captors didn't keep us gagged or in chains. They let us do whatever we wanted, except go home. We could go to the movies, cook four-course dinners, read Ibsen. We just couldn't return to the shore.

After a year underwater, a group of men came on a rescue mission. Most were graying, paunchy, fifty-something men, Monday-night football-watching types. But one was this beautiful, thirtyish, dark Daniel-Day-Lewis-like man. And I knew that he had come to rescue me. He would, of course, participate in the group effort while he was there, but I was the reason he'd come.

We all went home after our year under water. The home I went to was my childhood home in North Carolina, where I hadn't lived since I was eleven. I had, apparently, been engaged all this time, and my mother, in some stroke of faith or foolishness, had gone ahead and

planned my wedding, which was set to happen in three days. I stood
in the kitchen, hovering over the island in the middle of the room,
reading through the reply cards to the invitations she'd sent out. Donna
Bruni, a friend of my mother's from college, now moved to Texas and
married to a millionaire, couldn't come; she had written a long, cursive
note explaining why.

Neither my mother nor my fiancé (and whether or not my fiancé
was Dov remained curiously opaque) believed I had been kidnapped
by mermaids. They didn't flip out and accuse me of lying; they didn't
suggest I should be institutionalized; in fact, they didn't seem all that
curious about where I had been all year. They simply knew that mermaids didn't exist, so, obviously, I hadn't been kidnapped by any.

Still, kidnapping can be a fairly traumatic experience, and it would
have been nice to have had someone to talk to about it. So from time
to time I slipped off and went to meet the beautiful rescuing man, the
Daniel Day-Lewis look-alike, and we talked about the kidnapping,
nothing else, just my year as a mermaid, and then I would go back
home. End of dream.

I have bizarre and detailed dreams a lot. Recently I dreamed I had
to go to Japan, but first I spent the afternoon catching flying egg yolks
in a basement with my Uncle Bob. And I dreamed that a friend of my
sister's had gone on *Oprah* to talk about her boyfriend's infidelities,
but, in order to preserve her anonymity, she wore a giant bowling pin
made from pasteboard over her head. When she began to cry someone passed her a tissue and she had to maneuver it up under the pin
to get to her tears. I never try to interpret these dreams; I just remember what I can and then I get up, brush my teeth, hop in the shower.

But the mermaid dream was different. I knew, as soon as I woke
up, that the dream had come from God and it was about the reality of
Jesus. The truth of Him. That He was a person whose pronouns you
had to capitalize. That He was God. I knew that with more certainty
than I have ever known anything else.

God is a novelist. He uses all sorts of literary devices: alliteration, assonance, rhyme, synecdoche, onomatopoeia. But of all these, His favorite is foreshadowing. And that is what God was doing at the Cloisters and with Eudora Welty. He was foreshadowing. He was laying traps, leaving clues, clues I could have seen had I been perceptive enough. Dov saw them.

There had been other, earlier clues. There was the Christmas Eve in high school when I sneaked off to midnight Mass with my friend Nora (just because I remembered my sister, Leanne, going to midnight Mass one year with her best friend, and I wanted to be like her). There was the slender gold cross I asked my mother to buy me for my eleventh birthday (just because the pretty simplicity of a cross appealed to me more than the complex triangles of a Jewish star). There was the sandy-haired fundamentalist boy I met at a forensics match my junior year of high school. He came from Front Royal, and was trying to decide if he should go to Harvard or Liberty, Jerry Falwell's college in Lynchburg. We chatted. I was intrigued. I told him Christians mistranslated the verse in Isaiah that says that the Messiah will be born of a virgin. The Hebrew, I said, meant simply "young woman." I asked him to send me something to read about Jesus, a request that probably made his day. He mailed me two pamphlets and a tape of whiny Christian music. I skimmed the pamphlets and threw away the tape.

Nothing came of the pamphlets, or the cross, or the midnight Mass, but that is how the clues God leaves sometimes work. Sometimes nothing comes of them. Sometimes, as in a great novel, you cannot see until you get to the end that God was leaving clues for you all along. Sometimes you wonder, *How did I miss it? Surely any idiot should have been able to see from the second chapter that it was Miss Scarlet in the conservatory with the rope.*

. . .

So, BACK TO THE DREAM. All through the Bible and the Talmud and church history and Jewish history (and probably every other sacred history, too) God meets people in their dreams. There are Pharaoh's famous dreams about the corn and the cows, for example, and, in the Gospel of Matthew, an angel comes to Joseph in a dream. Still, it took me several years to figure out how to keep a straight face when telling people that *God communicated with me in a dream.* Biblical, sure, but also a little flaky.

At the time, in the days after dreaming the dream, I told only three people. First I cornered my roommate Beth, a curly-headed, blue-eyed Orthodox Jew who knows God more intimately than just about anyone. Her blue eyes got very wide and she said, "I bet the man who came to rescue you was Eliyahu HaNavi." Elijah the Prophet. The one for whom we leave the extra glass of wine at the Passover seder. The one who will announce the coming of the Messiah. *Close,* I thought, *but not quite.*

I told the dream to Dov. He was irate. He thought I was dreaming about another man. He thought I was being unfaithful in my sleep, or trying, subtly, to tell him I'd fallen in love with someone else.

Finally, I went to Virginia, to visit my tenth-grade physics teacher, the one devout Christian I really knew. The one who had come to faith reading the Gospel of Mark in her kitchen one morning. We sat in the garden at Monticello next to the fainting plant and I told her about the mermaids and the man who'd rescued me. "Do you have any idea who he was?" asked Lil. I was disappointed. I understood why Beth and Dov hadn't gotten it. But Lil, a full-fledged, born-again Christian? A woman who led a small group for teachers at her church? A woman who read her Bible every day? Why didn't she see it? "Well, it seemed pretty obvious to me that it was Jesus," I said. "Yeah, I think that's pretty obvious too," said Lil, "but I didn't know if you would be open to seeing Jesus in your dreams. You are an Orthodox Jew after all. An Orthodox Jewish life might not have very much room for Jesus."

She was right. I wasn't all that open to it. I had committed my life to Judaism. I was happily smitten with my Orthodox boyfriend. My day-to-day life in New York was all about Judaism; there was no room for Jesus there. So I told my dream to Lil, and then I shoved the whole thing in a drawer and fled. For about two years. Went to shul faithfully. Invested in more long skirts. Rid my kitchen of all its leaven at Passover. Baked Dov red velvet layer cakes on his birthdays.

But gradually, my Judaism broke. I couldn't remember why I was keeping Shabbat, why I was praying in Hebrew, why I was spending Friday nights and Saturday afternoons at long Sabbath meals, full of singing and wine, with people I loved. I called Rabbi M. and said I was having a *spiritual dry spell.* He said, *This is the beauty of Judaism. Even when you doubt, even when it doesn't feel like anything is happening, even when it seems like God is not around, you keep doing the mitzvot. You keep saying the prayers, you keep rinsing your hands every morning, you keep decorating the sukkah with fruit, and lighting the Sabbath candles, and making latkes at Hanukkah. The action will get you through the dry spells. Eventually the feeling that God is hovering in between your shoulder blades will come back.* So I kept praying, and decorating the sukkah with fruit, and lighting the Sabbath candles.

A week before classes started my senior year of college, I sat waiting for a friend in a bookstore. Though I had pledged not to buy anything, I picked up a book from a prominent display case just to read until Aaron showed up. It was *At Home in Mitford,* a novel by a woman who lived in western North Carolina. Mitford, it turned out, was a barely disguised Blowing Rock. The protagonist was Father Tim, fifty-something bachelor rector of a small Episcopal church, the Lord's Chapel. I read the first chapter, and walked out of the bookstore with the novel and its sequel in my knapsack. I spent the next week reading and rereading the Mitford books. They were no great works of literature, just vignettes about the people in Father Tim's parish, stories about ordinary Christians working out ordinary faith in their ordinary lives. Mitfordians frequently quoted Philippians 4:13, "I can do everything through him who gives me strength." They sang hymns I didn't know and prayed from a prayer book I had never opened. And I thought, *I want what they have.*

GETTING THERE WAS LESS CLEAR. I had that meeting with Pastor Mike, the Presbyterian pastor who told me I couldn't divorce Judaism. I bought that Book of Common Prayer and gave away my siddur. I still kept the Sabbath, but I started attending vespers at an Episcopal church. Dov and I broke up. I ate a bowl of Campbell's clam chowder. I went to Talbot's and bought two pairs of shorts, but I kept them in the back of a drawer. I kissed a Catholic boy and lay in bed with him, arguing about the role Polish workers played in the Holocaust. I read the autobiography of St. Teresa of Avila and wrote more papers about the Great Awakening. And I sat in on a mid-week "learning service" at an Episcopal church near Columbia.

The learning service drove me crazy. The church in question—let's call it the Church of the Resurrected Light—is a caricature of itself, the liberal end of the liberal end of the Episcopal spectrum. Each week at the learning service, a minister or lay-leader gave a talk and afterward there was a Q & A session, followed by Compline, the night-time prayer service. One evening, a stout, blonde woman, a member of the vestry and a sculptor of some repute, led the session. The minute she opened her mouth I knew she was from western North Carolina (Boone, it turned out). Her talk was about ecospirituality; and she spoke about Jesus, who, she said, was our cultural expression of the divine truth that all people yearn for, just as Kali was the Hindus' cultural expression. During the Q & A, I raised my hand. "Probably I missed something," I said, "but if Jesus is just our cultural expression of a universal divine impulse, why does one say the Creed?" One of the central teachings of the Nicene Creed, a fourth-century statement of faith that Episcopalians recite each Sunday, is the person of Jesus: that He is Lord, "the only Son of God, eternally begotten of the Father, God from God, Light from Light, true God from true God." *True God,* not one of culture's manifestations of the divine spark within us all.

The Creed, explained the sculptor, is our culture's vocabulary for giving voice to divinity.

I left the class furious. *I suppose I shouldn't be surprised,* I thought to myself, *that the Church of the Resurrected Light is serving up this wishy-washy liberal hogwash; after all, it's a place that hesitates to call itself "Christian," lest it offend its Buddhist or pagan neighbors.* It struck me as odd that it took an Orthodox Jew to ask questions about the authority of the Creed. Then, as I walked, it struck me as even odder that I cared so much. Surely I wasn't this angry just because the sculptor's presentation seemed intellectually inconsistent. "That church," I fumed to a friend later that night, "should be embarrassed that so many Christians are running from Christ."

Then I thought: *Maybe I should stop running.*

The class at the Church of the Resurrected Light concluded, and so did my college classes. I graduated, and I sweated through the summer teaching a high-school U.S. Government course in Durham. I spent Sunday mornings with black Methodists and somber Episcopalians. I met Hannah in that *W* section of a used bookstore. I drove through the neighborhood of the first Jewish mayor of Durham and cried. I decided that I would be baptized, but I also decided that I could not be baptized yet. That could wait till I got to England, where I was heading in the fall. I would find a church there.

England would buy me time. England gave me two years to be baptized and confirmed, to read about the Eucharist and the doctrine of the atonement, to learn a new liturgy and how to sing eighteenth-century hymns. England let me incubate my baby Christian self before I moved back to Manhattan, before I had to explain to people where all the long skirts had gone, before I had to come up with an answer to give a friend's mother when she asked me if I was still Jewish, before I had to figure out what it meant that I caught myself humming Hasidic *niggunim* in the car as I drove to church.

———— ❧ ————

IF, A HUNDRED years from now, a historian of American religion picks up my diary, she will scrutinize it for the real reasons I converted to Christianity. I know, because I have spent the last seven years learning how to be a historian of American religion, and I spend a lot of time trying to understand why people converted. Scholars offer lots of different explanations. Adolescent girls in the 1740s, one scholar suggests, converted to Christianity because they were allowed to do things in church, like speak publicly when under the influence of the Holy Spirit, that girls weren't usually allowed to do. Slaves, another historian offers, converted because they thought their masters would have to free them if they became Christians. Women converted, a third historian chimes in, because a Christian husband would treat you better than a whiskey-guzzling, barroom-brawling heathen.

A psychobiographer might scrutinize my life and say that in choosing Christianity over Judaism, I was choosing my mother over my father. The psychobiographer would note, correctly, that my mother and I had a fraught, fighting-filled time of it when I was a teenager, and that embracing the religion of her ancestors was a way that I, once we had come through adolescence, could re-cement our relationship. Or maybe the psychobiographer would say that I'd read my father's leaving my mother, as children often read divorce, as a rejection of me, and that rejecting his religion for hers was a way of getting back at him.

She converted, other scholars perusing my diary would suggest, because she couldn't figure out how to be Southern and be Jewish. She missed that pulled pork barbecue too much. She thought she'd stick out like a sore thumb at Carolina football games, clad in her long skirt and wig. Except, of course, she couldn't go to those football games anyway, because they're on Saturdays, when she couldn't drive or carry, when she would be in shul.

They'd have a lot of evidence to make that argument. They'd only have to cite my senior thesis, which was about a Jewish family who moved from Pennsylvania to Warrenton, North Carolina, in the early nineteenth century, a family named Mordecai. (Rhymes with "merrily." In Pennsylvania, the name was different; it rhymed with "key lime pie" or "clear blue sky." But when the family moved to North Carolina, the name got bastardized into something that would slip more easily off Southern lips.) Within a generation of their move, about half the Mordecais had converted to Christianity. In their letters, they write about God. They write about studying the Gospels, they write about Jesus invading their hearts. If you asked them why they converted, they would say, *Because God called us.* But in my thesis, I said that they converted because it was impossible for Jews to gain a foothold in Southern society.

. . .

THERE WOULD BE some truth in all those theories. But this is why those historians would be wrong, why all those scholars who try to explain away the Great Awakening are wrong, why my senior thesis is wrong. They recognize that conversion is complicated, that it is about family, and geography, and politics, and psychology, and economics. They just forget that it is also about God.

Shopping for a Crèche
with Hannah

First I try telling Hannah that I don't want to hear about her affair. "You can do whatever you want," I say, "but this is the oldest story in the book, and it is destined to lead somewhere bad. If you want to do it, go ahead, but I don't want to hear about it, so don't tell me anything. And don't ask to use my apartment as your love pad."

Then I realize that won't do. First of all, it isn't true. I do want to hear about it, out of voyeuristic curiosity if nothing else. Second, I realize that as much as I might want not to know this piece of information—that Hannah, one of the first Christians I had ever known and respected, might start cheating on her husband—I do know it, and I have some responsibilities. I figure she has told me for a reason, and maybe the reason is that she wants me to stop her from doing it, to hold her accountable for her baptismal vow and her wedding vow, to remind her of the cross dangling from her necklace. And, even if she doesn't want me to hold her accountable and even if I don't want to, I don't have a choice. Paul made that clear in his letter to the Galatians: "Brothers, if someone is caught in a sin, you who are spiritual should restore him gently. But watch yourself, or you also may be tempted. Carry each other's burdens, and in this way you will fulfill the law of Christ."

Hannah and I go to the gift shop at the Cathedral of St. John the Divine. We are looking at crèche scenes. The Cathedral sells chunky, brightly colored crèches from Peru, complete with donkeys and cows and tiny baby Jesuses. "Here's a thought," I say to Hannah. "What if you actually have sex with this man and then you get pregnant?" I realize I am grasping at straws here.

Hannah laughs. "I think that's really the least of my worries. There are other things I might not be able to prevent: Jim might find out. I might fall in love with him. All that is kind of out of my control. I think I can prevent getting pregnant."

Here is what Hannah finally tells me about the man. She tells me that they met at a dinner party, that Jim was there when they met, that Jim was actually sitting on the same couch with them, balancing his paper plate full of pita triangles and baba ganoush on his knees, just like they were. The three of them were drinking Shiraz. The man was charming. They talked about Gauguin, and they talked about literature. In particular, they talked about Latin American literature, which Hannah loves and Jim knows next to nothing about. It is her passion. Reading and writing about Latin American literature is what she does all day. She thinks maybe she doesn't want to have children because it will take away from the time she has to read and write about Latin American literature. This man, it appears, knows something about Latin American literature. They have a long conversation about Gabriel García Márquez, and finally Jim and Hannah get up to say hello to someone else and then the man calls her later that week and they meet for coffee. Then they meet for dinner, one night when Jim is out of town, and Hannah neglects to mention the dinner to her husband. "I've never had an affair," says Hannah. "Is this how an affair begins?"

"Yes," I say, although I do not know. But it sounds to me like this might be how an affair could begin. "Maybe you shouldn't see him again."

"But I want to," says Hannah. "I really, really want to. I can't stop thinking about him. I think about him all the time." *This sounds so pathetic,* I say to myself. *She sounds like an eight-year-old insisting that she wants chocolate ice cream even though dinner's in fifteen minutes. She ought to be able to hear how pathetic this is, that it's just about her wants, and snap out of it.* I don't tell her that, though, because it sounds too preachy, and also because, even though it's true, it's also not true. She does sound like an eight-year-old, and if Christianity teaches us anything, surely it is that we don't have to do the things we want to do, that God gives us the grace not to do them, that He gives us law, and then He gives us the grace to live His law. All that is true. But it is also true that desire is strong, euphoric, deadly. That it is not really as simple as telling her she sounds like she's eight.

She says it's not about the sex. "Sex might happen," she says. "But Jim and I have plenty of sex. I don't really care about having sex with him. I just want to talk to him all the time. I want him," she says, "to attend to me."

"I guess just having some nice, normal friendship is out," I ask. "Like, couldn't you have him over for dinner when Jim is home?" I feel hopelessly naïve. I feel like a schoolgirl. What do I know about marriage, and how to have friends once you are married, and how not to have an affair if you are somebody's wife?

"That's out," says Hannah. "He stares at me too wickedly to have him over for dinner when Jim is there."

"Hannah," I say, trying to sound gentle. "You haven't fallen in love with this man, you haven't slept with him, you simply have a crush on him. Just don't see him again. The next time you're tempted to call him, call me instead and we'll go to the movies." She doesn't say anything.

"You know how we ask God in the Lord's Prayer not to lead us into temptation? Well, I think He honors that best when we don't go marching into temptation ourselves." She still doesn't say anything. "Look. You made these promises at your wedding, and Jesus is very clear about adultery."

"I know," she says.

"That should be the end of it."

"You're right," says Hannah, "it should be."

Christmas

My Icons and Me

My Christmas this year is small. It is the first year that I have not gone to Charlottesville to spend the holiday with my mother and my sister.

Christmas morning was the one Christian ritual I had growing up. My mother would disappear off to church with her mother, the only time she went all year, and then she would come home to the Christmas tree and the packages and stockings. I remember the first Christmas after my parents divorced. It was the first year my mother bought a tree without my father's help. Picked it out herself, dragged it to the car herself, got it to stand upright in the green and red plastic tree-stand without the aid of my father. It was the same year we got a cat, which showed up on our friends' doorstep unwanted and unannounced. Our friends brought the cat to us. I don't think my mother had given much thought to adding a feline to our newly smaller household, but she took the cat anyway. "I suddenly realized I didn't have to ask anyone's permission," she said. Cats and Christmas trees. It was the year she read a book called *Tough Cookies Don't Crumble*.

This year I don't go to Virginia. I beg off with excuses about work, about my comprehensive exams coming up, and that is all true, but also I just cannot bear to spend this Christmas tense and overly polite and all the other complicated ways that families are. My sister, Leanne, calls me to say that she is disappointed that I am not coming home, and that I'd better come home next year. I can't tell if this is because she misses me, wishes I were there to delight in the red-white-and-green cream cheese dip she always makes just for me, or if really she is just annoyed that she has to play the dutiful daughter and do all the dutiful daughter things by herself, without me there to shoulder some of the filial burden.

So this Christmas is small. I go to midnight Mass, which at All Angels' we make at eleven o'clock instead of twelve. On the way home, I stop at the grocery store to buy a box of Lucky Charms. In line behind me is this sexy, blonde professor from my department. He is buying only healthy food, tofu and fresh mozzarella and some sort of wheat cracker. I am mortified. In the fall, I got drunk at a departmental party and came on to him wildly and I do not think I have spoken to him since, and here he is in line behind me at the grocery store on Christmas Eve, and of all the possible edibles I could have selected, I am buying Lucky Charms. We chat about the weather and I slink away home, and curl up on my sofa with a novel and a scratchy red afghan and fall asleep, novel in hand, under a crescent of light from my lamp.

CHRISTMAS IS THE closest a lot of people ever get to Christianity, but it is also Christmas, the truth of it, the radical secret of God becoming man, that puts a lot of people off. Sometimes I meet Professor Kerry, one of my undergrad advisers, and he looks at me and furrows his brow. He never did understand how this straight-A, Ivy League student could really believe that somewhere up in the sky sat a God who cared if she turned on a TV on Saturday afternoon; he finds it even less intelligible that the same student now believes that God took human form and walked around Palestine. "One day you'll have to explain to me how intelligent people can believe in something that sounds like a Greco-Roman myth," he says. "You know: Zeus, Demeter, Jesus."

Admittedly, it's a little crazy. Grand, infinite God taking on the squalling form of a human baby boy. It's what some of the old-timers call a scandal, the scandal of the Gospel. But it is also the whole point.

I've filled my bedroom with pictures of Jesus. Icons and paintings and church fans and other Jesuses dance all over my walls. Everywhere you turn, there He is, peering at you. Sometimes with a halo, sometimes on a cross, sometimes knocking at a door. When I don't much like Christianity, or when I can't remember why I am doing any of this, I look at these pictures of Jesus. Often I talk to them. I talk to them when I am too distracted, otherwise, to pray, and I talk to them when none of my friends are home and I am bored and alone. Eastern Orthodox Christians have an elaborate and sophisticated theology and practice of icons: they somehow enter into the icons, the icons become a window through which they see Him. My thinking about icons is a little more rudimentary. My icons are sort of like imaginary friends, only Jesus isn't imaginary.

In my more pompous moments, I describe myself, my Christianity, as *radically incarnational*. The Incarnation, that God took flesh, is the whole reason I am not an Orthodox Jew. The Incarnation is the whole reason I am not lighting a menorah at this time of year. I am a Christian because being a Christian gives me a picture of God to talk to during all these moments where, without the picture, I would forget that God exists. My old professor can't imagine how it can possibly be true that God became man, he can't imagine how I can possibly make sense of it, but I no longer know how to make sense of God, or anything else for that matter, without it.

Here is the thing about God. He is so big and so perfect that we can't really understand Him. We can't possess Him, or apprehend Him. Moses learned this when he climbed up Mount Sinai and saw that the radiance of God's face would burn him up should he gaze upon it directly. But God so wants to be in relationship with us that He makes himself small, smaller than He really is, smaller and more humble than his infinite, perfect self, so that we might be able to get to Him, a little bit.

Being born a human was not the first time God made Himself small so that we could have access to Him. First He shrunk Himself when He revealed the Torah at Mount Sinai. He shrunk Himself into tiny Hebrew words, man's finite language, so that we might get to Him that way. Then He shrunk Himself again, down to the size of a baby, down into manger finiteness.

Jane Vonnegut Yarmolinsky wrote, "The whole concept of God taking on human shape, and all the liturgy and ritual around that, had simply never made any sense to me. That was because, I realized one wonderful day, it was so simple. For people with bodies, important things like love have to be embodied. That's all. God had to be embodied, or else people with bodies would never in a trillion years understand about love."

Never, in a trillion years.

———— ⚬∞⚬ ————

CHRISTMAS MORNING, I wake up on my couch depressed and self-pitying. I am relieved that I'm not in Charlottesville, but I am not so thrilled with the alternative: Lucky Charms, studying, and my couch.

I lie here missing Steven. He is, I know, off gallivanting around New England with his new girlfriend. I know this because he sent me a gratuitous Christmas email, where he wrote, "I won't have time to call to wish you a happy holiday, but I wanted to let you know just how grateful I am for our time together. I'm sorry it didn't work out for life but I am so deeply grateful for what you gave me. I feel my current happiness and hopefulness is due in no small measure to you." Then he added that he was off to New England.

I know exactly what they are doing, Steven and this new girlfriend, because he and I planned the trip. We were going to go spend Christmas with his father in Northampton, then visit his mother in Boston, and then go borrow his cousin's farm in New Hampshire and just unfurl for a few days. I picture him introducing the new girlfriend to all the Northampton used bookstores. I picture him walking through the Isabel Gardner Museum with her. I picture him sitting in Back Bay drinking coffee with her, and traipsing through the snow on some wintertime New Hampshire nature walk with her. I feel I should have copyrighted the trip's itinerary.

After I tire of Steven, I start thinking about Hannah, and I am filled with loathing. I think about how she is waking up with Jim, snug in their bed like the couple in "The Night Before Christmas." They will unpack their stockings, and coo about Christmases past, and plan Christmases future, and go to church and come home and eat a nice joyful lunch. They might even sing carols. I am furious at her and jealous and dismayed that she gets all that while I just have this pathetic afghan and couch, and she is just going to casually toss it all away because some man who knows Latin American literature makes her pulse race. I should probably be grateful for the afghan and the couch. There are all those people in New York who have neither. But I am not grateful. I am mean and sad and spiteful and lonely.

Eventually, I pick myself up off of my couch. I determine to get dressed. Instead, I go into my room and scream at my icons. "Do something," I scream. "Make me feel better." Some part of my brain remembers that Jesus' primary task in coming to Earth was not to make me feel better, but I choose to ignore that part. "Other people have families they like and other people are in love and other people aren't this lonely," I scream.

So much for celebrating Jesus' birthday. I am more like the child who spends Mother's Day demanding to know why there is no Children's Day, not understanding that Children's Day is every other day of the year.

I pick up one of my icons. It is Rublev's Christ. Its official name is "The Savior," but I have never heard anyone call it anything other than Rublev's Christ. Andrei Rublev, a monk and iconographer, painted it in about 1420, one section of a seven-part icon for a church in Zvenigorod. It is a very simple picture, just Jesus with a massive mane and a flat beard staring out at you. Rublev's Christ is the Jesus I always talk to when I am most upset. He manages to look stern and sympathetic at the same time. "OK, Jesus," I say, "I'm in this because you came to Earth, and because you came to Earth I can somehow deal with my wretched loneliness and whatever comes along besides.

"You are supposed to be enough," I tell the icon. "That you came to Earth is supposed to be enough. Even if I never go to New England again, even if I never plan another trip with somebody, even if I never feel happy for one more minute, that you came to Earth is supposed to be enough." I glare at my icon.

"And," I say after a minute, "it is enough. It actually is. If this is all I ever have, this glimmer of knowledge that you were born in a manger, that really will sustain me.

"But," I add, "I really hope it doesn't have to sustain me." I really don't want it to be just me and the icons for all these Christmases forever.

Epiphany

Baptism

The season of Epiphany begins twelve days after Christmas. *Epiphany* comes from the Greek for "manifestation." In church we read Scripture passages that try to tell us just who Jesus is. We read, in John, about the miracles He performs. We read, in Luke, about His teachings. In the middle of Epiphany, we celebrate Christ's presentation to the Temple. But the first great clue about who Jesus is comes on the Sunday after Epiphany starts, when we celebrate His baptism. Jesus' is no ordinary baptism. After John washes Jesus with water, Luke tells us, "heaven was opened and the Holy Spirit descended on him in bodily form like a dove. And a voice came from heaven: 'You are my Son, whom I love; with you I am well pleased.'"

LOTS OF CHURCHES TAKE the celebration of Jesus' baptism as an occasion for congregants to renew their own baptismal vows. I find this hard. I remember what I pledged at my baptism and how badly I've done at keeping those pledges and I wonder if I dare make them again.

At the Clare College chapel in Cambridge, there was once a baptism of twins. I didn't know the twins, or their parents, but I went to the baptism anyway. It was a Sunday evening service, and afterward there was a special dinner, for all the baptismal guests and everyone else who had been at church. There were, waiting to be cut, four or five sheet cakes, all gooey white icing on top and orange marmalade inside. A few of us students busied ourselves at cutting the cakes, so that when the time came for dessert, there were two hundred square pieces, neatly laid out on small blue plates. It was tedious work. It was also, I thought, the most important thing I had done all month, cut cakes for those babies' baptisms. More important than any history I had studied, or any magazine articles I had written, or any prayers I had prayed. It was the drudge work of the church, and it seemed the best work in the world. Like sweeping the church, or setting out the hymnals, or making sure the sacristy held enough candles for the week's vesper services. The holy work of God's people, somehow. I told my priest, Jo, that I wanted to spend my whole life cutting cakes to celebrate babies' baptisms. I was, Jo said, an Altar Guild member in the making.

Sometimes people wonder how babies can be baptized; indeed, that very wondering is the genesis of the Baptist church. Baptists believe babies shouldn't be baptized. They say there's no scriptural precedent for it, that Jesus and John were both baptized as adults. Hannah, who's a Baptist, often says that a baby can't promise to do everything one promises in baptism. I have never found this a very persuasive argument. It strikes me as too individualistic. The very point is that no baptismal candidate, even an adult, can promise to do those things all by himself. The community is promising for you, with you, on your behalf. It is for that reason that I love to see a baby baptized. When a baby is baptized, we cannot labor under the atomizing illusion that individuals in Christ can or should go this road alone. When a baby is baptized we are struck unavoidably with the fact that this is a community covenant, a community relationship, that these are communal promises.

The other baptism I remember from Cambridge was mine. I was baptized the first March I was there, at a Sunday morning service in the antechamber of the chapel. I told Jo she had to use a lot of water, that I was descended from a long line of full-immersion Baptists, and the traditional Anglican sprinkling would not do. She made sure the water was warm, she doused me in it, and then she wrapped me in a big, striped bathrobe. "Like Joseph's coat of many colors," she said. Another Cambridge student was my godmother. She gave me the silver cross I wear around my neck. It is small and square, with slightly rounded corners.

A few days before my baptism, I met with Jo to go over the service. "Let's just read through this," she said.

Before actually baptizing me, Jo would ask a series of questions. The answers were printed out, right there in front of me, in my prayer book. Sitting in her rooms drinking tea, Jo and I practiced aloud. Jo's role was to ask questions like "Do you turn to Christ?" and I was to say, "I turn to Christ." "Do you renounce evil?" she would ask, and I would say, "I renounce evil." And so on.

We got to the third exchange, and finally I said, "This is ridiculous, I can't promise these things. Half the time I don't trust God one iota. I can't stand up there and promise that I will trust Him forever and ever. Who on earth makes these promises?"

Jo got up and went to the bookshelf. She found an American Book of Common Prayer, which is slightly different from the Church of England's prayer book. "Here, maybe this will make you feel better," she said, flipping to the baptismal service. "In the American prayer book, you don't just answer all these questions in the affirmative. You say, 'I will, with God's help.'"

I usually think the Church of England is much more together, insightful, and generally sane than the Protestant Episcopal Church of the U.S.A. But in this case, I think we Americans got it right. *I will, with God's help.*

Tu B'Shevat Muffins

When we taught Sunday school at Congregation Beth Israel, Randi and I were always desperate for activities. The chalkboard-and-paper lessons were boring. They bored the students, they bored us. So we took field trips, watched movies, and we baked. At least once a month, we sent home letters to the parents, cheerful notes that said, "Your ingredient assignment is eggs. Please bring three eggs to class next week." Or flour. Or oil. Or vanilla extract. We may not have taught our students much Hebrew, but we taught them how to cook —challah, hamentashen, carrot tzimmes, latkes, soup for the soup kitchen.

Randi and I always had an especially difficult time trying to figure out what to do with our Sunday schoolers on Tu B'Shevat. Tu B'Shevat (the name means simply the fifteenth day of the month of Shevat) is the New Year of the Trees, the trees' birthday. The holiday dates back to the time of the Talmud; it's not mentioned in the Old Testament. Its origins have to do with taxes. Every year, when the Temple stood, Jews' tithe included one-tenth of whatever fruit they grew. To determine what fruit counted for which year's tithe, there had to be a commonly agreed-upon date at which one agricultural year ended and another began. In the Mishnah, which was codified in the second century, there was a difference of opinion about whether this tree new year fell on the first of Shevat, or the fifteenth. The latter view, the view of Rabbi Hillel, was adopted. Hillel doesn't tell us why he insisted on the fifteenth, but later commentators have suggested it might have had to do with the moon. Judaism's is a lunar calendar, and the beginning of the month is always the new moon; the fifteenth would be a full moon, which, as Rabbi Arthur Waskow points out, "may have been a more practical and pleasant time for celebration than the barely glimmering new moon." And Tu B'Shevat falls six months after Tu B'Av, a minor springtime festival, a sort of Jewish Sadie Hawkins Day. Tu B'Av gives the Jews a springtime day of revelry, and Tu B'Shevat gives them a wintertime pageant, "exactly," in Waskow's words, "six months from the summery full moon of Av."

Tu B'Shevat presented special lesson-planning challenges. Fourth-graders were too young for reveling under the light of the moon, and they weren't interested in esoteric kabbalistic teachings about God as Tree. There were no good movies about Jewish trees. And Tu B'Shevat usually fell at the end of January or the beginning of February, when it was too cold for a field trip to a forest where we would plant our own baby oaks or maples. Every year Randi and I tried to be creative, and every year we fell back on old faithful: we baked Tu B'Shevat muffins.

───── ∞∞∞ ─────

WHEN I WAS IN high school and my mother had to go out of town for work, Randi came to stay with me. My mother paid her $25 a night, and left money for us to order a pizza. Sometimes I helped Randi with her Latin homework. Usually I just picked her brain about life. Had she tried cocaine? If she got pregnant, what would she do? Why hadn't she ever learned how to drive? How old was she when she first had sex? Why was she getting a Ph.D. in philosophical theology? What, exactly, *was* philosophical theology? I was always thrilled when my mother went out of town, because it meant I got Randi, undivided, for a whole evening. She had lived in New York, and was in her late twenties, and was impossibly cool.

A few months after I started college, Randi finished with her course work at the University of Virginia. Free to write her dissertation anywhere, Randi moved back to Manhattan. (Now that I'm trying to write a dissertation here myself, I often think that choice proves her insanity; why anyone who had other options would choose to dissertate in the world's most expensive, distracting city is beyond me— yet here I am.)

There were four years that Randi and I both lived in New York, before she moved to Ohio and I departed for England. During those years, a funny thing happened. I grew up a little bit.

By the time Randi was settled into her small Greenwich Village apartment, I was full in the swing of Orthodoxy, and Randi, who had grown up in Reform and Conservative synagogues and schools, found herself curious about how this Orthodox life worked, curious about the rabbis, curious about the holidays, curious about where one met God amidst all the halacha. Sometimes I would go to her apartment, carrying a Bible and a linear translation of Rashi, the eleventh-century rabbi whose commentary on the *chumash*, the Five Books of Moses, is the first you learn when you begin to read Torah as a Jew. Randi and I would make tea and study the weekly Torah portion, and one day, sitting on her couch, Randi looked up at me and said, with no more fanfare than if she were noting the rain, "You have become an equal dialogue partner for me." Meaning, I think, that we could talk to each other on terms approaching parity, on terms approaching exchange and encounter; it wasn't just me nagging her with questions about drug use.

I don't have childhood friends, not the kind of friends who were born two days after you and then you were in the same play group and you went to school together and now that you're forty-five you vacation together every year and you know each other better than chemists know the periodic table. Randi is the oldest friend I've got.

There are a few people out there with whom you fit just so, and, amazingly, you keep fitting just so even after you have growth spurts or lose weight or stop wearing high heels. You keep fitting after you have children or change religions or stop dyeing your hair or quit your job at Goldman Sachs and take up farming. Somehow, God is gracious enough to give us a few of those people, people you can stretch into, people who don't go away, and whom you wouldn't want to go away, even if they offered to.

THE RECIPE CHANGED a little each year, but the goal was to cram as many nuts and fruits into the muffins as possible. Into the usual mix of flour and baking soda and honey went yellow raisins and brown raisins, chopped walnuts, almonds, orange zest, grated carrots, the occasional fig or date or dried apricot or cherry, and whatever other fruit or nut we had on hand. "Like fruit cake," my mother said one year.

Baking these muffins with our fourth-graders was always a disaster. Every year, we forgot that assembling the muffins—chopping the walnuts and stirring the batter—took about half an hour. That left us with forty-five minutes to kill, while the kids waited for the muffins to bake and we waited for their parents to come take them off our hands. So every year we had to improvise a Tu B'Shevat lesson.

"Outside," Randi commanded one year. It was January 23. It was about thirty-five degrees out. "We're going to go notice the trees!" said Randi. "While the muffins bake. We will notice the trees."

So we bundled up our charges, helping with zippers and gloves, it-self a process that filled fifteen minutes. Then we walked the short block to Lee Park, so named because there is a giant statue of Robert E. Lee on his trusty horse Traveller, and tried to interest the children in the trees, which, because it was January 23, had no leaves.

"Trees," Randi began, "are extremely important. Think of every-thing trees do for us."

"Trees convert carbon dioxide into oxygen," I said.

"They give us apples and...carob," said Randi. Randi looked at me. I looked back. What else, exactly, did trees do?

"Topsoil," I said. "Trees often prevent topsoil from eroding away."

"We will now sing a song about trees," said Randi. *"Tu B'Shevat He-giah, chag ha-ilanot."* "Tu B'Shevat is here, the holiday of the trees." If anyone has ever really sung lustily, it was Randi in Lee Park. *"Hashkedia porachat ve-shemesh paz zorachat,"* she sang. *"Tziporim merosh kol gag, mevasrot et bo hachag."*

"Here is what the song means," Randi said. "Tell them, Lauren."

I glared at her. "The song means: 'The almond tree is growing. The sun shines'."

By now, the children had wandered off. They began to climb Trav-eller. "We need to reassert our authority," Randi whispered.

"Randi," I said, "we have no authority. I'm fifteen and you are four-foot-eleven."

"Who knows why we baked those muffins with all the fruit in them?" Randi asked the three students still assembled within ear shot.

"Because," our one teacher's pet said sweetly, "Tu B'Shevat is here, the holiday of the trees."

TOMORROW IS TU B'SHEVAT. In the morning, I will stand in my kitchen amid heaps and piles of nuts and dates and raisins, and I will bake the muffins. While they cool, I will call Randi and sing to her about almond blossoms and shining suns. Then I will take the muffins to church. I will set them out after the service, next to the doughnuts and cookies and bagels and juice that make up our coffee hour. And I will try to notice the trees.

Conversion Stories

I am spending the day in New Haven, where I sometimes go when New York City is too gritty and depressing to bear. I go to New Haven and drink coffee and visit friends and climb up on red East Rock. This afternoon I meet Beth, my college roommate, the one who saw Elijah the Prophet in my Jesus dream. I meet her today because I owe her an apology. The last time we saw each other was graduation. I tell her today that I owe her this apology, that I didn't know how to go about being her friend, these first Christian years; I ignored her emails; I skipped her wedding; I didn't call when I was in Connecticut. She forgives me. I knew she would. I imagine she already had, a long time ago.

We meet and walk, and, because it is crisp and perfect out, we sit on a bench in front of some large New Haven church and ten minutes later we are talking about *tzniut,* modesty, what the rabbinic texts say, and how to read them, and I remember this is what drew me to Judaism, in the first place, these words, turning them over like marbles in my hand, living inside these texts like clothes. Sometimes they are wool and they scratch and you want to take them off and maybe you do but you never stay naked for long.

THERE ARE LOTS OF WAYS to tell this story. I can tell a perfect Christian salvation story, about God's hand and foreordainedness and teleology. In that story, the telos, the end to which everything has always been pointing, is Jesus, is the church, is the Cross. That story tells of Jesus' dogged pursuit of me, of God's leading me through Judaism to Him, of everything matching and meeting and lining up just so. I can say, *I had this dream about some mermaids, and it changed everything,* and that would be true.

But there is another version of the story, one that is full of almosts and contingencies. Stop this story at any point and things look different. This story is harder to tell because it drips with more betrayal. It indicts. It reads more like a failure than a triumph. It is not the story of all the things that drew me to Christianity during my college years and before; it's the story of all the things that pushed me away from Judaism. It's the story I usually dismiss with a quick phrase: "And then, as I was growing increasingly disaffected from Orthodox Judaism . . ." This other story is harder, the truth of it and the telling of it, but it is also true.

By the time I moved to England, I could make a list of the things I couldn't stand about Orthodoxy. I didn't have enough perspective to know, then, that I had lived only a particular slice of Orthodoxy, an especially insular, strange, New York slice; I didn't know to qualify my list that way, that maybe life would have been different in New Haven or Harvard Square or Mea Sharim or a Williamsburg corner of Brooklyn. I knew only that I had lived as an Orthodox Jew and I had this list of things I could not stand, could not stand for one more minute, would have fallen right down under the weight of them if I'd had to try. The list was a list of half-truths, of exaggerations and imprecisions, but it was not a list of dreams I had made up out of whole cloth.

. . .

IF I WERE A DIFFERENT PERSON, I could tell a different, simpler story of dissatisfaction with Orthodoxy, a familiar story, one about feminism. I could say that I hadn't realized, dreaming about the Orthodox life from my high school perch in Charlottesville, what it would feel like not to be counted in the quorum for public worship; what it would feel like to sit and study texts that say (as Maimonides does in his Mishnah Torah): "A wife who refuses to perform any kind of work she is obligated to do may be compelled to perform it, even by scourging her with a rod"; and what it would feel like to know that I wasn't obligated to say all the prayers men had to say because the rabbis assumed I would be too strapped down at home caring for babies to make it to shul on time.

But that story wouldn't be true. Orthodox Judaism, at least in some corners, is changing its answers to feminist questions. Incrementally, and not in words that will satisfy all comers, but there is change, and, if anything, to be part of that change, to shape it and spin it, would have been exciting. I listen to Beth talk about *tzniut,* about how to teach high school girls about the laws of modesty, how she teaches them about skirts and sleeve-lengths without teaching them to despise their bodies or think they need to be shy and retiring and always stay indoors, and I catch the excitement, both in her voice and in the work she has before her, and it seems so much realer, so much more important and careful and honest than the endless debates in the church about God-language and headship. I am envious, faintly, and dream, briefly, about what it would have been like to spend my life being part of Judaism's work.

During college, those questions, feminist questions about Orthodox Judaism, didn't interest me. Feminism occupied a good chunk of my bookshelf; I read Catherine MacKinnon and Simone de Beauvoir and Luce Irigary and Charlotte Perkins Gillman. But the questions didn't translate. Even though I'd read all those issues of *Lilith* in high school, I didn't mind not being able to chant from the Torah in front of the congregation. I didn't mind that neither I, nor my brilliant, devoted women friends, could become rabbis. Maybe those are things I would have come to notice, to chafe and strain against, but the plain truth is, I didn't stick around long enough to find out.

So, anyway, when I tell the story of leaving Judaism, I can't begin with the small space for women.

The story begins instead with a lacrosse-playing, Prada-clad college classmate of mine named Sarah. Sarah was a biology major from New Jersey. She had long, curly black hair and a wonderful, toothy grin. We were at a party one night, a party where I met a beautiful older man, a man who had moved from New York to Israel as a teenager and served in the army and was just returning, and was full of desperate, drunken, profound stories about violence and rape and suffering. I was standing with the men, over by the window, and Sarah leaned over to a friend and, just loud enough, said that I had only converted because I wanted to marry a Jew.

There were lots of Sarahs, lots of petty Orthodox girls who snubbed me, the convert, never mind all the rules the rabbis piled up forbidding Jews to remind converts of their background. Those small snide remarks, which I should have been able to overlook, those, I think, are where this story begins.

Or possibly it begins with Hank Hirschfield. This was just weeks after the *mikvah*. He was the older brother of a friend of mine, and we met twice, three times, at a bar near Columbia called The Abbey, and he introduced me to his favorite beer, a sweet-tasting red brewed by Belgian Trappist monks. We talked, at that bar, about Torah and God and Tolstoy and the Rolling Stones, and then one night he turned up at my dorm and said really he couldn't do this, date me he meant. "Because of your conversion," he said. "Because, you see, I want my parents to dance with my in-laws at my wedding, I want my bride's family and my family to have giant holiday celebrations together, giant shared family Passover feasts and Purim *chagigahs*. So I could never marry a convert." I wept that night, cried myself to sleep for the first time ever, and when I woke up, I found that Beth had filled my wall with homemade, hand-lettered signs: *Lauren is a Jewess,* they said, *Lauren the Jew,* to remind me that I really was Jewish, pay no attention to what Hank Hirschfield said, or how he acted, or how I felt.

Then, of course, there is my college boyfriend's mother. As a hostess, a cook, a decorator, Dov's mother could put Martha Stewart to shame. At Purim, she baked her own *hamentashen,* the three-cornered pastries that recall Haman's three-cornered hat, from scratch, filled with lemon preserves she boiled down from lemons she plucked from a lemon tree in her own garden. (The only consolation I could ever find was that they hired a gardener — she hadn't actually *planted* the lemon tree herself.) When I spent time at Dov's parents' house in Westchester, she was cordial and kind and fixed the guest room up, setting out special lotions and soaps in a sandalwood scent she knew I favored. But she never liked me, and she made that clear to Dov, who made it clear to me. She worried because I was not familiar. I was not a proper Orthodox girl from Long Island who had been to the right Jewish summer camps and the right Jewish schools. I was some outlander from a state far away in the South, and my parents were divorced, and, worst of all, I was not a virgin, a detail Dov chose to divulge to her in what I originally thought was a curious lapse of judgment but later understood was an intentional barb, a strangely passive way to rebel against his mother, whom he adored, but who, I'm sure, suffocated him with her hugs and her *hamentashen*. When I visited, I often talked to her about recipes, and Dov eventually said she felt I was talking down to her and it was one of the few times I exploded at him. "What does she want?" I snapped. "She's a housewife and a superb cook. Am I supposed to talk to her about Hegel's theory of civil society?" Then, one day, she came out and said it plainly, she made explicit what we already knew. She told Dov that she didn't like me because I was a convert; I was pretty enough, and polite enough, but I was not what she wanted for her son.

The last time I saw her was a fine fall day, the day of Dov's going-away party. He had graduated from Harvard and was on to Oxford, to study politics for two years before heading to law school. He was tossing a Frisbee in the yard with his younger brother and some much younger cousins, and his mother and I stood on the porch, hands shading our eyes against the brightness, our summer dresses flapping in the breeze. "You know, I sometimes wish I hadn't married so young. I was so young when I married Alan," Dov's mother said. "I hadn't had time to develop into who I might have been. I never went to graduate school." I heard this for what it was, not a regret about her shiny Westchester life, but a warning about her son, that I shouldn't try to trap him now that he had his college degree in hand, now that he was off to England, now that he was both triumphant and poised for triumph.

I hear rumors that Dov is now dating a non-Jewish girl with some impossibly non-Jewish name like Maria. When this rumor first landed on my lap, I just laughed. I can't tell whom, exactly, I feel sorry for: Maria, Dov, or his mother in suburban New York.

To TELL THIS STORY, I would also have to talk about the crass materialism that snaked its way around New York Orthodoxy and the anti-intellectualism of the community. My five closest friends in college were the most intellectually capacious people on earth, but many of the other Orthodox Jews at Columbia were the worst breed of intellectually insular, mastering just enough knowledge to scatter their dinner party conversations with references to Freud or Kant, never mastering any more than that. I would have to talk about those things to tell the story of my leaving Judaism.

WHEN I MOVED TO ENGLAND, I flew there on an airplane, but I often imagine that I sailed there on a ship. I think that I associate England with ships because of all the pictures we were inundated with of Bill Clinton and Robert Reich on that boat, heading off to their Rhodes scholarships. Somehow I've learned from those pictures that everyone who goes to England after college gets there on a boat.

My imagination is wrong. I flew to England, as did Dov, and everyone else I know who did their time at Oxford or Cambridge. Still, when I think about moving to England, I imagine setting sail, and when I set sail for Cambridge, for Christendom, I expected Christianity to be different from Orthodox Judaism: I expected that what I disliked about Orthodox Judaism was somehow confined to Orthodox Judaism, not endemic to religious life, or a side effect of consumer capitalism, or just part of human nature.

I expected that, in Christendom, I would find an endless supply of, well, people just like me: devoted and hard-working intellectuals nobly spurning lucrative careers in law and medicine to hunch over desks in unheated, cramped garrets, furthering the pursuit of human knowledge and thinking rigorously about everything all the time. I was, of course, disappointed, in the church and in myself; Christians are just as anti-intellectual and materialistic as Orthodox Jews, and I'm no nobler than the rest.

Even once I figured that out, that the religious community I was entering was not going to be more or less to my liking than the one I was leaving, I still held on to the illusion that my relationship with God could be separate from the body of people I prayed with. That it could be separate from the community. That it is a vertical line, a silver puppeteer's string, keeping my head up straight and connecting me, straight up through the heavens, with God Himself. What draws me to a religion is the beliefs, the theologies, the books, the incantations, the recipes to get to God, and I like to imagine that they work in the abstract, that they are enough, that they exist, somewhere, pure and distinct from the people who enact them.

I learned, praying with the Orthodox Jews at Columbia, that I was wrong. I learned that Torah truths are shaped, for good and ill, by the people who live Torah with you. But when I entered the church, I entered under the same illusion, that the people next to me in the pews didn't matter, that it was new theologies and new incantations and a new God and I was going to climb up to Him on a new ladder, shimmy up a new rope, I would go out to the desert like Simon Stylite and stand on a pole and reach up to God alone.

I had imbibed centuries of stereotypes about Judaism being a religion about community, and Christianity, by implication, being a religion about God, about the individual believer sweating it out in solitude, like Jesus for forty days in the wilderness tempted by the devil. But when I stepped into Christianity, I entered a religion premised on community no less than the religion I was leaving. Judaism speaks straightforwardly about community. "When the community is suffering, one may not say, 'I will go to my house, eat and drink, and I will be fine,'" the Talmud tells us. "Do not separate from the community," Rabbi Hillel says elsewhere.

Christianity reaches for metaphor. The church, the community of faithful, is the very Body of God.

———— ❧ ————

EXPLAINING WHY I LEFT Judaism, then, also requires telling about me, about all my failures as a Jew.

To return to Pastor Mike's marriage analogy, or divorce analogy;

when I slid into that *mikvah* I was entering a marriage and to leave it would be to divorce.

If it was a marriage, me to Orthodox Judaism, I failed long before I met up with Jesus. I failed from the beginning. You could say I became a Christian because Judaism had stopped working for me, but the truth is that I had not done very much to make Judaism work.

For example, shul. Count all the many mornings I skipped synagogue so that I could sleep in.

Or consider Shabbat, the too-frequent shabbatot on which I managed to violate the letter of the law— didn't write, didn't underline, didn't shred or tear or kindle— but stayed home studying rather than *remembering the Sabbath and keeping it holy.*

Or take learning. Out in the real world, *learning* means to be taught something, as in *I am going to vocational school to learn how to fix cars* or *I am taking this translation course in order to learn French.* But among Jews, *learn* rarely means "be taught"; it rather means "to study," and it rarely has a direct object. It doesn't need one. We all know the direct object is *Torah.* You go sit in the *beit midrash,* the house of study, in order to learn. You go to yeshiva in Israel to learn for a year. In college, Beth ran a program called Wednesday Night Learning, where upward of three hundred Jews crowded into the top floor of Earl Hall, broke into pairs, and learned: learned *Shemirat Shabbat,* or *Masechet Brachot,* or some other slice of sacred text.

When people want the quick answer to "Why did you become a Christian, what attracted you to Christianity?" I tell them, "The Incarnation." When they want the quick answer to "Why did you become an Orthodox Jew?" I tell them, "Learning, text study." The more time I spent soaking up Judaism in my Charlottesville synagogue, the more I became convinced that the heart of Judaism, the most essentially Jewish thing, was a set of texts, and a particular, rabbinic, way of reading them— a canon and a hermeneutic, if you like. And I became convinced that the people who were reading those texts, and reading them the right way, were Orthodox Jews.

You would think, then, that I might have eaten up all the possible Jewish learning available at Columbia, eaten hungrily, as soon as I arrived. You would think I might have taken a Jewish Studies class, maybe fulfilled my language requirement with Hebrew rather than German, you'd think I might have taken a Tuesday night Talmud class at the Drisha Institute, or invested in an Aramaic dictionary. You'd think I would do the work and make that learning my own. But you would be wrong.

Not that I completely avoided the Columbia *Beit Midrash,* or the Drisha Institute. I did take one class, once a week for eight weeks or so, at Drisha, and Beth and I made a half-hearted attempt to meet every morning before services to study a text about *hilchot Shabbat,* the Sabbath laws. I did go faithfully to Beth's Wednesday Night Learning and studied, with a woman who is now a lawyer and a rabbi's wife and a mother of two, the Talmudic tractate that deals with Passover. But that's about it. I never really worked my Hebrew into shape. I managed to fulfill college requirements for religion majors without taking a single class about Judaism.

Maybe I thought the ethos was enough, that just being around the learning was as good as learning itself. Maybe I was intimidated by how much everyone else, fresh from a year in Israel studying at a yeshiva, knew about how to enter into those strange books written in strange letters, not even laid out on the page in a familiar, linear way. Maybe I was distracted by all the other subjects there were to study—American history and physics and Hobbes and Locke and Rousseau. Maybe I was just lazy. Probably all four, and then some. It was not a very good way to start a marriage.

· · ·

Sometimes divorce is the only thing to do. Sometimes it is the more loving thing to do. Sometimes, you have to do it. But before you divorce, you try every imaginable avenue to stay married. You quit your affair. You find a good marriage counselor. You tell your husband everything you should have told him three years ago, and you listen, stunned but listening, when he tells you the same, and then you get down on your knees and you ask the Lord to help you forgive your husband, and you remind all your friends who witnessed your wedding that they witnessed it and are supposed to hold you to the promises you made, and you do anything else you can think of to save your marriage.

To further the analogy: I had married Judaism and then I had an affair with a foreign God, another religion, I took another lover. And I realized I was in love with that other lover, and I wrung my hands for a while. I struggled through my own inner turmoil and angst and then I handed my shocked husband divorce papers, threw my stuff into some empty cardboard boxes, and moved out, setting up house with my new love before an even passably decent interval elapsed.

I did not do what I should have done. I never once sat my husband down and told him the cold, hard truth, that I had fallen in love with someone else but I wanted to try to make this marriage work and what, exactly, were we going to do about it? Not one conversation. I never said a word to Rabbi M. about Jesus. Nothing to Beth, no discussions at all. I never said, *I made that mikvah pledge and I am failing and I need you to help me.*

The marriage analogy cuts both ways. My husband was not really a hapless dope. Those divorce papers were not the first hint of my affair. There were the unexplained absences at dinnertime, the strange men calling on the phone, the lipstick stains on collars and the otherwise inexplicable cycles of ecstasy and depression: glowingly happy when I'd seen my paramour, morose to end the world when I hadn't.

I doubt Beth or Tova or my rabbi suspected I was out on the town with Jesus, but they knew, all of them, that I was around less and less. That I was going to shul less frequently, that I was spending Friday nights lingering over Shabbat dinner less often, that I was occasionally seen running around the city in a sleeveless dress, filmy blue India cotton, no sleeves. I doubt any of them thought I was filling my shul time with church, but they knew I was filling it with something, and none of them ever said anything. None of them ever said, *Hey, just checking up on you. Is something up? Is something the matter?* Or, harsher, *Lauren, you know, shul. You really need to be there.* I was part of their religious body; saying those things was their job.

So NOW I TELL ALL this to Beth, as we sit in the winter sunlight on our bench in New Haven. The words spill out fast with anger. I want to have been a different person back then, less cowardly, less scared. I want to have sat her down in our small New York dorm room and told her that all my Judaism was falling out of me, like intestines from a war wound, that I couldn't keep the promises I'd made.

But I want her to have been different, too. I want her to have tried to hold me to those promises. Instead, she stood pluralistically by and let me do what I wanted, because that is what college is about; above all, that is what college was about for Beth, who spent her Columbia years learning about cosmopolitanism and learning not to be judgmental, and sitting here on a bench in New Haven she sees that I want her to have been different, to have said something, to have asked me why I wasn't doing what I said I would do. I want her to have done the rude, invasive thing, the hard thing. I want her to have read my own words back to me and to have stood there in the silence till I somehow had to respond.

Taxonomy

I am sitting on the ninth floor of the Butler Library stacks, il-
legally eating a scone whose crumbs will probably sustain a generation
of silverfish, and reading a book about chocolate consumption in
Colonial New England. I am in the middle of a detailed discussion of
chocolate breakfast foods when I overhear two of my classmates,
Y. and Z., chatting away. As graduate students are wont to do, they are
gossiping about other graduate students, and I, of course, eavesdrop.

They are talking about the members of our nineteenth-century
history seminar. "I thought I was going to throttle him," says Y., and
it does not take too long for me to figure out that they are talking
about R., an overbearing Harvard grad who plans to write a dissertation about the history of the polka dot. In the current seminar, he is
writing about the polka dot during the era of the American Civil War.
According to R., the Civil War transformed the place of the polka
dot. His thesis, according to a rough draft he has recently circulated,
is that "the Civil War liberated not only slaves, but fashion." At the
start of the war, elegant ladies and foppish gents favored solids (and
the occasional stripe). By the war's end, polka dots were all the rage.
As R. sees it, this new dot fettish had something to do with the carnage

of war. Amid all the death, people wanted to affirm life, as symbolized by circles, or, *mutatis mutandis,* polka dots.

"What gets me most," Y. is saying to Z., "is that he simply has no fashion sense. If you are going to write about the polka dot, you should make an effort to look sort of snazzy."

After analyzing R.'s collection of fraying wool sweaters, Y. moves on to F., who is writing about a more conventional subject, the fiscal policy of DeWitt Clinton, an early New York governor best remembered for building the Erie Canal. I am beginning to fidget when Y. finally comes around to the subject I've been anticipating: me.

"You're pretty good friends with that Lauren girl," Y. says to Z. (This is true, although Z. and I are about as different as Felix and Oscar. Z. is leggy and elegant, always turning heads with the sexy gap between her two front teeth and her glossy black hair (hair that is black the way the blackbirds in the pie are black, hair that really demands the word *tresses*), whereas I only turn heads if I sneeze loudly, and my hair is so bland it doesn't even merit an adjective; she lives in a glam East Side apartment with her investment-banking husband, fifteen-month-old son, and French au pair, while I subsist in my grad school garret and wonder if I am responsible enough to adopt a cat; she studies New Deal elites and I study Colonial Anglicans; and she's about as interested in religion as I am in the finer points of antilock brake systems. Nonetheless, she is my closest friend at Columbia, and I will have to confess to her later on that I eavesdropped on her conversation with Y.) As Y. was saying, "You're pretty good friends with that Lauren girl. Is she some sort of fundamentalist Bible-thumper?"

I listen to Z. maneuver her way through. "Why do you ask?" asks Z.

"Well, there's her paper topic." Fair enough. I am writing a paper about the history of the Eucharist in nineteenth-century America. "And then, you know, she always seems to be quoting the Book of Romans."

"I think *Bible-thumper* is something of a derisive term," says Z., and "She is quite religious, though. I think she calls herself an evangelical. I don't think I've ever heard her call herself a Bible-thumper. Or a fundamentalist." Then Z. changes the subject back to the polka dot boy, and she and Y. walk away, leaving me to munch my scone and look around for a Bible to thump.

Z. WAS RIGHT. I don't call myself a fundamentalist.

David Brooks wrote a recent article in *The Atlantic* about the differences between red America (Republican, meatloaf-eating, religious, heartland) and blue America (Democratic, cappuccino-sipping, hyper-educated, urban). The folks in red America don't know that you never drink cappuccino after noon; many of them don't even know what cappuccino is. Many of us in blue America, confessed Brooks, are equally ignorant of red America's hallmarks. Blue Americans don't know what's said on Christian talk radio, or "what happens in megachurches on Wednesday evenings." Worse still, many in blue America "couldn't tell you the difference between a fundamentalist and an evangelical."

So, blue America, listen up. Here's the skinny.

In 1957, Billy Graham held a revival in New York City. The revival meeting, of course, was designed to bring unbelievers to Christ, and Graham was concerned about what would happen to those new Christians after the revivalists left town. He wanted to make sure the local churches were prepared to welcome and support the converts, so, as Graham and his people planned the revival, they met with local Christian leaders, helping prepare New York churches to receive what Graham hoped would be a large influx of new Christians. Graham was a Baptist, solidly evangelical, educated at the Florida Bible Institute and Wheaton College. He was ordained a Southern Baptist preacher, and as a young man he preached the gospel as a member of

Youth for Christ. In 1952, he began to reach hundreds of thousands of readers with his evangelistic newspaper column "My Answer," and, the year before his New York crusade, he founded *Christianity Today,* the country's leading evangelical magazine. His Christian credentials were impeccable.

Stilll, Graham's work with the local churches in New York sparked a huge controversy: for a while Graham met with fellow evangelical clergymen, he also worked with Catholics, liberalish Presbyterians, and others outside of the orthodox Protestant fold. Indeed, the revival was sponsored by the Protestant Council of the City of New York, an organization that represented 94 percent of New York's churches and was affiliated with the mainline National Council of Churches. In today's pluralist climate, such overtures may not sound terribly edgy, but at the time they were radical. Graham appeared to be granting some sort of imprimatur to Christians whose theology was more liberal than his. Bob Jones, John R. Rice (well-known for his 1941 book *Bobbed Hair, Bossy Wives, and Women Preachers*), and other powerful conservative Christians were outraged, and they denounced the rising young evangelist. Graham, however, stood his ground, insisting that "the fighting, feuding and controversies among God's people . . . is a very poor example," that "God has people in all his churches," and that "the one badge of Christian discipleship is not orthodoxy, but love." Graham's mild ecumenism and the brouhaha it inspired dramatized the split that is still pronounced between evangelicals, like Graham, and fundamentalists, like Jones.

Blue America has reason to be perplexed about the differences between evangelicals and fundamentalists. The differences, which are easier to intuit than to document, have to do with sensibility. Fundamentalists, like those who tangled with Graham, tend more toward separation from the rest of American culture. They tend to be more suspicious of interfaith and cross-denominational conversations.

Fundamentalist parents are likely to be more restrictive when it comes to what TV shows and rap songs their kids can be exposed to. There's the matter of science. Not all fundamentalists read the first chapter of Genesis as a textbook scientific account of the planet's origins, but almost all people who do read Genesis that way are fundamentalists. And there's gender. Fundies are more likely to include "obey" in women's wedding vows (though evangelicals aren't usually radical feminists, either).

One of my professors, who spends most of his scholarly time reading and writing about American Protestantism, has put it this way, only half in jest: a fundamentalist is an evangelical who is angry about something.

So I CALL MYSELF an evangelical rather than a fundamentalist because I don't think my temperament and my outlook is compatible with fundamentalists' general suspicion of, even hostility toward, the larger culture. (Actually, a similar dichotomy holds for my Orthodox days. I was part of the so-called modern Orthodox community, which, in contrast to the black-hatters of Williamsburg and Mea Sharim, tries to participate in the secular world without sacrificing halachic observance or Jewish communal life. The motto of Yeshiva University, the modern Orthodox college in New York, makes the point—"Torah u'Maddah," literally "Torah and science," but, more broadly, the idea that Jewish learning and ostensibly secular studies can be integrated. The motto would work well for evangelicals, too.)

Still, even as I recognize certain differences between evangelicals and fundamentalists, I acknowledge that our similarities may be greater than our differences. Theologically, evangelicals and fundamentalists have a lot in common. Both groups affirm the authority of Scripture (though fundamentalists are more inclined toward a literal interpretation of Scripture, and a doctrine called biblical inerrancy—the idea that the Bible, in its original autographs, is perfect and immaculate and free from error—is more central to fundamentalist identity). The person of Jesus sits at the center of both evangelicals' and fundamentalists' faiths. Evangelicals and fundamentalists understand that they are sinful and that they have been saved from their sin only through Jesus' blood on the Cross, and it means that they prize, in the parlance of both evangelicals and fundamentalists, *a personal relationship with Jesus.* Jesus is not remote and inaccessible, but profoundly involved with the day-to-day lives of His faithful. My Baptist grandmother's favorite hymn makes the point simply:

And He walks with me, and He talks with me
And He tells me I am His own.

Evangelicals and fundamentalists are Christians who are interested in walking and talking with their God, about everything from world peace to car insurance.

Sometimes I even feel equivocal about claiming the evangelical label. For, theologically, I am right in line with the evangelical mainstream, but what people want to know when they ask me whether or not I'm an evangelical is rarely theology. What they want to know is whether I vote for Pat Robertson, listen to Amy Grant, and believe the Earth is only five thousand years old. In fact, I've never voted for Pat Roberston, I prefer Mary Chapin Carpenter, and I think Darwin might have been onto something.

So, when one of my gin-swilling, scratchy-jazz-listening Columbia comrades asks me the e-question (a question people put to me with alarming frequency), my impulse is to temporize, to hem and haw, to split hairs and explain that my theological orientation is certainly evangelical, but culturally, intellectually, and politically, I am much more sophisticated than his stereotype of evangelism. I'm too insecure and worried about how I'm being perceived to risk correcting my interlocutor's presuppositions—by pointing out, for example, that 38 percent of Democrats in America are born-again Christians, never mind suggesting that not all Republicans or home-schoolers are numskulls. I simply want to correct his impressions of me, *No, no, I'm not one of them. I'm one of you. I believe that Jesus Christ is Lord, but I also wear fishnet stockings and drink single malt Scotch.*

I AM JUST AS LIKELY as the next person to consign people to tidy categories, and, without much evidence, I assume that my classmate Y. is among what nineteenth-century theologian Friedrich Schleiermacher called the cultured despisers of religion. I suspect that when Y. asked Z. about my Bible-thumping, he may have been after a little theology—he may have wanted to know if I actually believed the Bible was true—but he was primarily interested in sociology. Y. wanted to know if I was one of those people—you know, those tacky, benighted, intolerant people who shun PG-13 movies and own a few polyester pantsuits.

When I look around church on Sunday, I find myself wishing that Y. would ask me himself—*Hey, Lauren, are you one of them? A Bible-thumper?* If he would ask me directly, all my fine parsing would go out the window, and I would simply say *Yes,* even though Y. would probably, on the basis of that answer, assume that I think the public schools are godless and I have bad taste in art. I would answer Y. in the affirmative because I look around All Angels' at a motley crew of Christians, some of whom buy clothes at Wal-Mart and some of whom wear Vera Wang, and I know that these people are my people, polyester, Amy Grant, and all.

Family Values

At the end of the twelfth chapter of Luke sits a hard verse, words of Jesus that should trouble those Christians who unthinkingly invoke that catch-phrase "family values," and words that trouble me. "They will be divided, father against son and son against father." Sometimes I think this verse is very true.

I told my father about my conversion to Christianity only in tiny drips and drops. The week before I moved to England I spent a few days with him, and I said that I thought I might attend church occasionally when I got to Cambridge. This was, at best, a half-truth. I knew I would attend church, I knew I would be baptized, I knew I would do and become Christian things, but the most I could tell my father was that I might attend Evensong every now and again.

A few days after arriving in Cambridge, I received a letter, long and voluble, from my father. He is not much of a letter writer. The only other father-daughter letter I could recall was one he had sent my sister during her freshman year of college. She was almost eighteen, almost old enough to vote, and she was thinking of registering as a Republican. Out came my father's pen and writing tablet, and he wrote her a long, long letter explaining why she should sign up with the Democrats. I was ten, and he sent me a copy of his Democratic epistle, since eventually I would have to make a choice about political parties, too. I don't have that letter anymore, and all I remember of it is a line about bootstraps: that a major difference between Democrats and Republicans was how they treated the poor; Republicans wanted people to pull themselves up by their own bootstraps, but Democrats recognized that sometimes poor people couldn't afford any bootstraps on which to pull.

When I was twenty, this second letter came, also, in a way, about joining parties, also about shaping our lives along lines that look a little something like our father's life. The letter asked me, simply, not to become a Christian. There was a lot this letter didn't say, not explicitly. It didn't explain why, precisely, passing on Judaism was so important to a man who himself spent only a few days a year at shul, who could barely read Hebrew, who had married two Christian women. It didn't say that Judaism had to do with family, that it had to do with the first night of Passover spent around a table all together, our family. It didn't say that Judaism, even though my expression of Judaism was wildly different from his, was something we shared, the way he and my sister share a love of college basketball. It didn't say that my converting read like a rejection of him. Nor did the letter ask after my whys and wherefores. What the letter said was *please don't do this, your doing this will hurt me.*

I put the letter away, stuck it in the dust jacket of Robert Penn Warren's *Brother to Dragons* where I thought it would be safe and findable. But it has gone missing. When I went back to reread it, my father's letter was not there.

The letter made me sad, but it did not prevent my attending church; it only prevented me from talking about churchgoing with my father. I didn't tell him that I had been baptized until six months after the fact, and when I did, he asked me not to talk to him about it; that he could accept it, he wouldn't disown me or count me for dead, but that he didn't want to, or couldn't, hear the details.

So we don't talk much about church or God or prayer. And when we talk about other things, a creeping superficiality marks our conversations. I tell him about the papers I am writing for school, but I don't speak about *vocation*. I tell him about decisions I make, but I never speak about *prayerfully discerning God's will for my life*. I tell him about buying a new desk. I do not tell him about all the ways I am slowly turning into the person God wants me to become.

Lil, my high school physics teacher, the first Christian to whom I told my mermaid dream, Lil became a Christian ten years into her marriage. Her husband was worried and upset, scared that she would turn into some person he couldn't know or understand, scared that she would become a caricature, a small-minded, fire-breathing, Scripture-spouting crazy person. A few years after her conversion, he looked up at her and said, "You know, hon, you really haven't changed all that much." It was true in some ways. Lil still taught physics, still liked ballet and football games, still made a mean quiche crust. But her husband's comment also spoke volumes about their marriage, which, while solid, had turned somewhat surface-skating. Lil's husband could not see that, though she still baked quiche, what was most basic to her—why she got up in the morning, how she saw the world, what she did with her sadness—was all different, utterly.

Sometimes I imagine that my father sees conversion the way Lil's husband does. I imagine that he looks at me, several years into Christianity, and sees that I have not really changed that much. I am still a pointy-headed academic. I still work hard. I'm still boy-crazy and I still spend too much money on long-distance phone calls. I still would rather read than watch TV, go to the theater, or travel. I still keep an apartment that always looks like a hurricane has just hit, and I still hate to exercise. I imagine he must see all those similarities, and be comforted that he has not, really, lost his daughter to Christ. And I feel sad, because that very comfort is the proof of just how much has been lost.

Lowell House

Lowell House, the second oldest of the Harvard colleges, was built in 1930. It was named for the Lowell family, an old Massachusetts clan with a long line of Harvardians. John Lowell graduated from the college in 1721, and there were many other famous Lowells, like Amy Lowell, and James Russell Lowell, the poets, and Percival Lowell, the astronomer who founded Arizona's Lowell Observatory and wrote three turn-of-the-century studies of Mars. Lowell House is famous for its annual winter waltz; its Russian Bells that ring on Sundays at one; its annual performance, in the spring, of the 1812 Overture.

I am here on a magazine assignment, to interview the master of Lowell House, who has just written a new book about Buddhists and Hindus and Muslims in America. We meet in the master's residence, which is attached to the Lowell House dining hall. The residence is a striking mansionette, 50 Holyoke Street, reputed to have the widest door in Cambridge. The master, a scholar of Indian religions, has moved the portraits of the Lowells, which once hung in the entrance hall, to a blue drawing room. She has replaced them with elaborate, dark *pichhavais*, devotional hangings from the temples of Krishna in Rajasthan.

She has emailed me directions, but I know how to get there. Dov, the Orthodox Harvard undergrad I loved all through college, lived at Lowell House, and I spent more nights there than I can number. It shocks me to realize that he must be coming up on his five-year reunion, that it has been five years since he graduated, and I have not been to Cambridge, Massachusetts, since.

Standing here in the foyer of Lowell House, I suddenly miss him. I miss his broad, genuine grin, and the sharpness of his insights, and the way he swept me up into his arms, like Fred Astaire sweeping Ginger Rogers into some swirly, dancing embrace, every time I stepped off the train in Boston. I even miss his ridiculous habit of swinging the occasional imaginary golf club in mid-air, perfecting his soft draw as we walked down Mount Auburn Street. I think I would ride off on a horse to North Dakota with him if he pulled up on a steed right now. The missing pours out of my pores, extravagantly.

Dov was dashing, charming and clever, and we daunted each other, I think. I came home from my first date with him and I understood what people meant when they talked about being swept off their feet. I felt somewhere between floating and faint. I think the word I used then was *devastated*. I told him, on our second date, that I was devastated.

The first time I went to visit him at Harvard was a weekend in February, and it was somehow not too cold. I walked around, feeling every bit the hick from North Carolina, my mouth agape, my eyes big as ice cream scoops. Everyone at Harvard played squash. All of Dov's friends had been or would be Rhodes scholars. Dov took me to a dinner party at a shamefully well-appointed apartment; the hostess's rule was that everyone at the table had to recite a poem from memory. Shel Silverstein's "My Beard" was all I could come up with; the hostess, a fair-skinned, clever redhead whom Dov would later kiss behind my back, chimed in with "The Love Song of J. Alfred Prufrock." All of it. I knew my wide-eyed-ness was unseemly, but I was wide-eyed anyway. Had Francine Prose set out to write a parody of Harvard, she could not have pitched it this perfectly.

Gradually, the awe wore off. Harvard began to lose some of its shimmer. I found I could hold my own with Dov's friends at their symposia, in their parries. Indeed, I came to love visiting him at Harvard. I loved the used bookstores, more of them, I think, in Cambridge, Massachusetts, than anywhere else on the planet. I loved the river. Dov and I would walk down there at nights and he would kiss me, and it was picturesque. And I loved him, loved him with that startling, easy college love, the kind you can just fall into carelessly because you are only eighteen and you don't have any idea how much it will hurt.

I always looked forward to going to shul when Dov was leading services. He has this stunning, baritone voice, and perfectly formed Hebrew, and I would go to the synagogue, and sit on the other side of the *mechitzah*, the gauzy, filmy, white curtain, five feet high, separating the men from the women, and I would listen to him pray. Sometimes I would peer through the *mechitzah*, I would look across to the men's section, and pick him out, and watch him as he stood to pray, watch whom he sat next to, watch him, sometimes, stare at the ceiling and daydream.

The apologists for the *mechitzah* are right: there is something to be said for praying only with other women, for not worrying about what you look like or whether you might brush hands. The apologists say it would just be too distracting for men and women to pray together, all jumbled up together and close, that we would focus on one another, and not on God. I never would have prayed with Dov standing next to me. It was distracting enough just looking at him through the gauze.

A Winter Wedding

Hannah and I go to a winter wedding. The bride is Hannah's friend from college. Since Jim is attending a conference out of town, Hannah brings me as her date.

It is a lovely wedding, all tulle and perfect hymns and happy people. *Maybe*, I think, *Hannah will go away from this wedding with a renewed commitment to her wedding vows.* Maybe she will see the blushing bride and the goofily grinning groom and think about all the people who would be hurt if she had an affair. Maybe she will remember how light and hopeful she felt on her own wedding day.

When she meets me the next week for morning prayer, I expect her to say, *Watching Tanya and Bill exchange those vows was like watching a baptism; it helped me reaffirm my own commitments.* Instead she tells me that she drove home from the wedding, called Mr. Latin American Literature, had dinner with him, then had sex with him, and then went home and cried. After crying, she called him and told him she could never see him again, and then she ripped his phone number out of her address book, and then she stayed awake, smoking (which she hadn't done since high school) and drumming her fingers until Jim came home at four o'clock the next afternoon. She told him about the dinner and the sex and the address book.

"He looked like he'd been run over," she tells me. "He thought I was going to leave him. But this was never about me leaving. I was never going to leave."

I don't know what the Latin American literature man feels, but at least three people feel like failures. Hannah feels like a failure as a wife. Jim feels like a failure as a husband. I feel like a failure as a Christian, or a friend, or a witness. I feel like I should have been able to stop her doing this. I should have had better arguments, or more persuasive prayers.

Part of morning prayer is a confession and absolution. We humbly confess our sins unto Almighty God, and then the priest says, "The Almighty and merciful Lord grant you absolution and remission of all your sins, true repentance, amendment of life, and the grace and consolation of his Holy Spirit." The prayer book instructs, "A deacon or lay person using the preceding form remains kneeling, and substitutes 'us' for 'you' and 'our' for 'your.'" I am the lay person this morning, and I pronounce these words of absolution over Hannah and me.

Later in the week, I see Jim at a lecture. He smiles, but he looks unslept and his hands are shaking. I don't know how exactly he and Hannah will go about making their peace with each other, though I trust that somehow they will. It hits me, looking at Jim, that Jesus is the only person big enough to do this kind of forgiveness, that we can forgive only because He shows us how. I remember that He forgave my own sins, too, that when He hung on the Cross before slipping into death and said, "It is finished," He meant Hannah's adultery, and all my own sins, and Jim's and the Latin American literature guy's sins, and my parents', and my priests', and everyone else's, permanently, thoroughly, forgiven.

Lent

Ash Wednesday Evangelism

The imposition of ashes on Ash Wednesday is nothing if not bold.

The whole day is bold. There is a bold gash of ecclesiastical purple hanging on the wall of my Puritan-white simple Episcopal church, and our rector, Milind, wears an equally startling purple chasuble, which he will wear for all of Lent. It is a bold liturgy the Book of Common Prayer suggests we recite: to acknowledge that we are of dust and to dust we shall return, and to proclaim our chosen-ness as the children of God anyway.

But the ashes are boldest of all. A dark and undeniable slash across your forehead, a bold proclamation of death and resurrection all at once. You forget that it is on your forehead and you walk out of church, out into the world, a living reminder that Christ died for us. The cross Milind makes on my forehead on Ash Wednesday is no polite, small slice of silver dangling around my neck but easily slipped behind my blouse. The ash cross is bold, and undeniable.

I forget it is there, sashay out of church without thinking about it, until I get stares on the subway. There might be some neighborhoods in New York where forehead crosses on Ash Wednesday are commonplace. But on my subway, full of sophisticated Upper West Siders, I see only one other person on the whole train with ashes. Some people stare at me, one smiles sadly, and I shift, wondering what they wonder.

When I get to campus I feel truly uncomfortable. Columbia, its charming chapel notwithstanding, is a place devoted to different types of truths, not so eager to proclaim this one.

EVANGELIZING, IF IT MEANS handing out tracts, is not something I do. I don't ever casually swing my arm around a friend's shoulders, look meaningfully into her eyes, and ask, "Susie, if you were hit by a bus tomorrow, would you go to Heaven?" When I come face-to-face with Jesus' commission to the disciples—go and spread the word around the world—I wince, for I know I am not even spreading it around Morningside Heights.

I take comfort in the church's current affection for what is politely called "lifestyle evangelism." Being a lifestyle evangelist doesn't require handing out tracts; it just requires living a good, God-fearing, Gospel-exuding life. I like to assume that most people know I am a Christian and when they see that I am sometimes joyful and sometimes peaceful when they are not, they will want to know my secret.

Walking around with a cross of ashes on your forehead is another matter altogether. I feel unhidden, uncloseted; I feel embarrassed.

Late at night I dash to the library to return an overdue book, and I run into a classmate and as we stand chatting she fishes a tissue out of her purse. "You know, you have a smudge on your forehead; here, let me help you wipe it off."

"Ah, well, actually," I mutter, "actually, it's supposed to be there. It's Ash Wednesday today, you know." She looks at me blankly. "A Christian holiday," I say. Her gaze is still blank. "Christian," I say, louder, imagining I might be living before Constantine. "It inaugurates Lent, the season that culminates in Easter. The priest puts these cross ashes on everyone's forehead to remind us that Christ died for our sins."

It wasn't the only conversation I'd had that day sparked by my cross. A student I didn't know had approached me in the morning and asked me where she could go to church; another student, more hostile, wanted to know what business I had trying to teach undergraduates to think critically when I, an ash-sporting Christian, obviously didn't think critically myself. A third student, whom I knew only in passing, sat me down, burst into tears, and told me that her parents were divorcing. *Does this happen to nuns walking down the streets in their habits?* I wondered. And I ran into an old friend whom I hadn't seen since college. "When did you trade in Judaism for Jesus?" she asked, initiating a conversation in which I explained not only when, but why.

I had been prepared for Ash Wednesday to be intense. I had been prepared to feel something profound or moving when Milind told me I was dust. I was not prepared for it to be a day of unavoidable evangelism.

It may have been failed evangelism. None of these students, after all, knelt with me and prayed the Sinner's Prayer. But I consoled myself that it might not have been a total failure. After all, before I became a Christian, many people said many things to me that didn't result in my immediate conversion, but over time, they added up. Maybe just knowing that a normal-seeming graduate student at an Ivy League school is willing to proclaim, at least one day a year, that she is a Christian, will lodge somewhere in some student's heart.

The day reminded me, actually, of the Passover seder. I suppose that is fitting, since the seder is about commemorating liberation, and Ash Wednesday inaugurates the season that culminates in the greatest liberation of all, the resurrection of Christ from the dead.

At the seder, you do all sorts of strange things—you drink four cups of wine, you eat bitter herbs, you eat unleavened bread. There is a specific reason for each: The horseradish recalls the bitterness of slavery in Egypt; the unleavened bread helps you remember the Israelites who, in their haste to flee, did not have time to let bread rise. But the rabbis teach us there is a more general reason for all these curious culinary gestures. They are intended to stimulate the interest of children. Kids at the table will notice that something out of the ordinary is going on—they don't partake of bitter herbs and flat bread every night—and they will ask why the family isn't eating the usual dinner rolls or pumpernickel loaves. Then their parents will have an opening to tell them the story of what God did for the Jews in Egypt.

The cross on our foreheads is meant to be a dramatic reminder to ourselves—and it is that. When Milind looks at me and says, "Remember that you are dust and to dust you shall return," I know what God did for me. He not only created me, He then poured out His grace upon me in the blood of His son. Me, a bunch of dust!

But the cross also stimulates other people's questions. It provides an unmistakable opportunity—even obligation—to witness.

Since no one came to faith as a result of my ashes, maybe my Ash Wednesday evangelism wasn't a rousing success. But it was successful if success means that it did some spiritual work on me. I was brought face-to-face with my own discomfort about being a Christian on a secular campus, and I was brought just a few steps closer to shedding that discomfort. I sometimes daydream about teaching at a Christian college, where I wouldn't have to deal with this particular anxiety. It would be a given, rather than a surprise, that I called myself a follower of Jesus.

But God seems to have placed me, at least for the time being, at Columbia. I suspect He didn't place me here just to get an education and a fancy degree, but also to be a little salt, a little leaven to the loaf. The challenge, as I enter Lent, is to be this bold in my proclamation of the Gospel all year.

Reading Fast

It is the day after Ash Wednesday, and Milind and I are meeting for breakfast at a diner near church. I order eggs and he orders coffee. "So Lauren," says Milind, "what discipline have you adopted for Lent?"

I answer, with no small touch of self-righteousness, that I plan to fast every Friday. This seems like a big deal, far more serious than giving up chocolate or caffeine.

"Really?" says Milind. "Good for you." His Ash Wednesday homily, just the night before, had dwelt for a few minutes on fasting. He had spoken of the need to give up something that was truly important to you. To give something that was really truly yourself. He had encouraged us to remember what it was like to receive gifts from friends. So much of what made the gift meaningful, said Milind, was not the gift itself, but the spirit in which it was given. Say your friend has a beautiful green sundress. You have liked and admired that sundress for months. She gives it to you. If it's just a castoff—she has eighteen others just like it, so giving it to you is no real sacrifice—the whole exchange feels a little anticlimactic. But if your friend loves that dress, too, loves it dearly but wants you to have it because she knows it will make you happy, then you are thrilled. The dress takes on a whole new meaning. "That is how it is with the gifts we give to God," Milind said in his sermon. "I want to encourage you to give something to God that really matters. Something you really love. Something that is hard to do without."

Food, I think, happily, tucking into my diner eggs, is something I cannot do without. I feel sure Milind will praise me for this great sacrifice.

Milind sips his coffee. "Lauren," he says, "I want you to give up something additional for Lent." I raise an eyebrow. "I want you to give up reading."

I glance down at the book I had brought with me to the diner, just to fill the five minutes in which I might be waiting for Milind, who is occasionally late. It is *Soldiers of Christ,* a book about preaching in late medieval France. "You want me to give up reading," I repeat.

"I do," he replies. "Reading, it seems to me, is something you really love. It may be the thing you love most. I would like you to give up reading for Lent." I eat another spoonful of eggs. "I think books would be a gift you could give Christ that would be really meaningful," he says. I butter my English muffin. "Let me ask you," says Milind, "what do you do on, say, a Thursday evening once you have eaten dinner, rinsed your dishes, and quit working for the night?"

"I read."

"What about the occasional Thursday night on which you do not read?" asks Milind.

"I don't know," I say. "Usually, I read."

Then he says it again: "I'd like you to give up reading for Lent."

"Okay!" I say recklessly. "Philippians 4:13!" Philippians 4:13 is "I can do everything through him who gives me strength." It is that verse from the Mitford books. In Mitford, Episcopalians are always running around doing impossible things and chirping "Philippians 4:13."

"You know," I say to Milind, "reading really is my fallback activity. If I have time on my hands, nothing to do, what I do is read."

"No, no," says Milind. "Reading is *my* fallback activity. Reading is your life."

I EMAIL Jo, the Clare College chaplain. At Cambridge, I often asked Jo some theological question, and she often threw up her hands. "Can't you direct me to a book on this?" I would ask. Usually, the answer was no; Jo, even though she had a Ph.D. and headed up a chapel at Cambridge University, seemed to spend more time living Christianity than reading about it. My email to her is short. It says, "Dear Jo, My priest here has asked me to give up reading for Lent, and I said YES!!!!!!! Love, Lauren." She writes back, "Dear Lauren, Thanks for giving me a good laugh. Love, Jo."

On Sunday, Milind looks at me, radiating concern. "How are you handling the temptation?" he asks. You might think I have been suddenly stripped bare of my chastity belt and moved in with Tom Cruise. "Maybe you need to clear your books out of your apartment, just for Lent. So that you're not constantly tempted."

"Milind," I say, "I have three thousand books in my apartment. I can't just clear them out for Lent."

"Three thousand? You must have a huge apartment."

"No," I say, "I have a tiny, almost-affordable graduate-student apartment."

"But three thousand books? Where do you sleep?" he asks.

"On books," I say.

I USUALLY READ ON SUBWAY RIDES. For the first week of Lent, I people-watch instead. But people-watching gets old, and I find myself, instead of reading, instead of people-watching, preaching sermons in my head. I picture myself clad in a long, flowing chasuble, instructing my flock on the finer points of biblical interpretation, filling in fuzzy historical details they might not know, inspiring them to lead a more committed Christian life. In particular, I imagine the Lenten sermons I might preach fifteen years from now. They begin like this: "Fifteen years ago, my priest asked me to do something radical at Lent. He asked me to give up reading." There would be a few titters from the parishioners. "As most of you know, I love nothing more than curling up with a good book. At the time, I was also a graduate student and a Web-zine book review editor, so asking me to give up reading was a little like asking a pastry chef to give up flour. That first year, it was hard, at times unbearable. But I have renewed the practice every Lent, and I find, as we wind our way through Epiphany, that I look forward to my Lenten devotion. I look forward to the space it clears out in my brain. I look forward to the quiet time in which I hear only my words and God's words, not the printed words on the pages of all those books."

My real-life experience of giving up reading is not as grand or as self-satisfied or as easy as that imaginary homily. It is surprisingly hard.

IN HIS ASH WEDNESDAY SERMON, Milind had reminded us that the real test came in private. Would we adhere to our devotions when no one was looking? Were we doing this to impress our friends, or to offer a gift to God? Would we sneak that chocolate bar or Coca-Cola when we were at home alone? Would we be diligent, or would we cheat?

I am pretty diligent for a while, and then I cheat. At first my behavior is downright commendable. I don't read that out-of-print church history book by Rowan Greer, which I had finally tracked down through the Advanced Book Exchange. It shows up at my door two days after breakfast with Milind, and I unwrap it and put it on the shelf and walk away. I don't read Phyllis Tickle's memoir about her prayer life, even though I had been waiting for it to come out for a year. I'm not even fazed when the new Deborah Knott mystery turns up on my desk at work.

Then my friend's memoir about growing up with a preacher father in the segregated South comes out. The author sends me a copy and I add it to the growing pile of books I will delve into after Easter. It's in good company, sandwiched right in between Michael Dirda's *Readings* and Meagan Daum's *My Misspent Youth*. Every morning, I pass the shelf. I peer at my friend's book; it peers back. I take it off the shelf and run my hands over the smooth cover, and I inspect the photo on the dust jacket. But back the book goes, right between Dirda and Daum.

I try to convince myself that I have a legitimate reason for reading the book. I try to justify it on the basis of friendship. I am the author's friend, and as his friend I should call him and crow about how great the book is, but I really can't do that until I've read it. *Maybe*, I think, *it's actually hurting Charles's feelings that I haven't read the book. Maybe I should just read a few chapters, so I could have something to say to him about it. I bet Jesus would tell me to do that. It's probably the more loving thing to do.*

Even I realize this argument is painfully thin. But one Thursday night, I look at my bookshelf and say, "Screw it." I grab the book and dig in. I read all night. I feel like the dieter, long deprived of anything tasty, who decides to devour a gallon of Breyer's in one sitting.

I'M SAVING A LOT of money this Lent. I've only dipped into a bookstore once, to buy a birthday present for a friend in England. While squeezing some cantaloupes at the grocery, I see one of the clerks from Labyrinth Books. He asks me if I have been on a long trip. "Maybe to Barbados?" he asks.

· · ·

I'M NOT SURE IF Lent 2020 will see me giving a self-satisfied sermon about how much I look forward to my reading fast. But I do think I will give reading up again next year. Giving up books for six weeks did not just leave me with more free time. It did not just save me some money. It also left me starkly alone with my life. I read, I think, for many reasons. I read for information, I read for pleasure, I read because I want to figure out the craft of putting a sentence together. But I also read to numb any feelings of despair or misery that might creep my way. Sven Birkerts once wrote, "To read, when one does so of one's own free will, is to make a volitional statement, to cast a vote; it is to posit an elsewhere and set off toward it. And like any traveling, reading is at once a movement and a comment of sorts about the place one has left. To open a book voluntarily is at some level to remark the insufficiency either of one's life or of one's orientation toward it."

Even before Lent I had suspected that I used reading just this way, as a tonic or escape route. In late February, I wrote something in my journal about reading. "I feel myself entering a morose funk over this." ("This" was, of course, a man.) "I recognize this funk not because I want to sleep more or eat more, but by my desire to do what I always do when I get funked out: burrow into some feel-good small-town novel I've read a dozen times, usually Mitford, sometimes the Deborah Knott mysteries, now *Overnight Float*. It seems to be my always-cure."

During Lent, I don't have that always-cure, and I find myself, not surprisingly, praying more. At first I pray more because I have time on my hands. The Saturday after Milind and I had our diner breakfast, I was at home. I had finished my work and gone out to dinner with a friend. Then I had come back to my apartment, listened to some music, taken a bath, brewed a cup of tea, made a phone call, and generally felt aimless. I had nothing else to do. I said Compline. And I have said it every night since. I don't have anything else to do.

But I also find myself praying more because I don't have my usual distractions. When I am stuck in a puddle of sadness and mistakes, I cannot take them to Mitford. I have to take them to God.

I begin to suspect that Milind didn't want me to give up reading just because it was the equivalent of some dearly loved green sundress, but because it might move me closer to Jesus. It might move me to my knees.

Iola

A family of four, passing through New York en route to Niagara Falls, visits All Angels' for Sunday worship, and at the coffee hour I chat with the blonde and smiling mother, Violet. As she is telling me about the family's farm in Georgia, her small daughter, who looks about three, sidles up offering cookies. I coo. "You have quite a handful of cookies," I say, as my uterus skips a beat.

"Say hello to our new friend," says Violet. "Shake hands." Violet looks at me. "This is Iola Jane."

"Come again?" I say.

"I know, it's an unusual name," Violet says, and laughs a throaty laugh. "Iola. You probably haven't heard it before. It's a family name."

I explain that I have heard it before, but only once. Iola was my grandmother's name, my mother's mother. Iola Elizabeth.

IOLA ELIZABETH—MY SISTER and I called her Grandy— died seven years ago. The years before her death were narrow ones. She was in good health, but she rarely left her house, not even to go to church or get her hair done, two activities she had privileged above all else when she was younger. She had no friends. A woman from her church called her every morning, just to make sure she wasn't dead.

Visiting her was always tense and boring. My grandmother planted flower beds full of nasturtium and marigolds and never had a harsh word to say about anyone. She'd held herself and my mother together on her meager schoolteacher's salary after her son-of-a-bitch husband took off in 1945; she was pious, and frugal, and a teetotaler. Even after retiring she sent my mother to the liquor store to buy rum when she was making a rum cake, because she didn't think it looked proper for a Baptist schoolteacher to purchase alcohol, even for a cake. She played a mean game of Crazy Eights, and she loved us a lot. But I never had anything to talk to her about, and she was always hovering, offering food every time we turned around. I dreaded those visits. I resisted going. I always left her house as soon as I could.

That resistance began to change, gradually, when I was in college, the year or so before she died.

Usually I visited with my mother, but the last time I visited Grandy I was alone. I was a sophomore, and driving my car, and I felt suddenly grown up and able to do all the things I knew my older sister did when she went to visit—dust the living room while Grandy napped, go to the grocery store for her. At the Winn-Dixie, I bought all the food she had asked for, frozen rolls and canned green beans and fresh fruit and milk. And I bought a small, purple violet in a clear, plastic container, and cinnamon buns. On the way back to her house, I pulled into a strip mall and went into a shop advertising "Christian goods of all kinds." It was the first time I had ever been in a Christian bookstore, and I didn't know what I was looking for. Grandy's eyes were bad and she didn't read very much anymore, so I asked the clerk if they had any books on tape. The selection was small. I bought a tape of Billy Graham sermons and some gospel music. I had never heard of any of the artists: Doyle Lawson and Quicksilver, Steven Curtis

Chapman, Kim Hill. I bought a tape deck and some batteries. Six months later, Grandy died, in her sleep, the day before election day.

I think my grandmother was sad when she died that none of us, my mother or my sister or me, was a Christian. I think she thought every day about how Proverbs promises that if you raise your children up right, when they are old, they will not stray from the path of righteousness, and I think she was waiting for my mother to come back to church. I don't know what Heaven is like, or where my grandmother is now, if she is seated at God's feet, or if she is waiting, in some timeless in-between, for Jesus' return to earth and the final resurrection of the dead. But I hope, fiercely, that wherever she is, she can see me and know that I have become a Christian. I doubt that I will ever have the unwavering faith that she had. I will always be too embarrassed and too sophisticated and too modern to believe the way she believed. But I hope she is somewhere able to see that I believe just a little bit. I think it would make her smile.

A WEEK LATER, I get a postcard in the mail from Violet and Iola. Iola has crayoned a picture of a purple woman with pointy, feline glasses. Then, in her mother's loopy scrawl, "Wish you were here!"

Prayer Life

Last week, I met a man. His name is Bill, and he is tall and clever and knows interesting things, and I am taken with him. Quite taken. Very taken indeed. After our first date, which was one of those dates where neither of you is sure till halfway through that it even is a date and then it lasts until the wee hours of the night and you wind up feeling like you've taken a two-week trip to the mountains with him, not just had dinner and gone out to a bar. Anyway, after that date, he went out of town, and we were supposed to meet for a drink when he came back, which we did. He drank a 7 and 7, I think, and I drank Tullomore Dew, and the Yale Club, where we met, was deserted, except for a few college juniors on their way out of the country for spring break. I realized that he was the only person I had ever met who owned recordings of all the Dvořák string quartets, not just the famous ones, quartets 12 and 14; all those quartets impressed me no end. I felt like I could have listened to his peaty, scratchy voice for years. And then he went home and I went home and I was utterly fixated. Knocked flat on the ground, couldn't think about anything else but him him him. Couldn't work, couldn't take a shower, couldn't even go to the grocery store without thoughts of him, this-man-I-newly-wanted-to-marry-after-two-dates. Scrutinized his three-sentence emails.

Agonized about whether to call him, or would that seem too forward; on the other hand, could anything possibly be more forward than the half-drunk-Tullomore-Dew things I'm sure I must have meltily said in that deserted bar at the Yale Club?

Instead of calling Bill, I call Randi and say, "I'm just fixating, and I have to stop, this is ridiculous, I feel unmoored and it's ridiculous and I don't even know him and I'm not getting anything done and when I wake up in the mornings I think about him, very first thing." And Randi says what I knew she would say. She says, "Pray."

"Yes," I say, "but it's not really working. I tried it Wednesday night, when I was waiting for him to call and make these Yale Club plans, when I was waiting anxiously and couldn't grade my midterms and was just waiting, I did pray about it." (I actually got down on my knees on my dirty pink dhurrie rug and said, "Ok, God, I'm really getting out of control here. I don't want to feel this crazy over this man, I don't want to try to control a situation I can't control, so I'm going to just give it to you. You take it. You deal with it." I even — this is a little embarrassing — I even took a picture of the crucifixion down off my wall, and held it in my hands, and pictured myself laying this bundle of neurosis and anxiety and control-freakishness at Jesus' feet.) "So," I say to Randi, "I tried that on Wednesday, and it doesn't really seem to have worked."

"I think," says Randi, "that you have to do it every day, all the time, these prayers of relinquishment. I think it doesn't really do the trick to squeeze it in on your way to class, 'Hey God, I don't really have time to talk right now, but could you please just take away these kind of overwrought feelings, thanks, I really appreciate it, catch ya later.'"

"Well," I demur, "those squeezed-in prayers could work, if He wanted them to work. I mean, He's omnipotent. He could just zap these feelings away if He wanted to."

"I think you have to do it every day," Randi repeats. (She will say this again in a few weeks, when, after a third and fourth date, things with the peaty-voiced Bill fizzle out like flat ginger ale and I am crushed and don't want to get out of bed. She will say "I think you have to pray every day. Maybe twice.")

———— ❧ ————

I HAVE A HARD TIME PRAYING. It feels, usually, like a waste of time. It feels unproductive; my time would be better spent writing a paragraph or reading a book or practicing a conjugation or baking a pie. Sometimes whole weeks elapse when I hardly bother to pray at all, because prayer is boring; because it feels silly (after all, you look like you're just sitting there talking to the air, or to yourself, and maybe you are); but above all because it is unproductive. As Jo once put it, "If you spend a day in prayer, you cannot, at the end of the day, point to a pile of toothpaste tubes you made and say, *that is what I did today.*" Still, there are the weeks when I do pray, the weeks when I trust—or, at least, manage to act like I trust—that prayer does something, even if it is something I cannot see. Aquinas wrote, "Prayer is profitable because it makes us the familiars of God." I like that language. It conjures up God as a witch with a broomstick and a pointy hat, and me His little black cat, everywhere underfoot. Then Aquinas quoted Psalm 140: "Let my prayer be directed as incense in thy sight."

WHEN YOU ARE A JEW, if you are trying to be a righteous one, you pray three times a day, *shacharit, mincha, ma'ariv,* morning, afternoon, and night. You say those prayers in a quorum, in a group, at shul, or in a living room; and in between, all throughout the day, you sprinkle your other words with blessings, blessings over every crumb you put in your mouth, and blessings over rainbows and thunderclaps, blessings for when you see a dwarf or gnome or some other strange-looking creature, a blessing for when you meet a wise man, a blessing for after you pee, blessings everywhere.

The blessings are easy, short, and it does not take long for even newcomers to learn to bless habitually. What makes a blessing a blessing is the opening phrase, the six-word formula, which in English comes to ten words: "Blessed are you O Lord our God King of the Universe." King of the universe Who does something: Who brings forth bread from the earth; Who made the great sea; Who creates the fruit of the ground; Who sanctifies us with His commandments. In the second century, Rabbi Meir said that Jews should strive to say one hundred blessings a day. Sometimes during college I took the train to the Bronx Botanical Garden, just so I would have some flowers over which to say a blessing.

The prayers, the three-times-a-day prayers, are longer, and harder to learn, and require more discipline. I don't say them anymore, but I remember the lessons they taught me, which were two. One, it is important to pray with other people, in a group, a lesson that gives the lie to the lie I like to believe, which is that prayer is just about this vertical conversation between me and God and God and me. And two, liturgy is dull, and habitual, and rote, and you memorize it, and don't think about what you are saying, and it is, regardless, the most important thing on the planet. It is the place you start, and the place you come back to. I find liturgy, even Thomas Cranmer's beautiful poetry, as bland as macaroni and cheese, but I would have no prayer without it.

LITURGY IS ONE of the ways I stumbled my way into the Episcopal Church, and it is one of the reasons I stay put. When people ask how I came to be an Episcopalian in particular, why not a Lutheran or a Presbyterian or a Pentecostal falling down slain in the Spirit, I say that at the time I had not the foggiest idea why but I knew, long before I became a Christian, that if I became a Christian, I would become the Episcopal kind. "God's hand," I say. "God's hand guiding me." But God's hand in part because the Episcopal Church reminds me, over and over, in all its nooks and crannies and surprises and ways, of Judaism.

One way the Episcopal Church reminds me of Judaism is its hermeneutic, that is, its way of reading, in particular the way the Church reads the Bible. Jews read the Bible, the written Bible, the Five Books of Moses and the Writings and the Prophets, through a rabbinic scrim. They don't just sit down with the Book of Leviticus and figure out how to live. If they did, keeping kosher, for one thing, would be a lot easier. Leviticus, after all, just says to avoid boiling a kid in its mother's milk; it is the rabbis, speaking in the Talmud, who eventually determined the meaning of that verse: separate meat and milk completely, no cheeseburgers, no meaty lasagna, no hamburger on your pizza, indeed don't even eat them at the same meal, no hot fudge sundae after steak tartar, actually wait a few hours (some say one, others three or six) after eating meat before you drink milk or spoon some yogurt or cut yourself a piece of cheese bread.

Jewish tradition teaches that at Mount Sinai God revealed not just the written Torah, the Torah *shebachtav*, the first five books of Moses, but also the oral Torah, the Torah *she baal peh*, the Torah of the mouth, literally—the Talmud and all the other rabbinic commentaries. All of those elaborations, those readings, those interpretations, the cheese bread and the meaty lasagna, Moses received all that at Sinai. They are just as binding as anything in Leviticus, even though they didn't get written down till later. Jews who dare to read the Torah *shebachtav*, the written Torah, without the Torah *she baal peh*, are heretics of the first order, Karaites. These are the Jews who take literally the 613 commandments in the Old Testament, but disregard completely the teachings of the rabbis.

Anglicans, and other Catholic churches—that is, the Roman Catholics and the Eastern Orthodox—read the Bible like Orthodox Jews. Anglicans look at Scripture through the scrim of the church fathers, they balance the Bible with the weight of centuries of church teaching and tradition. This sets the Catholic churches apart from Protestants, who place less emphasis on, vest less authority in, tradition. Martin Luther, inaugurating the Protestant Reformation, called for *sola scriptura*, Scripture alone, and he translated the Bible from Hebrew and Greek into the common tongue so that layfolk could read it and interpret it for themselves, guided not primarily by centuries of church teaching, but directly by the Holy Spirit. If I had to do that, just secret myself away in my room, just me, King James, and the Holy Spirit, I don't think I'd ever open a Bible again. The task would be too awesome. I am much happier, much more comfortable, much more trusting, and much less terrified when I know that, instead, it's me, the Holy Spirit, and two thousand years of the church reading, arguing, teasing out, all together. This kind of reading is what I was used to. It's just the same as reading Genesis alongside a commentary by Rashi or the Vilna Gaon. Reading the New Testament without Jerome and Augustine and the Venerable Bede makes about as much sense to me as reading Hebrew Scripture without Rashi. So that is one of the things that drew me to Episcopalianism: reading with the church.

The other familiar thing, when I first walked into an Episcopal church, was the prayer book, the habit of fixed-hour prayer, the understanding that you were saying more or less the same liturgy as Anglicans around the world, that you would say the same prayers every morning, every evening, over and over and over, till you knew them by heart, and long after that, till they were rote and boring, comfortable as your best friend's kitchen and familiar as flapjacks.

RANDI'S GRANDMOTHER PAULINE is dying. She has Parkinson's. She's in a hospital in Maryland, and I don't think Randi has seen her in fifteen years, but death is still death, and it is hard any way you look at it. Pauline is ninety-seven, and I am not sure how to pray for her. For her healing? For an easy journey to the World to Come? In my prayer book, in the section called "Prayers and Thanksgivings," I find a paragraph for the aged. "As their strength diminishes, increase their faith and their assurance of your love."

A FEW YEARS AGO there was an article in the *New York Times* magazine about the Roman Catholic priesthood. Used to be that entering the priesthood was a smart, upwardly mobile move for the sons of Irish and Italian immigrants, a good way for kids kept out of the Ivies by quotas to get a good education and wind up with a good job. But, the article wondered, what kind of virile, normal man would enter the priesthood now? Who would take a vow of lifelong celibacy if he had any other options? The article focused mostly on the topics one might expect to find in the Sunday *Times:* homosexuality, celibacy, contraception. But buried in the middle was one paragraph about prayer. The seminarians, Jennifer Egan wrote, "talk about their prayer lives the way most people talk about their love lives."

I GET AN EMAIL from a near-stranger today, someone who has the distinction of being vaguely acquainted with both me and Steven, my ex. "I heard about Steve getting engaged," the acquaintance writes in her email. "I'm thinking of you. I'm hoping you're not too upset." The acquaintance, apparently, assumed Steven had had the courtesy to tell me about his engagement. That assumption—although, in our ongoing effort to have an amicable professional relationship, Steve and

I did talk for thirty minutes just yesterday about what caused the Montgomery bus boycott—was incorrect.

When your ex-boyfriend gets engaged less than six months after you break up, it is nice to learn that your friends cannot stand him. It is nice to have friends who insist that he just can't marry his equal, that Tiffany-the-part-time-Pilates-instructor no doubt has long legs but only about six brain cells. It is nice to have friends who say I am better off without him. It is nice to have friends who hold my hand and plait my hair and scoop chocolate ice cream into dishes for me when I can't possibly eat a thing, friends who say that Steve will be unhappy, their marriage won't last, she probably got knocked-up-by-accident-on-purpose, friends who say he is a creep and a cretin and all-around goon, friends who say the very fact that he could marry someone named Tiffany indicates that he's no prize.

It shakes me, their pending nuptials. I just don't get it. How he could have written me letters that said, "It is not that I can't envision my life without you. I have lived without you for twenty-six years (I don't need to envision it) and I know that in every particular, with you is better, realer, and more than without"; letters that begged me, in sticky-sweet-Valentine language, to "marry me, spend all your mornings and daydreams and nighttimes with me, be patient with me and help me love you better"; how he could have written me those letters, and then, six months later, marry Tiffany, the Pilates instructor with long legs.

And on top of that I am aghast and incredulous and just plain perplexed that we talked for half an hour yesterday morning and he didn't see fit to say, at the end of the conversation, after we had talked about Joanne Robinson and the Montgomery Improvement Association and why the Civil Rights movement began when it did, I am aghast that he didn't see fit to say, "So actually I'm really glad you called, because there's something I need to tell you." Two sentences is all. "Tiffany and I are getting married next week. I thought I should tell you that."

In my generous moments I think, *Well, he knew I had a lot of work these next few days. He knew I had these major exams coming up. He thought this might upset me and he didn't want to screw up my exam-studying, and he thought he'd tell me after.* Most moments, though, I am not so charitable. In those other moments, I think, *His craven heart just couldn't summon the reserves.*

I am a mean and petty person, and a terrible Christian to boot, and I spend all weekend hoping that Steven and his bride will be miserable, that his brilliant dissertation will turn to straw, that his roof will leak and his car will die and he'll be stuck in a loveless marriage in that god-forsaken town in Arkansas for the rest of his natural life. I hope, too, that she is not a Christian, that she'll lead him down a path of sin and restlessness, away from church and straight toward debauchery. I hope he forgets to baptize the baby all my friends imagine she's carrying.

I do have one friend who says something else, something other than the usual supportive Steven-is-a-cretin-and-I-am-very-angry-at-him cant. My friend Sam. He writes me a note. It says "Try to pray for Steven and his bride-to-be. Mouth the words even if all you feel is anger. Remember that the Spirit does our praying for us."

This advice at first sounds nauseatingly pious. But then somehow it doesn't. I am annoyed when I read his note, because I know he is right. It hadn't occurred to me to pray for them. But Sam is wise, and I pray for Steven and Tiffany, not so much for their sake, but for mine.

I pray the collect for families, which is nestled between the collect for the future of the human race and the collect for the care of children in my burgundy Book of Common Prayer:

Almighty God, our heavenly Father, who settest the solitary in families: We commend to thy continual care the homes in which thy people dwell. Put far from them, we beseech thee, every root of bitterness, the desire of vainglory, and the pride of life. Fill them with faith, virtue, knowledge, temperance, patience, godliness. Knit together in constant affection those who, in holy wedlock, have been made one flesh. Turn the hearts of the parents to the children, and the hearts of the children to the parents: and so enkindle fervent charity among us all, that we may evermore be kindly affectioned one to another; through Jesus Christ our Lord.

It is hard to pray this for them. I am not so holy. I start to cry every time I get to the word *dwell*.

GOD, I HAVE DECIDED, is not on call. That is what Randi means when she says I will have to pray every day, maybe twice. He is all powerful, so I suppose He could be on call if He wanted to be, and maybe, on rare occasion, He is. But in general, God doesn't just turn up when you page Him. He is right where He always is, and what regular, daily-maybe-twice prayer gives us is some more hint of just where that is, and how to get there, and one of the things liturgy gives us is a way to get there when all our other ways have given out.

When I am unable to pray, the prayer book gives me the words. Liturgical prayers, Edith Stein once wrote, "support the spirit and prescribe it to a fixed path."

Sometimes, I think I have come up with something poetic. One day, when I was full in the flush of agony about what I should do with my life, whether I would always be alone, whether I should become a nun, whether I should drop out of graduate school, and other high-pitch anxieties, I heard, reverberating around my brain, "Go out to do the work I have given you to do." *The work I have given you to do. The work I have given you to do.*

What an ingenious sentiment, I thought. *I can't believe I dreamed that up. Maybe I should drop out of grad school and enter a poetry-writing Master's of Fine Arts program.* All day, all week I heard those words, *the work I have given you to do,* heard them, and was deeply consoled by them, sure that God had given me work to do, that He had sent me out into the world to do it, that He even woke me up too early in the morning to do that work, it was mine, I was consecrated to it, and it was given of Him. I heard those words all week, and I felt peaceful. Not only had God given me work to do, He had given me little poetic snatches of reassurance, too.

Then I got to church on Sunday. We opened with a hymn. The crucifer and the priest processed in. We prayed the collect of the day, we read three passages from Scripture. Milind gave a rousing sermon about forgiveness. We sang some more, we prayed the prayers for the people, and exchanged the peace. Milind consecrated the Eucharist and we received it. Then we said the prayer of thanksgiving. "We thank you for receiving us as living members of your Son." And there, in the middle of that prayer, the words God had given me all week: "And now, Father, send us out to do the work you have given us to do." It was the liturgy that had lodged in my brain, words of the liturgy I barely noticed Sunday to Sunday when we said them, but here I was, noticing them raptly, in the middle of a weekday afternoon, when I needed them most.

Habit and obligation have both become bad words. That prayer becomes a habit must mean that it is impersonal, unfeeling, something of a rouse. If you do something because you are obligated to, it doesn't count, at least not as much as if you'd done it of your own free will; like the child who says thank you because his parents tell him to, it doesn't count. Sometimes, often, prayer feels that way to me, impersonal and unfeeling and not something I've chosen to do. I wish it felt inspired and on fire and like a real, love-conversation all the time, or even just more of the time. But what I am learning the more I sit with liturgy is that what I feel happening bears little relation to what is actually happening. It is a great gift when God gives me a stirring, a feeling, a something-at-all in prayer. But work is being done whether I feel it or not. Sediment is being laid. Words of praise to God are becoming the most basic words in my head. They are becoming the fallback words, drowning out advertising jingles and professors' lectures and sometimes even my own interior monologue.

Maybe St. Paul was talking about liturgy when he encouraged us to pray without ceasing.

IN CHURCH, ON Sunday mornings, we say the Lord's Prayer right at the heart of the service, right near the very peak, in the middle of the Eucharist service. After Milind tells the story of Jesus at the Last Supper, after he consecrates the bread and wine, and right before he breaks the bread in two, we say the Lord's Prayer. Milind prefaces our unison with these words: "And now, as our Savior Christ hath taught us, we are bold to say . . ." In newer versions of the liturgy, the words are a little different—"As our Savior Christ has taught us, we now pray." But I like the old words better. You lose something crucial in those newer, easier words. You lose how bold it all is, to stand there and remember that God is our father, even though He art in heaven.

There are lots of ways to make the words hard to say, to jolt ourselves out of memorization and into the shock of it all. Christian writers of all stripes have made a mint with slender books devoted entirely to the Lord's Prayer, taking it one verse at a time, clause by clause, breath by breath, trying to breathe meaning back into something so familiar and so old as to be outgrown, useless. I read many of those books when I first was baptized—not because I'd been saying the Our Father long enough to find it stale, but because reading about prayer was easier than actually praying. And I remember how stunned I was to read, in one of those books, that trespasses or sins—as in, "Forgive us our trespasses, as we forgive those who trespassed against us"—was better rendered as "debts." "Forgive us our debts, as we forgive our debtors."

I still have trouble praying that. I still think Steven, if he were a gentleman, would send me $800, for old plane tickets to Arkansas. I can forgive the tears and the fury and whatever it was he said one night that made me so mad I slammed a full wine stem down on his bookcase hard enough to shatter Chardonnay and glass all over my hand, but it's harder to forgive the debt.

In his book about religion in early modern Germany, David Sabean tells the story of Lienhart Seitz, a seventy-year-old man from Holzheim. In 1587, the chief magistrate of Goppingen summoned Seitz. Seitz, his pastor said, never came to communion, and he refused to pray. The pastor had invited Seitz to special prayer tutorials, but each time Seitz set out for the parsonage, he wound up somewhere different: a friend's house, perhaps, or a pub. "There was no question," writes Sabean, "but that the old man was mentally awake and alert; after all he was still able to make a sharp deal on a horse. It was just that he could not keep the Lord's Prayer in his head." When the magistrate threatened to send Seitz to jail for his failure to pray, Seitz promised he would visit the parson and try to learn the words. But Seitz was not optimistic: "No matter how many times he repeated the Lord's Prayer, he always got stuck at the passage where he was supposed to forgive his enemies."

. . .

EVEN IF YOU GROW UP Jewish, you learn the Lord's Prayer—
at least, if you grow up Jewish in the South. I learned it at summer
camp, the July after fourth grade, at Eagle's Nest, one of the dozens
and dozens of camps in or around Brevard, North Carolina. Far
enough away from home that I slept there overnight, but near enough
that my parents came on visitors' weekend, and other weekends besides, and signed me out of camp for the afternoon, and drove me to
town for ice cream.

I didn't like this camp. Renowned for turning girls and boys into
rugged, muscular outdoorsmen, Eagle's Nest offered all sorts of sporting, mountainous activities: hiking, canoeing, nature trail walking,
backpacking, rapelling. In the three years I went there, I never signed
up for one. I took arts and crafts, drama, Back Porch Cooking, anything to keep me inside. In drama the biggest role I won was one of
fifteen nameless orphans in *Oliver*. In arts and crafts I made yarn-
and-twigs God's eyes, which my mother proudly displayed on bookshelves at home, and in Back Porch Cooking I learned to make
bread-and-butter pickles, and Queen Anne's lace fritters, and black-
berry jam. I never did learn to like hiking. I was much happier when
my parents realized I was a hopeless, happy nerd, and started sending
me to academic camps instead, camps where I took poetry-writing
classes and German courses and generally made the summer as indis-
tinguishable from the classroom school year as possible.

On top of the cooking lessons, I also had my first lesson in prayer
at Eagle's Nest. Religion snuck into Eagle's Nest only on Sunday
mornings, when the camp gathered in an arc of wooden benches for
folk songs and Quaker-like silences. After the fifth Joan Baez tune, we
gathered around the flag pole, watched the Stars and Stripes fly up
to the sky, and recited the Lord's Prayer. There were no printed,
smudged ditto sheets, like there were for the folk songs; everyone
knew this prayer by heart.

After the second Sunday, I looked at Marianne, my Resident Advisor, whom I adored. She was a sturdy kind of beautiful. She had thick, shapely calves, and hair like a horse's tail, with blonde in it that didn't come from a bottle. They were wasting her in the grammar school cabin. She should have been with the teenage girls, so the fifteen-year-old soon-to-be-waifs could have seen they didn't have to starve themselves to be pretty. I bet Marianne never drank Diet Coke or worried about eating dessert. The last night of camp, she told me I was her favorite, and I was thrilled, but three weeks later, my parents separated and I didn't have any stamps and I never wrote Marianne a letter, as I had promised to do.

That Sunday morning I turned to her and whispered, "I don't know this prayer."

"I was beginning to notice that," she said. "I'll teach you."

Later that day, during nap-time, perhaps, or maybe when we campers were supposed to be tidying the cabin, she wrote down the prayer for me, on onionskin fragile paper, and we sat outside. She never mentioned Jesus, or where the prayer came from, how I could find it buried in a book on other onionskin paper, printed in red.

All Marianne said was that she had grown up saying this prayer daily, that one of the things she remembered from when she was my age was saying it every night at her bedside with her mother.

She didn't explain what every word meant, so there was much in the prayer that I didn't understand. I didn't know that *will* was a noun, I only knew it as a verb, so my grammatical reading of the second line of the Lord's Prayer—"Thy kingdom come, Thy will be done"—was a little off. I thought "will be done" the verb, so "Thy," the possessive pronoun, must be the subject. And I prayed fervently that *Thy* would be done.

Sometimes in church I think about that still, I think maybe that is what we should be praying for, not just that God's will be done, but that everything that is God's, everything that is His, everything that is Thy, will be done. *Yours be done*, I chant in my head. *Yours Yours Yours. Everything that is Yours.*

RANDI EMAILS TO SAY her grandmother is rallying. She says yesterday she floated into consciousness long enough to ask for some water. Randi says people around the country are praying for her grandmother, and she believes those prayers are making a difference. "Not that I think all that praying will make her live forever," she writes, "or even another year. But maybe it is giving her the strength to ask for water."

"That is a funny way to think of prayer," I write back. "I never know if I can think of it that way, that it makes differences that way, that it makes grandmothers eat or lovers stay true."

"I don't know," Randi replies. "I don't know how to think about it. I really don't."

She says she is lying awake nights, thinking about her grandmother dying and her beautiful baby girl and how she is turning thirty-seven next week. "I am taken aback by it all," she writes.

Augustine wrote that God sometimes does not give us what we ask in prayer. "Of his bounty, the Lord often grants not what we seek, so as to bestow something preferable."

Randi Waits Anxiously
for a Phone Call

Randi tends toward anxiety. She fixes on things and gets anxious about them, very anxious. Sometimes, when there is no cause for anxiety, she makes something up, just so she has something to feel anxious about. If her husband is three seconds late, she worries he has been killed in a car crash. If her daughter sniffles, she worries about tuberculosis. When she lived in New York, she taught, one semester, at a small college in Queens. It was an evening class, once a week, from six to nine, and finally in March, the janitor confessed that he had a crush on her, and Randi smiled and then spent the rest of the semester terrified that he would turn up in her classroom with a gun and gun them all down.

Randi also doesn't usually answer her phone. She screens her calls. If she answers right away, after the first ring, you know she is expecting a call from someone and you know it is not you. Today I call, and she answers before the first ring finishes ringing. "So who were you expecting to call?" I ask.

"Oh, you know," she says.

"No, I don't know. Who?"

"Well, I discovered this weirdness in my breast. A sort of bump. Or maybe a sort of line. A sort of weirdness." This is another thing she likes to worry about: breast cancer. "So I called the nurse at the women's health center and left a message asking her to call me to go over, you know, just what exactly I'm looking for when I do the monthly breast checks."

"So," I say, "you were waiting for the nurse to call you back."

"No," says Randi, "she already called. We just got off the phone, actually, about two minutes ago. She said everything was fine, of course, that I didn't need to worry." Randi sounds frantic.

"So," I say, "you were waiting for her to call back again and tell you she realized she'd overlooked some key symptom, and actually you have some rare inoperable form of breast cancer and will be dead in a week."

"Exactly," says Randi.

"You know," I say, "she could call back three more times to reassure you, and it wouldn't do any good. You could have eighteen conversations with the nurse, and they wouldn't do any good. Really, the only conversation that will work is the one with God." I sound pious. Randi sighs.

Later in the conversation we talk about what we want to be when we grow up: wives, mothers, professors at some nice college somewhere. Amazingly, sometime in the last five years, Randi became a wife, a mother, and a professor of Jewish studies. "It's odd," says Randi. "I spent so many years of my life aiming for these things and now I actually have them and I am just supposed to sit around having them. I used to feel anxious that I would never get these things. That I would never have a husband, or a baby, or a job. Now that I have them, I have to invent things to be anxious about."

"Well, you know, that is how God works," I say soberly. "He gave you all these things to trick you into relaxing a little so that in a few years He can really pull the rug out from under you."

Randi is quiet for a minute. Then she says, "You're kidding, right?" And I say that yes, I'm kidding. She says, "You just said what you said so that I would realize how ridiculous and crazy and ungrateful I'm being, right?" And I say that yes, that is why I said what I said.

Grinning Bananas, Teal Crescent Moons, and Other Body Art

All in all, I was a pretty good kid in high school. To wit, my ten o'clock bedtime, enforced until the day I left for college. I broke it only three times, each to stay up reading *Moll Flanders*.

And then there were the tattoos, four of them: a teal crescent moon on my ankle, a band of autumnal leaves braceleting around my left arm, a purple flower embedded in a purple star just over my left breast, and a small wreath of laurel leaves (which is what my name means) next to my left pelvic bone (which, teenage-girl readers should note, is a shortsighted spot for a tattoo, for while one's pubescent stomach may be flat as a refusal, eventually one gains the Freshman Fifteen, or one has a baby, or et cetera, and then your perfect, cunning tattoo stretches unrecognizably out of shape).

Tattooing was my one overt rebellion. Well, okay, it wasn't exactly overt. I hid them from my parents, and, when finally found out, I concocted some ridiculous story they appeared to actually believe about their being temporary tattoos, made of all-natural vegetable dye that would fade over an eight-month period.

This was the early 1990s. No longer the exclusive provenance of bikers, sailors, and construction workers, tattoos were becoming trendy. One could spy flowers, sunshines, and treble clefs peeking modestly around the ankles of middle-class high schoolers all across the country.

I am usually pretty out of it when it comes to popular culture, but this was one trend I wanted to be part of. A tattoo might offset my thick, nerdy spectacles, marking me as, if not exactly hip, at least neutral. (The same thinking explains my teenage nose-ring phase, and may, I hate to admit, also account for my flea-market glasses fetish these days.)

There was, of course, something slightly incongruous about a girl headed toward Orthodox Judaism getting tattooed. Leviticus 19:28 states, "Do not cut your bodies for the dead or put tattoo marks on yourselves," and Jewish law forbids tattoos, plain and simple. Indeed, getting a tattoo is faintly akin to committing suicide; both tattoos and suicide can prevent a Jew's being buried in a Jewish graveyard (and even the prohibition on giving suicides a proper burial can be fudged. Generous rabbis often declare the suicide insane, and therefore not culpable, and give him a proper Jewish burial).

At the time, I rationalized the tattoos. I knew that I was not, according to halacha, Jewish; I knew that in a year or two I would go to the *mikvah* with a triumvirate of rabbis; and I knew that nothing I did, in my pre-*mikvah* days, would really count. I knew that when I died the rabbis would look at the tattoos on my body and remember that I had gotten them before I was a Jew, and they would allow me to be buried in a Jewish graveyard anyway. This argument was a little tortured, but I was pleased with it; I thought I had actually applied a rather Talmudic style of logic to my own advantage.

THERE IS A LONG TRADITION of Christian tattooing. Procopius of Gaza, a historian who lived late in the fifth century, noted that many Christians in Europe wore tattoos of the sign of the Cross on their arms. In the sixteenth century, pilgrims to the shrine of Loreto in Italy got tattoos, often of the Virgin Mary or St. Francis, to commemorate their trip. Around the same time, European visitors to Palestine came home with tattoos of the Jerusalem cross. George Sandys, an Englishman traveling in Europe in the second decade of the seventeenth century, observed, "They . . . mark the Arms of Pilgrims, with the names of Jesus, Maria, Jerusalem, Bethlehem, the Jerusalem Cross, and sundry other characters." Christians not only associated tattoos with Christ's stigmata, but with two verses in the New Testament—Paul's words in Galatians 6 about carrying "the marks of Jesus tattooed on my body," and the prophetic vision in Revelation 19 about the writing on Christ's thigh.

Precedent notwithstanding, many conservative Christians have hang-ups about tattoos. Some Christians, pointing to the injunction in Leviticus, claim that tattoos are expressly forbidden, end of discussion. We tattooed Christians sweetly remind the Bible-quoters that if they want to take Leviticus 19 literally, they're also bound by Leviticus 11, which forbids eating scallops, bacon, and clams.

Even those Christians who recognize that the Old Testament's prohibition of tattoos isn't binding upon Christians still find permanent body art somewhat disconcerting. Tattoos seem to suggest some slippery slope toward an alien, dangerous culture. If your teenage daughter gets a tattoo, maybe she's also sneaking out of the house at night to guzzle tequila in some friend's pickup. The sixteen-year-old son of one of my friends came home recently with a grinning banana inked into his calf, and his mother flipped. I can imagine that it's a bit jarring to stare at that tattoo and remember your son's sweet-smelling baby body, perfect and pink. But I try to reassure my friend that, whatever her feelings about her son's aesthetics, a banana tattoo is not cause for alarm. "Getting a tattoo doesn't mean that one is dabbling in satanic ritual practice," I say. That middle-class teens at

Charlottesville High School had started sporting them under their J.Crew pea coats and flannel shirts meant that tattoos had become domesticated.

Still, I think there may be Christian questions about tattoos worth pressing. Christianity teaches the resurrection of the body at the end of time. Will I have tattoos on my resurrected body?

DURING COLLEGE I WENT once a month to visit residents at a Jewish old-age home. The very elderly have always scared me a little, and I always found these visits hard. The smells and the sadness of the place wore me down.

One afternoon in July, I sat reading to an old woman in a wheelchair. Her name was Flora. She sat with her head bowed and her back hunched over, and I wasn't sure that she heard me or even knew I was there. I was reading from *Pride and Prejudice*.

When I got to the passage in which Bingley's sister asks Elizabeth to take a turn in the hallway, Flora nudged my right leg. "What's a nice girl like you doing with a tattoo?" The edges of the teal moon peered out from behind the straps of my sandal. Before I could respond, she pushed up her sleeve, revealing a row of wavy black numbers. I stared at her, and then continued reading as if Flora hadn't said a word: "Her figure was elegant, and she walked well;— but Darcy, at whom it was all aimed, was still inflexibly studious."

Two years later, Flora died. Holocaust numbers are another exception rabbis make about tattoos and graveyards. Flora had a Jewish burial, in the simple shroud and plain pine box, in a Jewish graveyard in Queens.

Holy Week

Palm Sunday

It is Palm Sunday, the day we commemorate Jesus' entry, seemingly in triumph, into Jerusalem. He has been out touring the countryside, teaching in parables and making miraculous cures, and he rides into the holy city on a donkey. The crowd—the Jews—lines up to watch this donkey-riding healer, they wave palms and sing hosannas. It is the same crowd that, a few days later, will demand Pilate crucify Him.

At All Angels' on Palm Sunday, we march around the block, waving palms and singing hymns declaring our love for Jesus. I find this hard, embarrassing, out there on the streets of Manhattan proclaiming to all who pass by that I believe this stuff. I am chic and self-conscious. And I am worried that I will run into someone I know on his way to shul, Palm Sunday coinciding this year with the second day of Passover. Still, by the second verse of the hymn, I am swept up in it all, proud to declare my kooky faith, sure that this is part of learning to be (in St. Paul's phrase) a fool for Christ. I feel like an old-time Salvation Army lass, like Sarah Brown beating her big, round drum for temperance and for God.

Back in the church, we pick up our prayer books and hymnals and launch into the service, but instead of simply reading the Scripture passages, a drama team acts them out: Jesus healing babies in the Temple, the crowd welcoming him, then Pilate, dithering, confused, ambivalent, and the crowd—the Jews—crying, "Crucify him." It is something of a Passion play.

I never like these little bursts of theater, which pop up in church services every now and again. They feel infantalizing, like someone thinks the gospel needs to be dressed up and made entertaining rather than just being straightforward and read and dramatic enough in its own right. Skits in church annoy me.

But today I do not feel infantalized or annoyed. Today I feel stunned. I am stunned because of how the Jews look in this drama. The whole thing reeks of charges of deicide. The Passion play makes sharper what John's Gospel makes clear: Pilate is useless, the Jews are to blame, they turned into some bloodthirsty, chanting mob and killed Jesus. I look around me at the small children sitting in their pews, and I think, *When they leave, they will think the Jews are bad.* I expect Milind to comment on this, somehow, in his sermon, and he does not.

IT IS A HARD TEXT, and one I never know what to do with. The trial of Jesus, as recounted in the Gospels, is hateful to Jews, and has been picked up by generations of Christians as the reason to kill them. The early church fathers pointed to it, so did the medieval Christians, killing Jews and spreading fanciful tales of host desecration, and so did the German churches in 1933.

There is another hand, and it is this: this story is in the Bible. It is in the text the church canonized. It is in the book that is truer than any other book, the book we are not supposed to pick and choose from, the book we are not supposed to judge, but rather be judged by.

This morning in church is not the first time I have hit this wall about the Jews. Recently, a friend loaned me a novel about Pontius

Pilate published by a respectable Christian press. I read it, but my distaste increased by the chapter. This novel, I told my friend when I returned the book to him, was simply anti-Jewish propaganda, no way around it; it let Pilate right off the hook and said Jesus' death was all the fault of the scheming, grasping Jews. My friend found my criticism of the novel unwarranted. "This novel," he said, "doesn't say anything that's not there in the Gospels."

I don't know what to do with this text, but I figure this much should be obvious: it has been two thousand years, and we see that this story, this Jews-killed-Christ story, is a story with consequences. After two thousand years, it seems to me the church should take some responsibility for the way we tell this piece of salvation. I don't mean we should deny that this chapter of John is sacred writ, or stop reading it. But we shouldn't just act out charges of deicide, and then leave them sitting there.

❦

A FEW DAYS after Palm Sunday, I eat souvlaki and rice pudding at a diner with Esther. Esther is one of the other Jews at All Angels'. She is a vestry member, and a lay eucharistic minister, and on the missions board, and does so much at church that I often forget she has a day job.

Several years ago, when Esther was new to the church and there was a different priest, she made what people tell me was quite a scene one Sunday morning. It was the Sunday of Martin Luther King weekend; the homily was all about reconciliation and racial harmony and loving your neighbors even though they might be different, and half the music was borrowed from gospel choirs. After the sermon, the congregation sang a hymn set to the tune of "Deustschland Über Alles," which, before the Nazis co-opted it, was a theme in a Haydn quartet. In the few seconds after the hymn and before the recitation of the Nicene Creed, Esther stood up and said she was horrified, offended, devastated. The priest apologized for the church's insensitivity. Esther walked out.

So HERE IS THE QUESTION: how does the Church witness this Palm Sunday Passion play? Witness as in watch it, how do I sit there and watch it, but also witness as in testify, the way good Christians use the word, to offer your witness, to tell the story, to proclaim the truth of something. This, after all, is church, this is my church. This is the place that should be home for me, the place that should be the heart of truth.

Holocaust Fantasies

Sometimes I have these elaborate Holocaust fantasies. They run one of two ways. In the first fantasy, I am married to a nice Christian man and we have a beautiful quarter-Jewish child, we have a comfortable life teaching at some posh university and a beautiful house filled with beautiful furniture and many charming friends whom we are always inviting to charming dinner parties, and then the rules of exclusion, the rules that say Jews can't do this or that, hold elected office or work in certain professions, those rules start happening, and then violence and other terrible cruelties start happening, and I decide I have to leave. Maybe I go to Venezuela. I explain to the nice Christian husband that I am leaving, that I am fleeing, really, and that I am taking our daughter with me, and it is a test. A test of him, of his love for me—whether he comes to Venezuela, or whether he stays put.

In the other fantasy, the rules and violence start, and spiral, and spin, and it gets worse and worse, and in this fantasy, the church is on the wrong side. The church is cowed and cowardly and complicit, just like the Lutheran Church in Germany. I am somewhere dark, and there is mud, and there are trains and it is raining. Everything, all the clothes and scenery, are gray and olive and drab and brown. I have,

Edith Stein–like, pleaded with the church, petitioned every influential Christian I know, but the church sits still. And so finally I stand up and make a dramatic speech. I say, "If this is the best the church can do, if this is what the church is about, then I can have none of it." I declare that I am a Jew and go, calmly, wherever it is they are sending the Jews, to whatever tortures and death camps they have dreamed up this time. This fantasy is also a test, a test of the church, but more a test of me, of who I am, and where, finally, my loyalties lie, and where, finally, I live.

Seder Stories

Maundy Thursday. *Maundy* comes from the Latin *mandatum,* command, the command being Christ's command that we love one another. Jesus and His disciples have gathered together for the Last Supper. After the meal is served, Jesus, Who "knew that the Father had put all things under his power, and that he had come from God and was returning to God," fills a basin and grabs a towel and begins to wash His disciples' feet. "You should also wash one another's feet," Jesus tells the twelve. "I have set you an example that you should do as I have done for you." The disciples, as usual, are clueless, they don't understand that Jesus will be dead soon, that He is preparing them for that death, teaching them how to love one another, and how to remain in and unto Him once He is returned to heaven.

The Gospel reading for Maundy Thursday tells the story of the foot washing. In church, we also read a passage from Exodus. Our senior warden stands at the lectern and gives us the reading in his purposeful Georgia accent. "Tell the whole community of Israel that on the tenth day of this month each man is to take a lamb for his family," he says, "one for each household." It is Exodus 12, God instructing Moses and Aaron to tell the people to prepare a Passover sacrifice, to paint their doorposts with lamb's blood, so that God might spare Is-raelite homes when He strikes Egypt with the final plague, *makat bchorot*, the killing of the first born.

We read this because tomorrow is Good Friday, when God offers up to God the perfect paschal sacrifice. In our calendar, the Christian calendar, it is the middle of Holy Week, we are just edging out of Lent and down into the darkness of Crucifixion and then out into Easter resurrection. But it is especially fitting that we read this today, because in the Jewish calendar it is the middle of Passover. The two festivals do not always coincide, the church running on a Gregorian calendar and Judaism's calendar aligned with the moon, and when they do overlap it is breathtaking and sad.

FIVE BLOCKS FROM All Angels' is a tall, ornate, pre-war apartment building, where I spent many weekends, and most holidays, for most of college. In apartment 3B, an apartment that was designed to house a newly married couple and their maid, live a family of five. Actually, they don't all live there anymore, the kids are all off, in college or married and living in foreign places. This was the family, the Farmers, that more or less adopted me when I was in college.

I met Zev and Joan Farmer the high school summer I studied at Drisha. The family I lived with that summer, Liz and Arthur Good-man and their five kids, were Zev and Joan's best friends. By the time I met Zev and Joan, late that summer, I was already in love with the Sabbath songs I had learned, already getting used to the swish of long skirts around my ankles, already determined to live an Orthodox life, to be immersed in the *mikvah* and made really wholly a Jew, and the night Zev and Joan came over to the Goodmans' apartment, I sat with a large Hebrew tome open on my lap, searching for a name; I knew converts took new Hebrew names, like Catholics at confirmation taking on the name of a saint. I liked Hephziba, it means *desired one,* and Bathsheva, and Deganit. I chanted these names over and over that night, *Hephzi, Hephzi, Hephzi,* interrupting whatever it was Joan and Zev and Arthur and Liz were trying to do, study Talmud I think, every time I came across a new possibility. Joan laughed and said maybe I should choose something a bit less outlandish, something with a few fewer syllables, maybe Rachel, or maybe Shira.

The next time I saw Joan and Zev Farmer was about a year and a half later. In the meantime, I had started college; gone to *mikvah;* and gotten to know Joan and Zev's elder daughter, Rena, who was a year and a bit older than I, and a physics major at Columbia. She was down-to-earth and loved the Lord and waxed eloquent about Jerusalem, how much she loved the German quarter, how much she loved the soil. She exuded this quiet, take-it-for-granted faith. You met her and you knew she loved God, and that her loving God conditioned everything she did, every choice she made and every sentence she ever said. When I converted, I took her name: Rena. I didn't choose the name because I loved the sound so much, or even the meaning, which is *joy,* but because Rena Farmer was the very type of Jew I wanted to be.

My first year in college, just a few months after I went to the *mikvah,* Rena invited me to her home for Pesach. I remember how crowded the apartment was—Rena, and her parents, and her brother Aaron, just younger than me, and then Leah, three years younger; and a cousin visiting from Israel; and Joan's mother, who left Germany for America in 1934. I was put to work grating carrots the minute I arrived. And I didn't get much sleep that holiday. There were too many names to learn and too many books to flip through and too many conversations to have to bother with sleep.

That was the first holiday I spent in the Farmers' apartment; and for most of college, I spent every holiday there, every holiday and almost every Shabbat, and sometimes just the ordinary weeknight if I needed food and was broke or the laundry machines in my dorm weren't working or when I came down with a flu or when I just wanted to sleep somewhere where I wasn't surrounded by 9 million other eighteen-year-olds.

Once, I was sitting in the living room reading a novel and Joan pulled me into the kitchen and she said, "I want to talk to you about something you said the other night when you were here." She sounded urgent and serious and hushed. "You were leaving, after Shabbess. Aaron was trying to convince you to stay and go to the movies with him and Leah. You said, 'No, I have to get home.'" Joan paused. I narrowed my eyes and waited for her to get to the part where I'd said something that offended her or upset her or something. "It makes me sad to think of you thinking of your dorm room up at Columbia as home."

"But it is my home," I said. "It's where I live."

"I want you to think of this as your home," she said. She gestured around the kitchen. There were boxes of Entenmann's doughnuts on the top of the refrigerator and a stack of plates in the sink.

DURING MY SENIOR YEAR, after I had bought the Book of Common Prayer and after I had attended the Q & A at the Church of the Resurrected Light, I began telling a few people that Jesus seemed to be beckoning me his way. I talked to my friend Jana mostly. Jana was a convert, Presbyterian to Mormon, and I kept asking her, that spring, how she knew, finally, and how she had made the decision, and how she had told people and what they had said. That spring she came with me to one of the Farmers' seders. I remember almost nothing of the seder. I don't remember who else was there, or what we ate, or what I wore or which songs we sang. I don't remember walking back to campus with Jana, or where, in my cramped dorm room, she slept. I do remember that she loved the seder, and that she sat on my narrow twin bed in her cherry-red pajamas and said, "Are you really going to give all that up?" To become an Episcopalian, she meant.

I thought she meant giving up the seders. I thought she meant the singing and the Haggadah and the ritual and even the joy, and I looked at her and, haltingly, answered, "Yes; yes, I am going to give all those things up." But I am not sure I understood what all the losses would be. I'm not sure I knew that I would have to number the five people who lived in 3B among them. I have not seen them, except for Aaron, in four years.

───❦───

THE PASSOVER SEDER is the best kind of meal for a bookworm. It is the one meal all year at which we are not only allowed, but enjoined, to read a book at dinner. The Haggadah, literally "the story" or "the telling," guides the Passover dinner; it's both script and dramaturge's manual. The Haggadah is a wise book, and it has many perfect sentences and paragraphs. My favorite story comes near the beginning, just after the declaration that "we were slaves in Egypt." The story tells of five rabbis who make a seder at Bnai Brak. The rabbis are reclining at the seder table—reclining, as is the custom at Pesach, because only free people, only royalty, recline, slaves don't recline—telling the story of the Exodus. They're so engrossed in the telling that they stay up, sedering, all night, past dawn, talking and talking about the Exodus, and finally their students come around and tell them that it is time to pray, that the hours in which it is permissible to say morning prayers are almost over.

I love the devotion of those five rabbis. I love the sheer fun they must have had at their seder. And I sympathize with their headiness, with being so caught up in talking about God and talking theology and doing other cerebral things that the time for worship almost slips by. I recognize myself a little in those rabbis, so drunk on the thinking of it all, that you almost forget to pray.

WHEN I MOVED BACK to New York from England, I became a little fixated with talking to other Jewish converts. I made that trip to Baltimore to talk to the convert couple there. I vaguely remembered an ex-boyfriend had a friend whose father had grown up Jewish but was now a Lutheran pastor; I tracked him down somewhere in Iowa and called him up for a five-hour conversation. I read an article by a law student at Stanford who had converted from Judaism to Christianity in high school; I emailed her and we met for coffee when she was next in New York. And, through the friends of friends, I met a lawyer in the Bronx named Jeff. He grew up Jewish, had even considered entering the rabbinate, but had become a Christian about fifteen years before, at the end of college, like me. He and his wife, Amy, a scholar of medieval literature, invited me over for dinner in the fall.

I liked them both, though they couldn't be more unalike. Jeff is sloppy, paunchy, disorganized. He laughs with a great belly laugh and doesn't stand on ceremony. Amy is fastidious. Her study is organized to the point of obsession, custom shelves built to the exact size of her books. First thing in the morning her hair is perfectly in place. It's hard to imagine her padding around in a robe and slippers; I'm not sure she even owns a robe and slippers.

When we first met, Jeff and Amy were at the beginning stages of the long process of adopting a baby. "Thinking about rearing a child," Amy said precisely, "has raised all sorts of questions we didn't know we had." Questions about what to tell that child about Judaism; questions of how to resolve old, old hurts between Jeff and his parents, who had been horrified when he converted; questions about just what Judaism meant in the lives of Christians. "I've been surprised," said Amy at that first dinner. "Initially, I thought these were just Jeff's questions. He's the Jewish one. These questions don't really have anything to do with me. But I no longer feel that's true. If they are his questions, and if they are questions that will shape the life of our child, then they are my questions too."

"We are thinking," said Amy, "of creating some sort of Passover seder this year."

"A Christian seder," said Jeff. "Nothing too elaborate. But something that will give us the context for a conversation about some of these issues."

"Would you like to join us?" Amy asked.

ON THE NIGHT of our seder, I slip into my chair at Jeff and Amy's dining room table and I feel sure this is how the Jewish feminists making their feminist haggadahs for their feminist sedarim in the 1970s must have felt—pioneering and creative and faintly afraid that maybe it couldn't be done, that maybe they couldn't force this story into the shape they needed it to be.

Not that we are really all that pioneering. Christian Passover seders have been popular for years. Sometimes churches sponsor them, or members of a Bible study will get together for a Passover meal. Some Christians are interested in making a seder because they want to know more about the church's Jewish roots, they want to experience some sliver of Jesus' life as a Jew. This is what He did; we should do it too. And some Christians are interested in the seder because they appreciate the Eucharist, the Lord's Supper. Churches that used to celebrate communion four times a year or once a month are now celebrating every week, with more and more Christians seeing that the Lord's Supper sits at the center of Christian worship. It was at a Passover seder that Jesus instituted the Eucharist: it was matzah He held up when He said, "This is my body," and it was seder wine that

He drank when He said, "This is my blood. Do this in remembrance of me." Christians growing into the Eucharist sometimes want to recreate that meal.

So we aren't doing anything new in making this seder, but it is new to me. I have never been to a Christian seder before.

There are eight of us at the table: Amy and Jeff and me and Martha, a friend of theirs from Georgia who is visiting, and a couple from their church, Alice and Albert, and Albert and Alice's twin daughters, Alicia and Amelia Ann. The service we follow is the traditional Jewish service. We have left the Hebrew haggadah more or less unchanged, and we follow it straight through. We bless the wine. We eat a fresh spring vegetable. We break the matzah, Jeff lifting up three pieces of matzah, pulling out the middle one, and breaking it in half. Later he will hide one half of the matzah, a game for the children, to find the missing piece somewhere in the apartment, and once they have found it, Jeff will ransom it back, giving them each a present in return for the missing matzah, and then we will eat that missing hidden piece for dessert.

Amy watches Jeff break the middle matzah and she begins to cry. "It's His body breaking," she says, and everyone at the table knows what she means. We see in the three pieces of matzot the Trinity, the Father, the Son, and the Holy Spirit, and see that we are taking the middle matzah, and breaking it, and we see that this is the way Jesus' body will break, on the Cross, and then over and over, every day for the rest of time, in the Eucharist. I think, *It is we Christians, we, who do this, not the Jews.* At the seder, it is so clear: *The Jews didn't break his body. Our sins broke his body. Break break break. They didn't kill Him; the weight of our sin killed Him.*

FRANZ ROSENZWEIG WAS a German-Jewish philosopher who almost converted to Christianity. For years, he carried on a tortured, and fascinating, correspondence with his cousin, Eugen Rosenstock-Heussy, who had himself become a Christian. In 1913, Rosenzweig himself finally decided to convert. But, he said, he wanted to—felt it imperative to—come to Christianity as a Jew. So, before heading off to church to be baptized, he went to a synagogue. It was Kol Nidre, the evening of Yom Kippur, the Day of Atonement. And there, in synagogue, Rosenzweig realized that Judaism could provide a vital path to God. In a sort of inversion of Paul's moment on the road to Damascus, Rosenzweig committed his life to Judaism. What was supposed to be a route to Christianity turned out to be his destination. Rosenzweig went on to write the most influential work of Jewish philosophy in the twentieth century.

In *The Star of Redemption*, Rosenzweig discusses time and calendars and holidays. About Pesach, he writes, "The welding of people into a people takes place in its deliverance." And that, it seems to me, is what both Passover and Maundy Thursday are about—making a people. In the Exodus, the Jews are transformed from people into a people, and at the Eucharist, instituted there at the Last Supper, we Christians are transformed into a people, too. This, after all, is what we say in the liturgy of the Eucharist: "May we be one body, because we all partake of the same bread." The body of Israel is constituted at the Exodus, and the Body of Christ is constituted at the Eucharist, through the very consumption of the Body of Christ.

The question of the Christian seder is how to constitute these two bodies at once. Can they inhabit the same body?

⚬⚬⚬

ALL WEEK I think about my family. When I'm in church, listening to the reading from Exodus; when I'm at Amy and Jeff's seder; when I'm walking down the street or cleaning my kitchen. I think about my family celebrating Passover in North Carolina, and I think about the

Farmers' seder on Riverside Drive, and I think about Beth and her husband in New Haven, and I think about Randi and her husband and baby making a seder in Ohio, and I feel sad.

The Passover seder gives thanks to God for delivering us from bondage, but it is also shot through with longing, with messianic expectation. It is a service that ends, finally, with the recognition that redemption is not yet complete. During *Nirtzah*, the concluding prayers, you say the words, *"Bkarov nahel nitai kana, p'duyim l'tzion b'rina."* "Soon will you lead the shoots of the stock that you have planted, redeemed, to Zion, in joy." I think about my family and the Farmers and Randi and everyone else saying those words, celebrating this holiday of liberation, and I want them to realize that Jesus celebrated this same memorial of our redemption from Egypt, and then he died to liberate them eternally.

I WAS HALF-SMITTEN with Aaron Farmer all through college. I have never known if he was half-smitten with me. If circumstances had been different, we might have been married years ago, with a baby already and living here in New York and visiting his parents all the time. It was never possible, though, because the Farmers are *cohanim*. They are descended from the line of the high priests of Israel, those men who, when the Temple still stood, performed all the most important sacrifices, and on the holiest days, soaked in a *mikvah* and removed their shoes, and entered the *kadosh kadoshim*, the Holy of Holies, what Latinists call the *sanctum sanctorum*. They entered that spot, and they uttered God's ineffable name. There is no Temple anymore, but Jews know that one day there will be a Temple again, so the *cohanim*, the priestly class, must be kept distinct, and pure, and separate. Priests must be found and called on when the time comes. *Cohanim* are subject to all sorts of special rules that don't apply to other Jews. They cannot enter cemeteries, lest they become contaminated by the impurities of the corpses, and they cannot marry converts. That I had grown up thinking I was Jewish did not matter; I was a convert, and Aaron Farmer was off-limits. We bantered and conversed endlessly but we rarely talked about what I took to be our kindredness. We never kissed. I never told him I sometimes looked at him across his mother's table and just wanted to touch his face. Joan and I discussed it once, discussed how it could not be, and I wished—because I wanted to be her daughter as much as because I fancied being his wife—that it could be.

When I moved back to New York from England, Rena was already married and living in Jerusalem, but Aaron was in school here, at Columbia, majoring in religion and taking classes with some of my old professors, and I wondered if I would see him on campus. I half-hoped I would and half-hoped I wouldn't. And for months I did not, never saw him, never ran into him in the library, never crossed paths with him at the bookstore. And then after all the months and months of not seeing him, I began to see him every time I turned around. I passed him one day on College Walk, the concrete tree-ringed sidewalk that cuts through the center of the Columbia campus. He was walking east and I was walking west, he was walking alone and I was walking with a friend, and he and I looked at each other, and I waved, as though just seeing someone from class whom I recognized but whose name I didn't know, and he smiled, his eyes heavy like sleep, and his smile a bit sheepish, and neither of us slowed our walk, and after he passed, or I passed, I said to my friend, "That was Aaron Farmer," and I began to explain who he was, and we were quiet for a minute or two and then resumed our conversation, which was good mindless academic chatter, about the New Deal, I think, and why Robert Wagner had cared so very much about labor.

The next day, I saw him on College Walk again, and he saw me, but pretended not to. The day after that, we passed each other outside

Kent Hall, and then, that same afternoon, I was coming out of the newly built library coffee shop, and Aaron Farmer was tripping down the steep Butler Library stairs, a portrait of Lady Liberty behind him, and if we had taken three more steps we would have crashed straight into each other and I said, "Hey, since when is it okay for you to ignore me on College Walk?"

And he said, "Well, I think it's quite understandable. Given what's happened." He paused. "I don't think I can talk to you, it's a little uncomfortable, and that seems understandable given what's happened."

And I, feeling like a first-grader who'd been spurned at recess, grew icy, and said, "Well, I'm sorry to inconvenience you. I'm sorry to make you uncomfortable. It won't happen again," and I spun around and stalked off back into the coffee shop, wishing already that I had been more mature, more graceful, more poised. Or more poisonous. *More like Dorothy Parker*, I thought.

Last week, I got an email from Aaron asking if we could meet. I replied right then, before I had a failure of nerve. "Sure," I wrote back, "let's meet."

He comes to my apartment, and it's not at all clear, initially, why he has come. He asks me about my coursework. He tells me about his after-graduation plans. I ask him if what he wants is an explanation, if he wants me to tell him why I had converted, or how I had come to convert, or what it meant to me, something like that, but he says no, he doesn't want to know those things. Then he says what he has come to say: "Even a Jew who sins is still a Jew," an old rabbinic truism that reminds even the most reprobate sinners that they cannot shed their Judaism. A call for repentance, perhaps. "I just thought you should know that," he says. "I felt I had to tell you that." He wants to be sure I understand that my halachic conversion to Judaism, my morning at the *mikvah*, had not been undone by my apostasy. He wants me to understand that, in the eyes of the Torah and the Jewish community, I am still a Jew, albeit a Jew caught up constantly in sinning.

"I already know," I say. "I know what the rabbis say about Jews like me." Then I ask after his parents, and he says that they are well, but that they can't talk to me. "They think about you sometimes," he says, "the whole family talks about you sometimes." But his parents feel too hurt, too betrayed, that this was too much, this thing I had done, and they cannot talk to me. "Because," he says, "because you were family."

We leave my apartment and walk to campus. We talk about the weather. When we get to the library, I want to create some scene from a movie, some melodramatic parting that will either resolve things (perhaps we'll run away together and join a secular Israeli kibbutz), or definitively not resolve them, me weeping and giving a speech on the steps about how it devastated me to hurt his family, about how this is the great unresolved puzzle of my life, the cross I will have to bear; Aaron confessing that he was crushed when he'd heard I'd been baptized, that he shouldn't have come to see me, but that he just couldn't stay away.

Of course, that's not what happens. We stand outside the library and Aaron says, "I wish you the best. I wish you every happiness. I really mean that." And he really does.

"Me too," I say. And then he heads into the library, and I head east toward Broadway and I call out over my shoulder, "Aaron, I'm glad you came by. I really mean that." And I really do.

———— ∞ ————

MY MOTHER HAD a saying when I was growing up. When she was frustrated, piqued, vexed, and undone, when she was wondering why half the world lay up nights thinking of ways to make her life difficult, when she really had just about had it, she would say "I declare! I am losing my religion." Forget about coming to the end of your rope. Who needs rope? Losing your religion means you are really coming apart.

Then when I was in middle school, R.E.M. released a single, and they called it "Losing My Religion" and teenagers around the world came into that quaint Southern expression.

This is one of the things that happens when you convert: it happens when you grow up a God-inclined half-Jew who abandons her parents' ways for the rigors and requirements of Orthodoxy, and it happens when you are a long-skirted, long-sleeved *frum* Jew who somehow turns and kneels at the foot of the Cross. One of the things that happens is, you feel family-less, even if your own family doesn't cast you out, and you lean on your friends and your classmates and all the people in your new religious world more than you should. Your roommates, and their parents, and their friends, you gobble up their lives, adopting and being adopted and fitting yourself in just so. You need a family and you love them like a family and you make them love you back just that way, and they do. And so, should you convert again, you lose all sorts of things: not just your library and your vocabulary and your prayers, but also your family, all the people who made you their own and who you made yours. It's a good reason to only convert once, if you can help it. Because it is more than just your religion that you lose.

I LEARNED THE WORD *suture* in a summer school class I took with Rena Farmer. It was a course on the human skull, which we were taking to fulfill our science requirement. The text was *Gray's Anatomy,* and every day we came to class, sat down in a pair, and played with a skull. We took it apart and put it back together. We were trying to learn to identify all the bones. Sometimes we were quizzed, orally. The professor would hold up a bone and we were supposed to name it and find the bones that were its neighbors. I always did worse on these quizzes than anyone else.

That summer school class was the first time I had realized the skull was not, in fact, one circular bone. It is twenty-two bones, all pieced together. The line, the place of fusion, between any two skull bones is the suture.

When I think about Joan and Zev Farmer now, the word I think is *suture*. I write Joan letters in my head. The letters are mature and restrained and ask if we could meet. They explain that her absence leaves an unfinished gape, and I would like to see her, even though I know better than to imagine that one hour of conversation and a cup of coffee could suture that gaping.

The Viaticum

Every Sunday at about 11:30, I stand in front of Milind and cup my hands and he says, "The body of Christ, the bread of Heaven," and I say, "Amen," and lift the bread of Heaven to my mouth and chew and swallow. I believe this receiving the Eucharist is the place where I most really meet Christ, the place where reality is most real. I believe it is the most important thing I do each week.

Naysayers sometimes dismiss the eucharistic rite as hocus-pocus. You say some formula over a slice of bread, and it becomes flesh, poof, magic. (In fact, *hocus pocus* derives from a parody of the Latin words a priest says at the Eucharist: *"Hoc est corpus meum."* "This is my body.") But it is not a magical formula that the priest says over the wafer and wine. He tells the story of Jesus instructing his disciples to do this in memory of him. Actually he does more than tell it. He enacts it, he reenacts it. Milind doesn't just intone; he moves. He lays a table for us. He raises a goblet. And, after he consecrates the bread and after we say the Lord's Prayer, then comes the moment of the service called the fraction, which comes from the Latin *frangere,* "to break," like a number broken into mathematical thirds. There, he raises the eucharistic wafer, and carefully, over the chalice so no stray crumbs go flying into any strange corners, he breaks the wafer in two. At that moment, it is always Good Friday. Christ's body is broken on the cross, again.

I have never, not once, felt anything at the Eucharist. Not a thing. I have never felt stirred, or joyful, or peaceful, or sad. I have never felt closeness. I have never felt God at the communion rail. Steven once said that after receiving communion, he felt woozy, as if he'd drunk two bottles of magic wine, not just one tiny sip; but I have never felt woozy.

I keep hoping one day God will give me some feeling at communion. In the meantime, I figure He is helping me become something else. He is calling me to know Him in the Eucharist even though I don't feel Him there. He is calling me to a place where He is truer than everything else, truer even than how I feel.

WHAT YOU NEED for this sacrament is simple: just some bread and some wine, or grape juice. Grape juice became popular in the late nineteenth century, when temperance-advocating evangelicals realized they couldn't call for a complete ban on potables if they were imbibing themselves at the altar on Sunday. They mounted all sorts of complicated arguments about the different Greek words for wine, and they suggested that Jesus hadn't been drinking fermented wine, but rather unfermented, nonalcoholic, wine at the Last Supper. The people in the pews found these arguments bizarrely persuasive, and then churches were faced with a new problem—producing enough unfermented grape juice. The ladies of the Women's Christian Temperance Union circulated "receipts": "Express the juice of the grapes as you do for jelly; heat immediately to the boiling point, bottle and seal exactly as you do fruit. Adapt the size of the bottles to the number of communicants, as the wine will ferment if left over from one communion to another." Women labored over their stoves, churning the stuff out, week after week. Thomas Welch, a Methodist dentist from the strip of upstate New York so given to religious revivals that it earned the moniker "burned-over district," saw a great business opportunity. In 1869, he found a way to mass produce nonalcoholic grape juice and, in 1875, his son Charles Welch founded a company.

You don't have to have any particular type of bread for the Eucharist. A priest I know was once backpacking with his wife in Washington state. They celebrated communion with a pizza crust.

I spent the June between my two years in England teaching at a high school summer camp in Maryland. I attended Sunday morning worship at a little stone church out in the country. They were a bit depleted that summer—most of the Altar Guild was vacationing elsewhere, gone, perhaps, to a little stone church in the mountains for the hot summer months. I volunteered to help Viv, the lone Altar Guilder left at home, bake Eucharist bread.

Viv is a widow in her mid-sixties; she adores church and adores her garden and adores playing on her computer. "I email my grandson at college every day," she chirped. When I turned up at her house on a Wednesday evening, she had everything laid out on her yellow kitchen counters: whole wheat flour, white flour, and bottles of sparkling water.

"Perrier?" I asked.

"Oh, yes," said Viv, "I always use Perrier in the eucharistic bread. Mark 14:7, don't you know."

I wracked my brain. I had no idea what Mark 14:7 was.

"It's the story of Jesus and the woman at Bethany," Viv explained. I gave her a blank look. Where was Bethany? "The story where the woman comes to Jesus just before Passover and anoints His feet with the most expensive perfume. All the onlookers grouse that she shouldn't have wasted such nice perfume on Jesus' feet. They tell her she should have sold the perfume and given the money to the poor, but Jesus says that she did the right thing, spending her rich perfume on Him. 'The poor will always be with you,' He says, 'but I will not always be with you.'" Viv ripped open a bag of flour and a white cloud burst out with a poof. "I take from that story the lesson that when we do something for Jesus, especially something as important as the Eucharist, we shouldn't just use ordinary ingredients. We should use the finest ingredients! Making eucharistic bread with tap water would be an insult, don't you think? So I always use Perrier."

Goodness, I thought, *Jo wasn't exaggerating when she said that gradually the Gospel would come to shape even the smallest details of my life.*

Making the bread was easy. We stirred together half a cup of whole wheat flour and half a cup of white flour with half a cup of Perrier, and then we pressed the dough onto a cookie sheet. "Three seventy-five," said Viv, sliding the cookie sheet into the oven. "Preheated." After fifteen minutes, we flipped the dough over, baked it for five more minutes, and then flipped it again. "Five final minutes," said Viv. "Then you're done."

Viv sent me an email a few weeks after I left Maryland. She wrote to tell me that she had just finished reading a novel she thought I would like (*The Cape Ann* by Faith Sullivan), and that Pastor Rose had preached a wonderful sermon about evangelism. Then she wrote, "P.S. I was just pulling your leg about the Perrier. I don't really use it because of Mark 14. I use it because the bubbles make up for the missing leaven. I wanted to be sure to tell you that, in case you one day decided my reading of Mark wasn't convincing. Always use sparkling water in your eucharistic bread."

⸺⸺⸺⊷⊶⸺⸺⸺

WHEN I BEGAN ATTENDING CHURCH, I didn't know much about the Eucharist. I didn't understand what it was, exactly, or how it worked, but I knew, deeply, that the Eucharist was somehow essential, that it was the heart of what we do in those spired buildings. Since I hadn't been baptized, I couldn't receive Communion, but, still, when I started going to church, I only went to churches that offered Communion every Sunday, not those that celebrated once or twice a month. Even though I couldn't receive, I didn't think there would be much point in going to a church with a Eucharist-shaped hole carved out in the middle of its Sunday worship.

After my baptism in England, I began to slip into church at noon, every day, for the short eucharistic service: a scripture reading, a confession of sin, consecration of the bread and wine, tasting them, prayer of thanks. Twenty-five minutes. Forty, if you factored in the brisk walk from my rooms to church and back again.

"What is really happening at the altar?" I would ask Jo. Jo would murmur about mystery, or about remembering what Jesus said at the Last Supper, remembering his sacrifice for us. "Orthodoxy," I would say. "Right doctrine. I want to know what's really going on. Does the cup of wine, really, actually become Christ's blood, or not?"

Finally Jo pulled down her *Oxford Companion to the Christian Church* and turned to the entry on "Eucharist." "This article outlines about eight different understandings of the Eucharist," she said, "and you can find Anglicans who believe any and all of them."

Hearing that I could believe just about anything and still remain a good Anglican didn't help much. So I did what I always do: I read. I read guides to Anglican thinking about the Eucharist, which laid out the positions of Thomas Hooker, Thomas Cranmer, John Tillotson. I read surveys of medieval Eucharistic thought, which explained that theologians like Thomas Aquinas, seizing upon Aristotle, said that the "substance" of the bread and wine became Christ's blood and body, but that the elements' "accidents," that is, the appearance of the bread and wine, remained the same. I read about Martin Luther's doctrine of consubstantiation. Finally, I lit upon some twentieth-century

Catholics who put forward a view called transsignification, which affirmed the Real Presence of the Lord in the Eucharist, but focused on the symbolic, rather than the purely phenomenological, change that happened at the altar. This was a theology of the Eucharist that made sense to me. One Tuesday afternoon, I burst into Jo's rooms carrying a thin orange paperback, *The Eucharist,* by Edward Schillebeeckx, a Dominican from Antwerp. "This is it," I said triumphantly. "This is what's really happening at Communion."

"Great!" said Jo. "Now that you've read up on the Eucharist, would you mind participating in the Eucharist?" She handed me a bundle of purificators—the squares of linen with which ministers wipe the rim of the chalice while serving communion. They needed laundering by Sunday.

———— ❦ ————

AT ALL ANGELS', I teach the five-and-six-year-old Sunday school class. One day we sit in a circle on the dusty green rug and talk about the Eucharist. "Then Milind stands up and prays for a long time. He gives a long speech, doesn't he?" I ask, referring to the consecration of the bread, when the priest tells the story of the Last Supper. "What do you think is in that big goblet?"

"Apple juice," cries out one student, evidently swayed by weeks of Sunday school snacks. (She may also think the Eucharistic wafer is a graham cracker.)

"I know," says a boy in a daringly pastel T-shirt. "Milind is giving everybody wine to drink." That was the correct answer, of course, but I kept calling on students.

"I think," says a pensive girl with black corkscrew curls circling her face, "that Mister Milind is pouring God into the cup for us to drink."

That, I think, is what Jesus must have meant when He said we need to be like little children. He was talking about this very corkscrew-curled little girl, who doesn't care about transsignification or consubstantiation or substance and accidents. She just knows that the priest pours God into a communion cup.

THE SERVICE OF BREAD and wine has many names. *Eucharist* comes from the Greek for thanksgiving, and that name makes a straightforward kind of sense. Jesus gives us this gift in the Eucharist, the gift of his real, indwelling presence, and we, in return, give him thanks.

We also call this service the Mass, from *missa,* meaning, "You are dismissed." One must be baptized before receiving the Eucharist, so, in England, during the months before my baptism, I stood in church and watched the handful of Christians who gathered in the chapel on Sunday mornings receive. Usually, the Eucharist was passed around from communicant to communicant, each person feeding the bread to the person in line next to him. Each week, when the small silver paten with the circles of bread came to me, I stepped back, not partaking, not participating. In the early church, I wouldn't have even been allowed to watch. Anyone who was curious could attend the beginning of worship services: Scripture, homily, prayer. But when it came time for the Eucharist, for the bread and the cup, the priest said to the onlookers, "*Ite, missa est.*" "Go, you are dismissed." *Missa,* that is how we came to call that part of the service, the secret, precious, inner part, the Mass.

It doesn't sit well with our modern sensibilities, the idea that you could be excluded from a group, asked to leave, shut out because you didn't believe something, or hadn't been doused in the right water. But there is something fitting to the privacy of a members-only Eucharist. The Eucharist is intimate. Watching it is a little like spying on a couple making love. This may be the place where Christ loves us best.

Holy Communion is another name, and there are good reasons to speak of *taking Communion.* Those words remind us that we are not only drawing near to God, but that we are doing that most basic and social thing, we are eating together, we are drawing near to one another. This has been a long, slow lesson for me. I am just starting to learn that the people I take Communion with are the people who count.

I didn't like most of the people at Clare College chapel. I loved my priest. And I loved Becky, my godmother; Anna, the ordinand sent over by her seminary to be our priest-in-training; and Helen and Olivia, two short-haired eighteen-year-olds with lively minds and brassy giggles. Other than those few, the people at chapel weren't people I would have chosen to socialize with. They weren't up to my standards. I didn't think them clever enough, entertaining enough, whole enough. Mostly, at the Clare chapel, I met broken people, needy people, people who were in church for a reason.

In fact, some of the chapel people repelled me. They were pale and pasty and watery drips of people, inarticulate and shy and nerdy and downright tedious. I had nothing to talk about with any of them, though Lord knows I tried, not even theology, a concept that seemed foreign to these students, students for whom everything about Jesus was perfectly clear-cut. "These are not," I sniffed to Jo, "people I would ever invite to a dinner party."

Jo, in her wisdom, didn't point out the obvious fact that I was, indeed, having a dinner party with them every Sunday morning. She pretended to sympathize. She pretended to be every bit the snob that I was. She said whole days elapsed where she had to speak, hour after pastoral hour, to people she did not like very much or find terribly interesting. "There aren't too many people around here like you," she admitted conspiratorially, as though it were just us two charming and sophisticated Christians pitted against the rest of the sorry, benighted church. Then she sighed and said, "But I realized awhile back that if I built a church filled with my friends, it would be a rather small and homogenous church." I blinked. "Dull, really," said Jo.

So much for sympathy.

The day before I left Cambridge for good, I saw Paul and Gillian, two of the most annoying of the annoying Christians, on Clare bridge, and I hugged them. I said I would miss them. I thought I was lying, to be polite. But I wasn't. I have missed them. I do. No one else I ever meet will have pledged to support me in my life of Christ, which is exactly what Paul and Gillian pledged at my baptism. My friends at Columbia, the friends I meet for drinks at trendy bars in the Village, the friends with whom I chat about post-structuralism and Derrida — those people didn't witness my baptism. They didn't cheer at my confirmation, they didn't pray with me every Sunday for two years, they didn't hand me Kleenex when I burst into inexplicable tears in the middle of the Lord's Prayer. They aren't my brothers and sisters in Christ. They are merely my friends.

EUCHARIST, MASS, and *Communion* all have their place, but I want to start a campaign to revive an older name for the Eucharist: the Viaticum. *Viaticum* was a Roman term; it designated the food, clothes, and money that a Roman magistrate took with him when he traveled on state business. It was the necessaries he needed to get him through his trip. In the early church, Christians called the host you gave to one who was on the verge of death the Viaticum. Like the money and food that outfitted the Roman envoy for his journey, the host was the provision dying Christians needed as they stepped out on their journey from this world to the sweet hereafter.

Sometimes, early Christians used *Viaticum* to designate not just the deathbed Eucharist, but any Eucharist. The Eucharist, the Viaticum, was the necessaries for our journey through this life. It was, in the words of one minister, "the sacrament of maintenance." It is like what the angel said to the exhausted and broken prophet Elijah, collapsed in a sleep under a broom tree. The angel waked him and said, "Arise and eat, else the journey will be too great for you."

And that is the Eucharist. If I did not eat, the journey would be too great.

Opal's Easter

On Friday morning, before heading to church for an afternoon and evening of Good Friday prayer and sermon and thought, I pay a visit to Opal. I am sitting in Queens, in her living room, on the sofa with the white slipcover. From behind her lattice of cigarette smoke and beside a vase of bright tulips, Opal asks me a question she has asked before. "Lauren, I really do not understand why you feel the need to throw yourself into this religious group that I spent my twenties escaping." (What lies behind Opal's question is her own autobiography, which involves growing up an evangelical and leaving Christianity in the seventies, when she discovered both Doris Lessing and sex.)

I want to answer Opal's question by simply pointing upward, by saying that I do this because of God. I know this answer will inspire only a sigh and an eye-roll from Opal. It is, I acknowledge, a tautology: God because of God.

I have spent my whole life since middle school, and actually even before that, seeking God. As a child in bed at night, I made up prayers to some God up there somewhere, then I was led into and through Judaism, and then I converted to Christianity, in particular, because I came to understand the Christian story about God being the True

One. And when I dreamed about Jesus and read Paul's letter to the Galatians and Edward Schillebeeckx's orange paperback about the Eurachist and the Mitford books, and all that theology, gradually, over the shifting time of a few years, I came to understand that what the Gospels said about Jesus, about God, was True, and, so, there you have it: I became a Christian.

So I try it out on Opal. I say, "Well. I became a Christian because God gave me the grace to do it." I tell her that Cyril, Bishop of Jerusalem, said that people think they are coming to church for all sorts of reasons, but really the only reason they are coming, *even if they don't know it yet*, is that God has gotten them there. He wrote, "Perhaps some man among you has come because he wants to win the approval of his girl-friend. . . . Perhaps a slave has wanted to please his master or someone has wanted to please a friend. I accept this as bait for my hook and let you in. . . . Perhaps you didn't know where you were going or recognize the net waiting to catch you. You have swum into the Church's net. Allow yourself to be caught; don't try to escape."

This answer does indeed inspire Opal to sigh and roll her eyes. She has asked me why I took up this one particular religious vocabulary, and I have answered her in that vocabulary, which means I have given her an answer that both utterly satisfies and does not satisfy at all. Then Opal asks something else. "Is it just that you take comfort in the idea that when you die, you will go to Heaven instead of becoming lunch for a worm?"

GOOD FRIDAY IS WHERE that one grave and theological term, *incarnation,* most pointedly meets that other grave and theological term, *atonement.* Hanging there on the Cross, bleeding and in pain, He (and the capital *H* is especially important, as not just anyone's suffering would have had the same result) atones for our sins. Theologians have endlessly debated theories of the atonement, but on this basic fact all orthodox Christians can agree: through Christ's atoning work on the Cross, we fallen sinners are reconciled with God. (The word "atonement" was coined by sixteenth-century English theologian William Tyndale, as a translation for the Latin *reconciliatio*.) In His crucifixion, as Paul puts it bluntly, Christ ransomed us from death.

This curiously good day is long, sad, and exhausting. We fast. We sit through three hours of somber mediations on Jesus' last words from the Cross. We inch toward Christ hanging on the Cross bleeding and drinking vinegar and in pain. I leave church feeling supersaturated. I am not sure I can go to church the next night for Easter Vigil. I am not sure I can ever go to church again. I feel ground down by liturgy. I don't want to pray anymore. It is all I can do the next night to force myself out the door and down the street for the vigil that heralds in Easter, as Saturday turns to Sunday and Jesus shades from death to resurrected life.

Our service begins in the darkest, deathest darkness, the church building becoming Jesus' tomb—we are entombed with Him—and then, in this darkest, deathest dark, Paul J., who's been a member of All Angels' forever, lights the Paschal Candle, which will burn all of Eastertide. And as he and Milind and the candle process in, everything lifts and I am giddy. I glimpse why it matters that Christ rose again. I know in the candlelight that His suffering on the Cross is not the end of the story. I know that He is risen, and that His being risen is a marvelous thing.

During Lent, we do not say the word *Alleluia*, from the Hebrew for "praise God." But at the Easter Vigil, the word bursts back into the liturgy, right as Milind begins to celebrate the Eucharist. "Alleluia," he declares. "Christ is risen."

"The Lord is risen indeed," we reply. "Alleluia!"

You can tell we are a people deprived of Alleluias for two months. We say it over and over. We say it with exclamation marks.

ON SUNDAY MORNING, I join Hannah and Jim at their little Baptist church. I am the only woman here without a hat. The woman sitting in front of me is wearing a fetching blue cloche. Even Hannah (who, frankly, can't really wear a hat) is sporting a straw boater. "Why didn't you give me a sartorial heads up?" I whisper to Hannah.

"You're from the South," she says, "I thought you knew these things."

One thing I do know is that I'm in for a long sermon. I've worshipped here with Hannah and Jim four or five times, and the shortest sermon I've heard Pastor Bob deliver lasted sixty-two minutes. Bob may have been the only person in the country to enjoy Clinton's nomination speech at the 1988 Democratic National Convention. In his sermon, Pastor Bob drives home that the resurrection that Jesus experienced was real, that it was literal and embodied. "No metaphor, no parable," he says. "He actually got up from his tomb, once dead but now alive, enfleshed. Seems like a Christian basic—indeed it *is* a Christian basic—but we can no longer take for granted that even churchgoers are on board with this central event of Easter." A 1995 poll, Bob tells us, revealed that 35 percent of born-again Christians say that Jesus never had a bodily resurrection. "Apparently, we moderns, soaking in our culture of scientific proof and Enlightenment cynicism, find the idea of Jesus rising from death too hard to swallow. It is the core of the Christian story, it is the sine qua non, and yet, somehow, it is easier for us to believe in the Easter bunny than in the Easter resurrection."

And with that (at minute forty-seven of the sermon), Pastor Bob gave me one very concrete reason to be glad I grew up on old-fashioned Judaism instead of on cynical Enlightenment: Judaism taught me daily to expect God to resurrect the dead. True enough, over the centuries the rabbis have debated the details of Jewish after-life, but it boils down to what you say every day in prayer. And what you say every day in prayer, in the middle of the *Shemoneh Esrei* (literally, the "eighteen," because it comprises eighteen blessings), is that God "heals the sick" and "releases the prisoner" and is "faithful to raise the dead."

Easter, it seems to me, is the most profoundly Jewish of all Christian holidays. For a Jew becoming a Christian, bodily resurrection is no surprise. It is what we had been expecting all along.

EASTER, THE CHURCH TELLS US, is the most important day on the Christian calendar—the day that celebrates Jesus' resurrection, the day that proclaims (pace all those Hallmark cards that suggest that Easter is about the Triumph of Crocuses over Winter) the Triumph of Christ over Death. On Easter we celebrate not just the time-bound miracle of Christ's resurrection, but the timeless truth of eternal life with God forever and ever unending, on and on.

Easter gives the next piece of a story begun at Christmas and continued into Good Friday. He lived for us and then He died for us and then He rose for us. His death atoned for our sins and His resurrection opens the door to everlasting life. In this way the task of Easter is to presage eternal reality.

This is a theme that C. S. Lewis, the Oxford don and Christian apologist, sounded again and again. This earthly life, even for church-goers, is a mere shadow land, but soon we will live resurrected in the bright glory of reality. *The Last Battle,* the final volume of Lewis's Narnia chronicles, pictures the end of time. Aslan—the lion who represents Jesus—has returned, folding all of culture and humanity into his kingdom. In the novel's last pages, he tells Lucy, a child from London, that everyone she knew back in Blighty is dead and raised to new life. And as Aslan spoke, writes Lewis, "the things that began to happen . . . were so great and beautiful that I cannot write them. And for us this is the end of all the stories, and we can most truly say that they all lived happily ever after. But for them it was only the beginning of the real story. All their life in this world and all their adventures in Narnia had only been the cover and the title page: now at last they were beginning Chapter One of the Great Story, which no one on earth has read: which goes on forever: in which every chapter is better than the one before."

On Easter, we glimpse the beginning of Chapter One.

OPAL WANTS TO KNOW why I have landed myself in church, and I can give her a list, knowing, though, that the sum of the parts will never capture the whole. For the fierce hold of that net about which Cyril spoke; for the knowledge that Jesus' blood ransomed me from death; for the ongoing meeting of Him in the people at church, and many other reasons besides; and one of the many other reasons besides is the promise of Heaven, which is the place where we have that resurrection from the dead, we have it because Jesus rose, and in Him we are raised. The Heaven that I prefer to Opal's worms may or may not have pearly gates; Heaven may or may not be, as Fitzgerald has it, one long party at Gatsby's; in Heaven, I may see my dead, saintly grandmother again, or I may not see her in a way I recognize, but I may be so preoccupied with God's nearness that I won't quite care.

This returns, inevitably, to the same tautology, because this with-God-in-Heaven was this end I was created for. I was, as St. Ignatius of Loyola said, "created to praise, revere, and serve Him"; I believe, with Augustine, that people desire to praise God, that God "prompts" that desire in us and that the end toward which we restlessly ever move is rest in Him. Or, again, there is what Cyril said, right after he instructed his catechumens to allow themselves to be caught in God's net: "Jesus is fishing for you, not to kill you but to give you life."

Eastertide

Contraband Party

The Monday after Easter, Hannah and Jim throw a party. We've all been instructed to bring our contraband, whatever we gave up for Lent. Beer. Chocolate. Something caffeinated. A friend of Jim's turns up with a case of retsina. Sherri, a woman from Hannah's church whom I know slightly, brings a bag of teddies, push-up bras, silky slips, and garter belts. "You gave up lingerie for Lent?" I ask.

"No," Sherri says. "I gave up sex." She leaves all the lingerie with Hannah. She is giving up sex for good. "Well, at least until I get married." Sherri grins. "This Lent was the beginning of my new chaste life."

The party was really just a fancy pot-luck. Hannah and Jim assumed that most people had given up some edible for Lent. So I bought a bag of gummy worms to bring with my book. "The bookworm," says Hannah, "is back."

Bede

Of all the company of heaven, my favorite saint is the Venerable Bede. Today is his saint's day, and I am making a picnic to celebrate. Just me, my picnic basket, and a book of Bede's homilies for Lent. (I couldn't read them during Lent, since I was on that reading fast, so I am reading them now.)

The Venerable Bede was an eighth-century priest and monk. In *Paradiso*, Dante places him in the Sphere of the Sun, the heaven of wisdom, dancing in a circle with Thomas Aquinas, Solomon, and nine other sages. Bede was prolific, a scholar's scholar, writing more books than he lived years. In icons Bede sits at a desk over an open folio, writing implement in hand. His most famous book is the *Church History of England*. To the end of *Church History* he appended a vita, over seventy titles, and then he added this prayer:

> I pray You, noble Jesu, that as You have graciously granted me joyfully to imbibe the words of Your knowledge, so You will also in Your bounty grant me to come at length to Yourself, the Fount of all wisdom, and to dwell in Your presence for ever.

That prayer is why I love Bede. Because he knew that knowledge and books were just a nice way to fill the time until he came to dwell with Jesus. It is a good prayer for a graduate student.

Ascension Day

Luke doesn't linger over Jesus' ascension to heaven. He gives us the scene in just six verses at the beginning of the book of Acts: After Jesus rose again, after He was resurrected and enfleshed on earth for another six weeks, He promises His disciples the Holy Spirit, and He instructs them to carry the Gospel to the ends of the earth. Then, Luke tells us, as the disciples were watching, "he was taken up before their very eyes, and a cloud hid him from their sight." The disciples stand gawking at the sky, and two men in white robes appear and explain what has happened: "This same Jesus," they say, "who has been taken from you into heaven, will come back in the same way you have seen him go into heaven." Every day, we repeat what the white-robed men said when we recite the Apostles' Creed: "He ascended into heaven, and sitteth on the right hand of God the Father Almighty. From thence he shall come to judge the quick and the dead." He was born incarnate, and He will come again, but right now He is up in Heaven.

The church celebrates Ascension Day forty days after Easter. It is always a Thursday, and we always read the same Scripture passages. At church, we read the passage from Acts. At home, guided by the lectionary for the daily office, we read the Gospel of Matthew, Jesus charging the disciples with evangelism, and telling them that He will be with them always, until the end of ages; and we read the reminder in the Epistle to the Hebrews that, "It was fitting that God . . . in bringing many children to glory, should make the pioneer of their salvation perfect through suffering"; and we read four psalms. Of all the readings for today, it is the last four verses of Psalm 96 that tell me best about Ascension Day:

> Say among the nations, "The Lord reigns." The world is firmly
>   established, it cannot be moved; he will judge the peoples
>   with equity.
> Let the heavens rejoice, let the earth be glad; let the sea resound,
>   and all that is in it;
> let the fields be jubilant, and everything in them. Then all the
>   trees of the forest will sing for joy;
> they will sing before the Lord, for he comes, he comes to judge
>   the earth. He will judge the world in righteousness and the
>   peoples in his truth.

Those lines make the point. Jesus is up in Heaven now, but He will come again. His work is not yet finished. He will come again to judge us.

Ascension Day is not a festival we spend looking up at the sky, looking after Jesus, wondering where He has gone. It is also a day that forces us forward to the time when He will come again.

THERE IS A JEWISH SAYING, found in *Avot d'Rabbi Natan:* if you are planting a sapling and someone runs by shouting that the Messiah has come, finish planting the sapling, and then go to greet him. The saying is a favorite of liberal Jews, who want to emphasize the Torah's imperative that we do social justice, that we don't sit around being otherworldly, pining for the messiah; while he tarries, we get to work repairing the world.

Christians have sometimes made similar arguments. In the nineteenth century, most American Protestants were postmillennialists. The *millennial* in *postmillennial* refers to the thousand-year reign of holiness promised in Revelation 20, and the *post,* the "after," refers to Jesus—postmillennialists believe that Jesus will return only *after* the millennium of peace and perfection. Postmillennialism is an optimistic theology, one that suggests that human beings can make the world a better place; indeed, it not only encourages us to improve the world, it obligates us to improve it, which is why most of the reform efforts of the nineteenth century—from temperance and abolition to women's education and opposition to dueling—were headed up by evangelical Protestants.

The instructions to finish planting that sapling can be taken too far, of course: it is easy to become so proud of our work that we begin to think that our planting the tree is the Messiah. Still, it is a good reminder that we need to plant as well as pray. Indeed, today's Gospel reading makes a similar point. Jesus' last instructions to his followers are not to spend twenty hours a day in prayer, but to "go and make disciples of all nations, baptizing them in the name of the Father and of the Son and of the Holy Spirit, and teaching them to obey everything I have commanded you." He tells them to carry on the work of redeeming the world.

PEOPLE THINK JUDAISM and Christianity are radically different from one another, and that the difference is straightforward—one religion has a messiah who has come, and the other religion doesn't. But on Ascension Day, I am struck by the deep similarity that lies just underneath that difference. Both Jews and Christians live in a world that is not yet redeemed, and both of us await ultimate redemption.

Some of us wait for a messiah to come once and forever; others of us wait for Him to come back. But we are both stuck living in a world where redemption is not complete, where we have redemptive work to do, where we cannot always see God as clearly as we would like, because He is up in Heaven. We are both waiting.

Confession

My mother taught me, early on, how to write proper thank-you notes, how to set a table, and how to tell people I'd done something wrong. It was grueling, that third lesson. I came home from kindergarten, smart in my new green rain-slicker, which I adored and wished to wear even in the loveliest weather, and presented her with a quarter. "Where'd you get that?" she asked. "Did you forget to buy your milk at lunch?"

"No," I beamed, "it came from Mrs. Smith's desk." I did not pretend embarrassment, for I had done nothing wrong. I had just found something valuable and brought it home for the family coffer.

I was a teacher's pet, even then, and Mrs. Smith had asked me, and second-pet Christina, to tidy out her desk drawer during recess. I never much liked recess, hating the outdoors and preferring to stay inside and read even then, and tidying a desk wasn't reading, but it was better than kickball. I was thrilled.

We tidied and straightened, rounded up all her stray paper clips, and cornered them into one rectangular compartment on the right-hand side of her desk drawer. We banded together all the rubber bands and tucked them in the back. We lined up her pencils. We stacked stickers and capped pens. There was one quarter, just there alone, no other quarters. I scooped it into my pocket.

My mother handed me my green coat, steered me toward the car, and drove the four miles to Ira B. Jones Elementary. We walked to my classroom. "Why Lauren," exclaimed Mrs. Smith, "did you forget something?"

I squirmed. "No," my mother said, "but she has something to tell you."

I pulled the quarter out of my slicker and handed it to her. "I took this from your desk today. I'm sorry," I managed.

Mrs. Smith smiled kindly, and hugged me and thanked me for coming back and giving her the quarter. "It was probably not a very easy thing to do, to come back to school in the middle of your afternoon and give me this quarter. I am very grateful that you did. I forgive you for taking my quarter." The next week, at recess, Mrs. Smith asked me if I would like to clean out her desk drawer.

I think God is a little like Mrs. Smith. I think He forgives us the way Mrs. Smith did: only a fool, God, or a saintly kindergarten teacher would allow a known, convicted, desk-drawer quarter thief to tidy her desk not seven days after the first crime. Mrs. Smith did, though, because she believed repentance had been done. I was truly sorry, she had truly forgiven me, and that was all there was to it.

———— ✂ ————

ABOUT ONCE A MONTH, I take a train two hours upstate, hop into a cab, and ride a few more minutes to a small, brick Episcopal church, and there I meet Father Peter, my confessor. There are, of course, many priests in Manhattan who could hear my confession, starting with Milind. But I don't want to confess to him because I don't think I'd say everything. I'm too eager for Milind to like me. If he were my confessor, I think I'd skip the hard sins. So, instead, I trek upstate to Father Peter.

I picked Father Peter because I had friends in his town, and I figured I could kill two birds with one stone: confession, followed by lunch with folks I don't get to see very often. When I first rang up Father Peter's church and asked if he heard confession, he said, "Why, yes," but he sounded rather taken aback. "I have to admit that there aren't too many people in this parish who seek that service, but I would be happy to hear your confession." He paused. "Is this some sort of emergency?" I wasn't quite sure what he meant: was I on my deathbed?

"No, no," I assured him. "Any time this month would be fine."

He told me to meet him Tuesday at four, and asked me to come prepared—with a list of everything I planned to confess. "That way you won't forget anything," he said.

I spent the next three days praying with my eyes open and a legal pad in hand, asking God to call to mind all the sins I needed to repent; I can't remember if Father Peter told me to do that, to pray with a legal pad. Someone must have told me. I don't think I would have thought of it on my own. On Tuesday afternoon, I walked down to his church, clutching six long legal pages, yellow paper made blue on both sides with ink.

"Well, now," he said, "I'm pleased to meet you. Since we've never met before, I thought we should spend a few minutes getting to know each other." So we stepped into his office, and began to chat—about where I was in school and what I was studying and where he had gone to seminary and what our favorite books were. It was one of those fabulously bookish conversations where, twenty minutes in, you are both pulling books off the shelves and reading things aloud and recommending favorite authors and favorite titles, absolute must-reads. I liked him, this priest, and I wanted him to like me.

"I can't possibly confess everything on this list," I thought, as we traded book notes. I could tell I had impressed him, that he took me, even, as a kindred spirit. And that was precisely what I wanted: for him to think well of me, to be impressed, to approve. *He won't possibly still like me after he hears this list,* I thought, and I began ticking off the things I would skip. *I'll have to tone down the stuff about failing to pray,* I thought, *and the last paragraph of page three, I'll have to skip that entirely.* The last paragraph of page three, of course, was the sexual stuff. The last paragraph of page three detailed how I had failed to walk the chaste straight and narrow after being baptized. Sex with my boyfriend. Sex with an ex-boyfriend I then lied to my boyfriend about. Not behavior that was really in line with Paul's instructions to the Thessalonians: "It is God's will that you should be sanctified: that you should avoid sexual immorality."

As I was mentally deleting items from my legal pad list, Father Peter and I began to talk about the theology of confession. "I'll tell you," I said, "I don't really understand about confession. I mean, I've already prayed about most of this stuff just to God directly, secreted away in my closet. Presumably, if I repented then, He's already forgiven me. So what am I doing here? It's like double jeopardy." Father Peter nodded. "On the other hand," I said, "maybe confession actually does something, maybe you are really truly forgiven only once you go through the rite of confession. But that doesn't make any sense either, because it means that praying to God directly, alone in my bedroom, isn't good enough." Meanwhile, I offered up a confused prayer, that if I was really supposed to confess all those awful-sounding things, all those things that would make me just look ordinary and normal and not impressive or kindred in Father Peter's eyes, that I would go ahead and confess them; but I didn't have any intention of having that prayer be answered; I intended to skip the last paragraph of page three.

Father Peter allowed that he didn't totally understand how confession worked either. "Some people say it's important not for theological reasons, but for psychological ones. You feel you've truly confessed and truly been forgiven only after you go through some semipublic rite."

"That may be," I said, "there may be a psychological benefit. But the church hardly called something a sacrament just because it made people feel better."

Father Peter nodded. He seemed to agree. He didn't seem to have any magical answers, however.

Father Peter put on his purple—purple is the color of Easter, but also the color of secrecy—and he reminded me that anything I said to him in this confession would go, as it were, under the purple, to sit in secret and never be repeated. We walked upstairs to the sanctuary, and we knelt at the altar. "Usually," Father Peter said to me, "a priest knows his penitents a little better than I know you. We've just visited for half an hour and I don't know you very well at all. But this is a sacramental moment, and we must both believe that we have been called by God to be here."

It is a simple service, The Reconciliation of a Penitent. It opens with the penitent (that's me) saying, "Bless me, for I have sinned." And then Father Peter said, "The Lord be in your heart and upon your lips that you may truly and humbly confess your sins." And then I did; I tried, anyway, to be humble and true, and I read my long list from the yellow pages, and talked about all the sinning I had done in the short while since I was baptized, since I'd pledged to renounce Satan, wickedness, and sinful desire. When I came to page three, to the sins I had hoped to skip, I was caught up enough in the spirit of the thing that I didn't skip them; but I was still so conscious of myself, and of Father Peter there in purple, that I blushed.

And then the priest, as the Book of Common Prayer has it, "pronounces absolution." "The Lord has put away all your sins."

"Thanks be to God," I said.

"Go in peace," said Father Peter, "and pray for me, a sinner."

I thought, then, that we were done, but Father Peter said, "One more thing. I'd like to have your lists." He held out his hand. I clutched my yellow sheets. I had thought it might be nice to keep a record of these sins. And why did he want them anyway: did he want to read them, checking up on me to see if I had said everything I was supposed to say? Father Peter smiled, and, reluctantly, I handed over my sins, and then I watched as Father Peter ripped my six sheets into shreds. Apparently, this is common. A priest friend of mine in Minnesota tells me that he burns people's lists after they confess. "It's funny," said Father Peter, as we walked out of the church, "it happens whenever I hear a confession. After I leave the altar, I can never, for the life of me, remember a single thing the penitent said."

THE LORD HAS PUT *away all your sins.* I think that language is perfect, God folding my sins neatly and putting them in the dresser drawer next to the sweaters and the turtlenecks and the socks. It means the God who worries about our sins is not only God the judge, but also God the caretaker. He worries about sin because He craves right-eousness, but also, simply, because He loves us.

TODAY, I AM ON THE TRAIN, off to see Father Peter. I feel, on these train rides, a little like I felt the one time I hired someone to clean my apartment. I hadn't vacuumed in about eight months. The dust bun-nies had morphed into dust mastodons. The kitchen floor was sticky with jam and brown with dried coffee. I was having a dinner party, and begged my friend to loan me her Friday maid. As soon as Lucy had agreed to come, I began to panic. Surely she had never seen an apartment this dirty. What would she think? I would have to do the thing my mother had always told me to do when I was growing up, the thing she instructed me to do every Thursday night, the thing that made no sense whatsoever: I would have to *clean because the maid is coming tomorrow.* I got on the phone to Randi. "I am so embarrassed," I said.

"Get over it," Randi said. "This woman is a professional. This is what she does. This is her job. She's seen it all." That's a little how I feel about Father Peter. I feel chagrined and awful every time I go to see him. But this is his job, and he has seen it all.

The chagrined awfulness must be part of the point of this confession. Things done in private, seen in private, and known only to God, now become known to someone else. "The lot of penitents," Joseph Martos once wrote, "was not a happy one, nor was it meant to be."

In a few minutes, the train will pull into the station, and I will head to church. It is chilly, but the rain has stopped, so I will walk from the train station, past small shops with gourmet tasties in the windows, past several dozen fine houses, even past one small stone cottage, all gingerbread-like, down to the gumdrop flowers that angle around the yard. By now the church secretary knows me as "that confession lady."

Father Peter and I will not make chit-chat. We will head straight for the altar, where we will pray, and I will read my long list like a litany. When I finish my list I will sit in silence and see if God has any other sins He wants to call to mind.

Father Peter will grant me absolution, but confession isn't just about absolution. It's not some kind of antinomian free-for-all, where, since we know Christ has already forgiven us, we can just keep sinning. The change, I think, that conversion gradually effects on your heart is this: you come, over some stretched-out time, to want to do the things that God wants you to do, because you want to be close to Him. So the point is not just to be forgiven, it is to be transformed. The religious languages have better words for this than English—*teshuvah* in Hebrew, and *metanoia* in Greek. A complete turning around.

I doubt I will achieve a complete turning around here on Earth. I will always need this ritual of confession, because I will always keep screwing up. And God somehow will keep forgiving me, and pulling me closer to Him. He will, over time, make me sadder and sadder when I spit in His eye. He will make me love Him better. And that might mean, maybe, that I will sin a little bit less.

After he tells me to pray for him, a sinner, Father Peter and I retreat to his office and talk. We talk about how much repetition there is, how I seem stuck in the same old sins. My confessions seem usually to concern two familiar topics: prayer and sex. Not enough of one, too much of the other. We talk about what I can do.

Today we will talk mostly about praying. I keep making these pledges to pray more regularly, more devotedly, more attentively, but I continue to pray irregularly, inattentively, with precious little devotion.

Father Peter will say, "But you have made real progress regarding chastity," by which he means that I am no longer turning up here all the time talking about all the sex I've had. He's not saying this to make me feel better. He's saying it because he wants to know what worked. He wants to know how I have managed to live (as he puts it) "content without intercourse" for these many months but I can't make myself stick to a simple regimen of morning prayer.

But Father Peter does not always say easy, helpful, pastoral things. He does not always ask gentle questions. The first time I met with him, I hemmed and hawed and then finally got up to the part about having had crazy sex one night with an ex-boyfriend who was in town for the weekend. "Well, Lauren," he said. "That's sin. That is sin."

───── ∞ ─────

ON YOM KIPPUR, Jews confess their sins, both privately and corporately. Before the holiday begins, they go around asking the forgiveness of everyone they have wronged; the Talmud teaches that God forgives the sins we've done against Him freely, but He will not forgive the sins we've done against our neighbors until they have forgiven us first. One Jewish prayer book puts it this way: God's forgiveness for us is our forgiveness of other people running through us.

And on Yom Kippur, people pray, corporately, for God's forgiveness. Part of the Yom Kippur liturgy is a long confession, *Vidui*, a long list of sins committed: bribery, slandery, lust, gossip, insolence, envy, theft. Once, a Jewish man went to his rabbi and asked, "Why am I confessing all these sins? I didn't commit half of them. I haven't stolen anything or bribed anyone or told lies." The rabbi looked at the man and said, "If you understood the glory and grandeur of God, you would realize you had committed each of these sins, every day of your life."

CONFESSION IS NECESSARY because something has gone wrong in the world. Baptized Christians keep sinning. As the Anglican theologian John Macquarrie wrote, "Post-baptismal sins . . . from a theological point of view, are strictly an anomaly. In baptism, sins are forgiven and the baptized person receives the gift of the Holy Spirit. That ought to be the end of sin as far as that person is concerned." But it's not the end of sin. We sin, as the Book of Common Prayer puts it, in what we have done and what we have left undone. And the church gives us confession to deal with those sins.

I am not sure I understand the sacrament of confession much better than the first time I sat down with Father Peter. I say confession because the church teaches that we should, and I say it because, when I don't, I feel over full—not in a good, cup-overflowing way, but in a sticky, sweaty, eaten-too-much way.

Confession makes sense to me because it is incarnational. In the sacraments, the Holy Spirit uses stuff to sanctify us. In the Eucharist He uses bread and wine, and in confirmation He uses oil and in baptism He uses water. In confession, the stuff He uses is another person. In that way, confession teaches us about the Incarnation all over again.

As Dietrich Bonhoeffer wrote, "Christ became our Brother in the flesh in order that we might believe in him. . . . Now our brother stands in Christ's stead. Before him I need no longer dissemble. Before him alone in the whole world I dare to be the sinner I am. . . . Christ became our Brother in order to help us. Through him our brother has become Christ for us in the power and authority of the commission Christ has given to him. . . . When I go to my brother to confess, I am going to God."

Here, in confession, God is connecting us to Himself not through bread or oil or water or wine, but through another broken body, one who absolves you, and then says, "Go in peace, and pray for me, a sinner."

Family Reunions

This weekend, my family is holding two small reunions. In Virginia, two cousins, Sylvie and Betty May, are coming to visit my mother. They are her first cousins, and my mother has not seen them in many, many years. They have been planning this visit for months. They will go to Monticello, and a craft fair, and the farmer's market. They might go to Vinegar Hill, the artsy movie theater, and watch a Merchant-Ivory film. A few weeks ago, Betty May called my mother and said, "Sylvie and I thought we should tell you . . ." And then her voice dropped. "We thought we should tell you that we drink wine."

"Oh?" asked my mother. She drinks wine, too.

"Well, you know how we were all raised," said Betty May, meaning, *You know we were all raised as teetotaling Baptists.* "We didn't know how you'd turned out."

ALSO THIS WEEKEND my father will visit New York, one of his regular trips to see me and go to the opera. I think about stripping my walls, taking down all the Jesus pictures and all the crosses. I know they will upset him. I know he will glance at them and his vein will start popping out, the vein in the middle of his forehead that always jumps up and down when he is distressed. I think maybe taking them down would be the respectful thing, the honoring-thy-father thing. So Thursday night I unhang all the crosses and fold up all the batiks, and put them in a big box at the foot of my bed.

And then Friday morning, before he arrives, I decide it cannot honor your father to not let him know you as you really are, and I hang them all up again.

Two Funerals, and a Wedding

It is the end of May, and Randi's grandmother dies. She is buried in a cemetery in New Jersey. I borrow Hannah's car, and try to drive to New Jersey to meet them, but her alternator dies before I am over the George Washington Bridge, and I spend the morning at the mechanic's instead.

Two days later the woman I roomed with the summer after my freshman year of college dies. She had very quick-spreading cervical cancer that, her mother tells me over and over, the doctors just didn't catch in time. For this funeral, also in New Jersey, I take a train.

MAY ALSO INAUGURATES the season of weddings. I gear up for one a week for the rest of the summer. These weddings are fine when you are dating someone, someone you think you might marry, because you daydream the whole time about your own wedding with him, you feel soft and hopeful and excited. When, however, the last man to kiss you was your dad, then the weddings get to be rather a drag. You try to be happy for your friends. You fail.

Marriage has always been my synecdoche of choice, a wedding-cake part for the whole of my life. And I'm not the only one in my family obsessed with marriage. My stepmother once told me (after I'd badgered her for about twenty minutes, demanding to know how upset, on a scale of one to ten, my father was about my conversion to Christianity) that my father once asked her, apropos of nothing, if she thought I would want a church wedding. A church wedding, thought my father, would seal it. It would fix Christianity in my life the way thiosulfate fixes a photograph. Forget about baptism and pledging my life to God. Once I'd pledged it to a Christian man, I was in it for life.

There is something tempting and true about that line of thinking, because social bonds are real; they are forceful. It is easier to pretend that an invisible God is imaginary than it is to pretend that your husband is imaginary; if you are a Christian and you marry a Christian man, if you stand up in a church and make your vows before a minister and not just a magistrate, then keeping your vows to your husband becomes tangled up with keeping your vows to God. If being a Christian might help a couple stay married (a debatable premise, according to sociologists of American religion, but one that I feel should be accurate nonetheless), being married might help a couple stay Christian, too.

I sometimes wonder what shape my religious life would have taken if I had married Dov. Jesus, being omnipotent, could have gotten to me regardless, but the scenario is a little hard for me to imagine. All that seems certain is that had I married Dov, and had I somehow become a Christian anyway, Dov's mother would have, understandably, flipped her lid.

THE FIRST COUPLE on this season's wedding docket is the soon to be Mr. and Mrs. Jonathan Thyme, aka Jack and Donna. Jack was at Cambridge with me, and Donna knows Hannah from college, though we didn't have a hand in introducing them. Jack and Donna are getting married at a big church on the East Side. I sit with Hannah and Jim in a pew near the front.

I think back to that wedding this past winter—the one after which Hannah slept with Mr. Latin American literature. I hope now, at this wedding in springtime, to see some sort of spark between Hannah and Jim, some bit of renewal. I hope to see her touch his leg or sneak a kiss or smile and giggle or something, but I don't see that. They don't look grim, exactly. They just look determined.

I wonder what Hannah and Jim are thinking as they sit there listening to our friends make these crazy, extravagant promises to each other. I wonder if they think these promises are un-keepable, or if they think no one should ever try to be married, or if maybe they are glad they are married, grateful they are married, because it is only God's glue, promised to them in the sacrament of marriage, that kept them from spiraling apart, Hannah to the excitement of the Latin American literature man and Jim to wherever he would have spiraled after that.

All the Questions You Might
Want to Ask about Angels

Angels are all the rage these days. They have their own TV shows, and people wear angel pins and buy angel cards. When you attend a church named after angels, you find yourself thinking about them sometimes.

I don't go in for the TV version of angels, the cloying guardian types who are more interested in making us happy than in serving God. But I do believe in some other, winged, real type of angel, the type that was in the Bible, the type that showed up at odd times and made strange announcements to stunned virgins.

In college, Beth and I often argued about whether it was better to be an angel or a person. I said that I wished I had been born an angel, because angels, according to one Jewish teaching, do nothing but stand around praising God, and that is what I would like to do, praise God. If I were an angel, I would praise Him all day. As a person, I generally manage about three or four minutes of praising, then I get caught up in doing all the other things I want to do, like going shopping or reading novels or toasting toast.

"But if you were an angel," Beth would always reply, "you wouldn't have a choice about it. You would have to praise God all day because that's what angels do. As a person, your praises are so much more meaningful, even if they're less frequent, because you have free will, and you are making the choice to praise God. Angels," she would say mournfully, "don't have free will."

"I'm not all that interested in free will," I would say. "Seems to me that praising God is the best thing you could do with your time, and if that's the trade-off—more praise, less choice—that would be fine."

<hr />

WHEN I GO to the Metropolitan Museum of Art, I generally stick to two galleries, which, happily, are right next to each other: medieval art and the American wing. Even when I go with the best intentions of viewing a special exhibit or looking at Monet, I always wind up sitting with portraits of George Washington or stark thirteenth-century icons.

You walk through the medievals first. You walk past stained-glass scenes of the Passion, and past illuminated Psalters swollen with Latin. You pass a case filled with enamel from Limoges, chrismatories and pyxes, the small circular homes for consecrated eucharistic wafers. You pass silver reliquary crosses and square ivory diptychs of the Virgin, and then you push through glass doors, and you're in another century and on another continent. In the American wing are the hand-pieced quilts, the voluptuous deco furniture, the re-created Shaker bedrooms and Victorian parlors. It's rooms like those that made me an American history major; I spent so many grammar school afternoons hanging around the Biltmore Estate and Monticello, and loved being carried back, loved the shiny wooden tables with the spindly legs, loved the brocade and the velvet, loved the dim, historic kitchens, and the moldings and the banisters and the gilt.

The middle of the American wing is a courtyard, an indoor sculpture garden, benches to sit on and fountains to find soothing, and over to the right, in limestone and oak, is the choir rail and pulpit that used to sound the sermons of All Angels' Church.

The church was incorporated in 1859, and it stood, proudly, at West End Avenue and 81st Street for over a century. By the 1970s, the church's numbers were dwindling, and its coffers were low, and finally, in 1979, the congregation deconsecrated the building, sold the property, and moved a block away, to the smaller building in which we worship today. Before the original building was torn down, the choir rail that wrapped around the inside of the first All Angels' Church was saved. Commissioned by Sarah Cornell in memory of her husband, carved by the Vienna-born sculptor Karl Bitter, it now lives here, memorializing the Cornell clan, in the Met.

The choir rail is a chain of dozens of angels, seductive in their robes of limestone gray, swaying across the balustrade up to the pulpit, carrying harps and triangles and other instruments that angels play. At the top, above the balustrade, above the empty space where a preacher should be standing, perches one giant angel with a trumpet.

A group of schoolchildren is in the courtyard today, an early September field trip, and I eavesdrop as I sit on my bench looking at the sculptures. Their teacher is explaining the façade that fronts one of the period rooms. She tells them about the Ionic column, and the triangle-shaped pediment, and the windows. Next, the teacher points out a sculpture of Diana and quizzes the students on Greek mythology. She is beginning to usher them into another room when one of her charges asks about the angel.

"Who is that man with the trumpet?" the boy asks. At first, the teacher seems to think he's asking after John Quincy Adams Ward's sculpture of August Belmont, much more manly in his suit and regal chair than the angel. But only the angel has a trumpet.

"That is a decoration from a church," says the teacher. "Remember the stained-glass windows we saw? Those were decorations from a very old church, and this is a decoration from a more recent church."

"Why does he have that trumpet?" asks the child. "And why is he so high up?" The angel could almost reach to the ceiling, if he stretched a little.

"All angels play instruments," the teacher says. "And he is high up because his real home is not the museum, but Heaven, up above the clouds."

We have a copy of that angel at church, in the southwest corner of the sanctuary. I am glad the original is here at the Met, surveying the courtyard, rising triumphant above Edward Kemeys's *Panther and Cubs;* out above banker Belmont, bulbous and green with oxidized age; floating over even tall, golden Diana, poised with her bow. Above all that is the angel, caught in singing flight, trumpeting his good news to the courtyard and to all the world.

Pentecost

Shavuot

Pentecost, which means "fifty days" in Greek, was once just another name for Shavuot, the Jewish holiday that comes fifty days after Passover. Shavuot is an agricultural festival, first commanded in Exodus 23:26 to commemorate the harvesting of grain. The Jews in the time of the Temple offered loaves of bread to God, in thanks.

But shortly after the death of Jesus, Pentecost took on special meaning for Christians. The Book of Acts tells us that when Jesus' disciples gathered together to celebrate Shavuot, a remarkable thing happened: the Holy Spirit descended upon them, just as Jesus, minutes before His ascension to heaven, had promised. On Pentecost, in the church, we don't celebrate the original harvest holiday. We celebrate the anniversary of God's giving the Holy Spirit to His church. Pentecost is one of the three great Christian festivals, alongside Easter and Christmas, although we've fallen away from according Pentecost as much attention as the other two. And, today, the term *Pentecost* denotes not only the holiday, but also the liturgical season it inaugurates, the season after Easter.

Jews no longer celebrate Shavuot as a primarily agricultural festival either. Though it began as a holiday about grain, by the rabbinic era

Jews commemorated God's revealing the Torah to Moses at Mount Sinai on Shavuot. The story of the revelation is recorded in the middle of the book of Exodus. The Israelites, freed from slavery in Egypt, had been wandering in the wilderness, led by God, who hovered in a cloud ahead of them, and fed by manna that God sent from the sky. When they come to Mount Sinai, God tells Moses to prepare the people: "Go to the people and consecrate them today and tomorrow. Have them wash their clothes and be ready by the third day, because on that day the Lord will come down on Mount Sinai in the sight of all the people." On day three, the Lord descended upon Mount Sinai and met the people. Then He called Moses to the top of the mountain. Moses stayed for forty days, and the Lord revealed the entire Torah to him; not just the written Torah, but also the oral Torah, the Torah *she baal peh*—the Talmud and all the other rabbinic commentaries. Moses received every scrap that would be set down later in the Mishnah and the Gemara; he received all the glosses, all the layers and layers of interpretations through which Jews read the words of Genesis and Judges and Job.

To mark the revelation, Jews have the custom of staying up all night learning Torah. It's called a *leil tikkun Shavuot*, a set order of study for the night of Shavuot. You stay up all night as penance for the Jews' sleepiness—on the morning that God was to reveal himself at Sinai, the Jews overslept, and Moses had to roam the camps, rousing them.

Centuries later, God's people still hadn't learned. On the night before He was to be handed over, Jesus went to the garden of Gethsemane to pray. He took Peter and the sons of Zebedee with Him, and He told them He was "deeply grieved, even to death," and He asked them to stay awake with Him. Then He went off to pray, and when He returned He found His disciples sleeping. He woke them, and gave them instructions to stay awake. A second time, He found them asleep. More waking, more instructions, more sleep. This third time Jesus wakes them with sharp words: "Are you still sleeping and taking your rest? See, the hour is at hand, and the Son of Man is betrayed into the hands of sinners. Get up, let us be going. See, my betrayer is at hand." *Could you not stay awake with me for one hour?*

My life is like a disciple's nap in Gethsemane: I have promised, over and over, to be vigilant for the things of God, to be awake to Him, but I seem to spend much of my life sleeping.

A FEW MONTHS BEFORE I left for college, we made a *leil tikkun Shavuot* at Congregation Beth Israel. Even though there were just ten or twelve of us gathered, we knew we were doing something exciting. We were a Reform synagogue, but we were taking this mysterious Orthodox custom and somehow making it our own. We had each prepared a text that we would teach to the others. I taught on the story of creation in Genesis, and a history professor taught on a passage from the Zohar, the medieval work of Jewish mysticism, and a lawyer who'd just moved to town taught about Maimonides' approach to *tzedakah*, charity.

The *tikkun* broke up before sunrise, but Randi and I were determined to stay up all night. We found a diner near the university and we split a giant ice cream sundae, our version of the traditional Shavuot meal, which is always heavy with dairy products. Randi raised a spoonful of Butter Brickle in a sort of toast. "May the Torah be as mother's milk to you," she said.

⁂

IF ONE WERE DRAWING parallels between Jewish holidays and Christian holidays, one would pair up Shavuot and Christmas. At Shavuot, God reveals Himself to His people in the Torah, and at Christmas He reveals Himself to His people in Jesus Christ.

But I have never been able to shake the sense that if God hadn't wanted us to make some connection between Pentecost and Shavuot, between the gifting of the disciples with the Holy Spirit and the revelation of the Torah at Mount Sinai, He would not have given those gifts on the same day.

I call Jeff. "Want to do it a second time?" I ask, as if he should know what I'm talking about.

He doesn't. "Do what?" he asks.

"Another Jewish-Christian holiday thing. Like our seder."

Jeff pauses, and I'm sure he's counting in his head to the next holiday. "A Christmas-Chanukah bash would be a bit premature," he says. "You want to throw a Pentecost party?" he asks.

"I want to study," I say.

Jeff laughs. "You want a *leil tikkun* Pentecost."

"That's exactly what I want."

So Jeff and I spend a Sunday afternoon at the Columbia library, armed with tape and glue sticks and scissors and quarters for the Xerox machine. We paste together a two-inch-thick packet of texts we will study on Pentecost. The passages we have pulled together are from disparate sources—from the Bible and the Talmud and snippets of the Church fathers. Jeff has even snuck in a few paragraphs from a novel by Phillip Roth. Our one guiding principle is to figure out what Pentecost and Shavuot have to do with each other. To figure out why they are the same day. "I realize," I say to Jeff, "that I sound like I am trying to write a term paper for an eleventh-grade English class. But it seems to me that if you were reading a novel, you would figure the novelist hadn't made two things happen at the same time just by accident. You'd figure he wanted you to see something in their proximity. If the Christians had been rabbis, they would have taken for granted these two events happened on the same day for some reason."

Sometime around four o'clock, I have Xeroxed a passage from Abraham Joshua Heschel, and I am trimming it down to size, pasting it onto a sheet of paper next to a passage from the Book of Acts. There is glue in my hair and scraps of paper stuck to my sweater. There's even some glitter under my right thumbnail, although I don't know where it came from—neither Jeff nor I brought any glitter. "You look as happy as a kindergartner at arts and crafts," says Jeff. From eleventh grade to kindergarten in a few hours.

The night before Pentecost, I steep a strong pot of black tea, and Jeff and Amy turn up at my apartment armed with cheese blintzes, cheese and crackers, and a cheesecake, and we camp out in the den.

We had decided beforehand that each person would teach one of the passages in the packet. Amy starts, sensibly, with the story of the first Pentecost in Acts. The disciples were gathered for Shavuot, and "a sound like the blowing of a violent wind came from heaven and filled the whole house." The disciples began to speak in foreign languages and the hubbub draws a crowd. Each person in the gathered assembly, Scripture tells us, "heard them speaking in his own language." Romans, Mesopotamians, Phrygians and Pamphylians, Egyptians and Libyans all heard the disciples "declaring the wonders of God in our own tongues!" The crowd was awed, but there were some hecklers who said the disciples were just drunk. *These men are not drunk!* declared an indignant Peter. *It's only nine in the morning! You're not hearing wine; you're hearing the Holy Spirit.*

FOR A LONG TIME, the Holy Spirit stumped me. I understood something of the Father—the Father seemed basically to be the God of the Torah—and something of the Son. But who was this third person of the Trinity? The Spirit seems the least easily defined person of God, the person who never speaks in words to us from the pages of Scripture, the person whose body is never described, the person we never get to see.

One day, I was talking to Hannah about something mundane, a birthday present for my father. "And the Spirit moved me to pick up this book," I said. Hannah didn't notice, but I was surprised. I had just ascribed the choice of a birthday present to the Holy Spirit. And I knew it was true. I knew that the Spirit had led me to that book, and I knew the Spirit had, in fact, put that sentence in my mouth; as Jesus said to His disciples in the Gospel of Luke, "The Holy Spirit will teach you at that time what you should say." And that was when I began to understand what the Holy Spirit is. The Holy Spirit is the way God dwells in us, works on us, even though we are down here on Earth and God the Father and the Son are up there in heaven. The Spirit is what Elijah the Prophet calls the still small voice of God. But not always still and small. At Pentecost, the Spirit comes in tongues of fire to the disciples; and the Spirit is what will cause, in the prophet Joel's famous phrase, "Your sons and daughters [to] prophesy, your old men [to] dream dreams and your young men [to] see visions." In the Gospel of John, we see that the Spirit will be with us forever, will guide us in all truth, will teach us, and will take what is Christ's and make it ours. In church history, the Spirit helps us formulate creeds, helps us interpret Scripture, helps us make decisions. In our own humble houses, He helps us pray. He helps us know what to say when we open our mouths. The Spirit is the reason we Christians can do anything, the reason we do not live paralyzed in fear of messing up. The Spirit is how we unfold God's will this side of eternity. The Spirit is the reason we can build a church and have confidence that we will get it at least a little bit right.

Amy and Jeff and I don't get to a much more precise understanding than that of who the Spirit is and what the Spirit does, and eventually Amy looks at her watch, and looks at her husband, and says, "Your turn." Then she reaches for a blintz.

Jeff teaches a passage from the commentaries of the Israeli rabbi

Eliyahu KiTov. KiTov is commenting on *parshat Terumah*, the twenty-fifth, twenty-sixth, and twenty-seventh chapters of Exdous. In *parshat Terumah*, God tells Moses how to build a tabernacle. God gives all the details: how much wood, and what kind, and how to craft a candlestick from pure gold, and how to twist together blue and purple and scarlet linen for the tabernacle's ten curtains, and how to hold those curtains together with fifty golden clasps. KiTov, in his commentary, asks after the nature of revelation. The Book of Exodus, he writes, makes clear that God gave the Torah once — once and forever. But the rabbis teach that "every day the Voice of God issues forth from Sinai." How, asks KiTov, can the revelation recorded in Exodus be a unique event if God's voice is always sounding forth from Sinai? Because, KiTov says, what God did at Sinai was not speak something new, but silence all the background noise that usually covers up his divine voice. God is always talking at Sinai. He talked long before the revelation of Torah, and He is talking still, if we could figure out how to tune out the buzz and hum of everything else and listen.

"Maybe," I say, "that is why the first letter of the first word of the first commandment is *aleph*, a silent letter. In speaking *aleph*, God quieted all the noise." I stir my tea. "Maybe that is what the Holy Spirit does. Maybe He silences all the voices in our head that keep us from hearing God."

Somewhere in the middle of our discussion of the passage from Ki Tov, I remember, in my fingers and the arches of my feet, why we spend Shavuot studying. I understand that we study Torah because to do so is to experience revelation all over again.

IT IS ALMOST ONE in the morning when we come around to the passage I am supposed to teach, and before we turn to it in our packet, I make another pot of Ceylon.

The passage I picked is from the twenty-ninth page of *masechet*

Menahot, the Talmudic tractate dealing with Temple sacrifices of meal. In the story, Moses ascended to Mount Sinai and found God sitting, drawing small three-pronged crowns on the tops of the letters of the Torah. Moses asked him, "Lord of the universe, why are you putting crowns on the letters of your already perfect Torah?" "In many generations," replied the Lord, "there will be a man named Rabbi Akiva, who will expound upon each small crown heaps and heaps of laws." Moses asked to see this great rabbi. "Turn around," said God, and when Moses did, he found himself in Akiva's classroom. Moses sat down in the back and watched the students arguing about the Torah. Moses could not follow their arguments at all; he grew more and more uncomfortable and felt more and more stupid. Then Rabbi Akiva offered an especially astute, but esoteric, point, and one of his students said, "Rabbi, how do you know?" "It is in the law that God gave Moses at Sinai," said Akiva. Hearing that, Moses felt a little better. He turned back to God and exclaimed, "Lord of the universe, you have a brilliant man like Akiva, and yet you give the Torah through me." God replied, "Hush. It is my will."

"I've always wondered about those crowns," says Jeff. He turns to Amy and explains. "Even today, Torah scrolls are written in elaborate calligraphy, with crowns decorating the tops of the letters."

"Apparently," says his wife, "those crowns do more than just decorate. Do Torah scholars really interpret them?"

"Well, they interpret just about everything," says Jeff. "There's even an elaborate numerology, where each letter is assigned a numerical value and then the rabbis try to figure out what those numerical values mean."

"Like *chalav*," I say, looking at the remains of the cheesecake, "the Hebrew word for *milk*. If you add up the numerical values of the letters that spell *chalav*, you get forty. That's one of the reasons you're supposed to eat dairy products, milk foods, on Shavuot, because Moses spent forty days on Mount Sinai."

Jeff asks why I put this midrash, this Talmudic tale, in our packet. I like the story about the crowns, I say, because one of the church's oldest anti-Jewish tropes has been that Jews read literally, that Jews miss the truth of Jesus because they don't know how to read allegories. The interpretion of crowns makes clear that Jewish reading isn't about literalism. "But I chose this midrash for tonight," I say, "because I think if there's a parallel to be found between Pentecost and Shavuot, it's going to be found in this story."

Amy squints at the passage in front of her. "I don't see it," she says. "Go on."

"Well, we usually say the Incarnation is the parallel moment to the revelation at Sinai—God giving himself in Torah and then in Christ, right? But what's being given here, in this story? The Torah?"

"The giving of the Torah is the context for the story, but that's not really what's going on," says Jeff. "What's being given is a vision of the future. A vision of how God's revelation stays alive after the moment of revelation at Sinai is over."

Which is precisely what happens at Pentecost. God gave us the thing that would make His revelation stay alive for us, stay with us, even though that moment of revelation is over. He gave us the Holy Spirit to help us build the church even though Jesus has ascended into Heaven.

"And what God gives at Sinai," I say, "is not a Holy Spirit, exactly, but an exegetical process. A way of reading his one-time revelation so that the revelation will keep revealing forever."

In giving the Holy Spirit to his church in Jerusalem, God gave the continuation of His word in the community of His faithful. He gave the ongoing work of the church. So, too, in giving the Torah, God gave a living tradition. He gave not just a book, but a way for His children to read and interpret that book. He gave three-pronged crowns, full of meaning, and He gave classrooms and students and teachers who will interpret those crowns, who will transform the Torah Moses thinks he knows into a wild sea animal, something that leaves Moses bewildered, something that Moses cannot even recognize. The established kingdom of God on Earth looks different from the perfect moment of revelation.

JEFF AND AMY AND I finally call it quits at about three o'clock, having made it through about an eighth of the packet we put together. They collapse on my fold-out couch and I crawl into bed.

The next morning at church we sing songs about the Holy Spirit, and in the collect for Pentecost, we ask God, "who on this day taught the hearts of your faithful people by sending them the light of your Holy Spirit," to "Grant us by the same Spirit to have a right judgment in all things." We need right judgment, and I am glad we are asking God for it in this Pentecost prayer. It is a dangerous thing He gives us, the freedom and innovation of continuing His work here on Earth after the moment of revelation has passed. Without that right judgment, the freedom God's community has to carry out His work becomes the freedom to undo ourselves.

Sitting in church I think again about the story from *masechet Menahot*, the story about God decorating the letters of the Torah with coronets. It's a story that's often quoted in works of Jewish scholarship and in popular books about Jewish spirituality. Often the storytellers end with Moses' asking God why He doesn't just reveal his Torah directly to Akiva, and God's saying it is His will. But in the Talmud the story goes on for another few lines. Moses says, "Lord of the universe, you have shown me Akiva's Torah. Now show me his reward." Again, God tells Moses to turn around, and when he does he sees salesmen weighing out Akiva's flesh at market stalls, for Akiva, who participated in Bar Kochba's rebellion, was martyred by the Romans. Moses is horrified by this vision of Akiva's fate. "Lord of the universe," he asks, "how can such a brilliant, God-fearing man be rewarded with such a horrible death?" Again God silences him. "Quiet! This is my decree."

That ending leaves us with a rather different story. Without the picture of Akiva's death, we have a bedazzled and slightly sheepish Moses and a God who comforts him, who tries to make him feel better, a God whose will encompasses the innovative brilliance of Akiva and the humble service of Moses. In this second ending of the story, God says the exact same words—in Aramaic, *Shtok, kachalah hemachshava lifanai*—but they mean something different. They mean that God's will encompasses not just the enigmatic choice to reveal his Torah to Moses, but also the enormity of Akiva's flesh weighed at market. At Pentecost and Shavuot, revelation becomes a human responsibility, but God's decree that Akiva die a martyr's death puts that responsibility in a somewhat different light. At the end of the story, God reasserts His rule. The authority of the rabbis to interpret, the authority of people to unfold revelation here on Earth, will always be held in check by His will.

The Bible I Use

The Bible I use, most days, is a white-jacketed, stout book, Hebrew on the right pages and English on the left. Benjamin, my Orthodox friend from Washington, D.C., gave it to me when I was fifteen. He had won some award at his high school, and the prize was a gift certificate from the local Judaica shop, and what he bought with that gift certificate was a Bible for me.

He didn't inscribe the book. He wrote a card, which still sits lodged in the middle of the book of Numbers. The card is gray, heavy, textured like raw silk, and he wrote in red ink, his handwriting arched and dramatic. There is a great red slash on the frontispiece of the book, where his pen spilled off the card and onto my page.

THERE'S NO NEW TESTAMENT in this white Bible, of course. For that I have a separate book, the New Jerusalem, an English translation of a French Catholic translation of the Greek, which I bought in high school. The day I decided to go to Columbia I celebrated with a trip to the William's Corner Bookstore on the downtown mall in Charlottesville where I bought this New Testament, and Ben-Sasson's *History of the Jewish People,* a book about medieval women and food, written by a Columbia historian, and the diary of Mary Chesnut, a Confederate congressman's wife who chronicled the Civil War from her parlor in South Carolina. That afternoon, riding around town with my mother, I read aloud, first from Chesnut and then from Romans. My mother laughed. "That can't be the Bible," she said. No *thees, thous,* or *begats.* It didn't sound anything like the King James of her growing up. "The language is so simple," she joked, "that you might imagine they want us to understand it." The Reformation had come to Charlottesville.

Reading Ruth

On Shavuot, Jews traditionally read the Book of Ruth. Ruth has always been my favorite name. It comes out harder in Hebrew, *Root*, like the root of a tree, no sighing *h* to round off the end. I have always loved the name, both in Hebrew, and in English, and in its diminutive, Ruthie. And Ruth has always been my best beloved character in the Bible, mostly because she is a convert, a Moabite who marries an Israelite and eventually pledges herself to the Hebrews' God, and she is the great-grandmother of King David, and it is through his line that the Messiah comes. In the months before I went to the *mikvah*, I read and reread Ruth all the time. And every year in college, at the *leil tikkun Shavuot*, I studied only Ruth, the Book of Ruth itself, and what the rabbis had to say about it, and sometimes modern recastings of it, women rabbis' retelling the tale in feminist terms, or Jane Hamilton's novel about a twentieth-century Ruth trying to piece together her wretched life in Honey Creek, Illinois.

Then, for about two years after becoming a Christian I didn't read the Book of Ruth at all. I didn't set out to avoid it, I just never came around to reading it, somehow, and I only gradually realized that I was avoiding the Book of Ruth the same way I was avoiding all my Jewish friends, that I felt I had betrayed Ruth, this dead woman from the Bible, just as surely as I had betrayed Beth or Rabbi M.

During my last months in England, I started buying commentaries on Ruth, painstaking works by Old Testament scholars determining just how many inches she gleaned and just what Boaz's name meant. The commentaries sat unopened on my shelf, a growing stack of books I wasn't reading about a book I wasn't reading. I even bought a commentary on Ruth written in French, even though the only French I know is *pommes frites*. I just wanted to have it around.

Now I am reading Ruth again, and I find I am reading her differently. Ruth is still my favorite. Not because she is a convert, but because she is a bridge, genealogically and literarily, to Jesus.

It is no surprise, I guess, that I read Ruth differently than I used to. All the stories look different through Christian glasses.

⁂

THE BIBLE IS A BOOK for minimalists. The Book of Ruth is a spare short story, four chapters, ninety-five verses in all. It opens with the Biblical equivalent of "It was a dark and stormy night." The first six verses, prelude and background rolled into one, tell us over and over that all is not well.

The very first word, the Talmud points out, presages disaster: *vayhee*, "and it came to pass." *Vayhee*, the Talmud explains, often crops up when the Jews are about to stumble into trouble, as in the Book of Esther, which tells of the Persian Jews' near destruction at the hands of Haman. Esther begins, "*Vayhee yimai Ahashverush.*" "And it came to pass in the days of Ahasvherush." (What the Talmud neglects to mention is that, like the Book of Ruth, the Book of Esther tells the story of disaster ultimately overcome, and overcome by the cunning of a young woman.) So we know things are off to a bad start.

Then we learn when the Book of Ruth is set: "*bimay shifot hashoftim*," "in the days when the Judges ruled." This story happens sometime during the era of Judges, a time when the Jews didn't follow their leaders; the community is plagued with idol worship and infighting; the tribes of Israel rise up against the Benjamites, killing all but six hundred of Benjamin's descendants. The days when Judges ruled were the nadir of pre-Diaspora Jewish history.

Next we learn that there was a famine in the land, *"vayehi ra'av b'eretz."*

We meet a man, Elimelech, with a wife and two sons; they flee famine-stricken Bethlehem (the "house of bread" is starkly empty of food) and head to foreign territory, Moab. In case the reader hasn't yet realized that things are terribly wrong, the text gives us clues in the characters' names. *Naomi,* the wife's name, means "pleasantness," but her sons' names are worrying: *Mahlon* and *Chilion* mean "sickness" and "ending."

And then, in three verses, all the men are dead: Elimelech dies, Mahlon and Chilion take Moabite brides, and then they die. The three women are left widowed. As scholar Rachel Adler notes, the Hebrew word for *widow* derives from the etymological root meaning "to be unable to speak." "The man who spoke for her," writes Adler, "who provided for her, who gave her a place in society, is dead. Her new designation depicts her as a mirror of that death, mute, helpless, adrift. Small wonder that the prophets keep reminding people to remember the widow. Along with the stranger and the orphan, she is a disconnected person, unclaimed by any and having claims upon none."

All that in the first six verses.

Naomi decides to go back to Bethlehem, and she and her two daughters-in-law, Orpah and Ruth, set out. But Naomi is now left saddled with responsibilities she can't discharge. She has no way to care for herself, let alone Orpah and Ruth. She tells them that it is in their best interest to return to Moab, to their own people. She doesn't have any more sons for them to marry, and she is too old to have more babies. Orpah, the Bible tells us, "kissed her mother-in-law." That is, she kissed her good-bye, followed her instructions and headed back to Moab. "But Ruth clung to her." *Clung, davka,* the same word Jews use to describe a cleaving to God, *devekut,* and the same word used in Genesis to describe what a man does to his wife after he leaves his mother and father—*vdavak b'ishto,* "he cleaves to her."

Ruth cleaves, and then she makes her most famous speech, the one that often turns up at weddings: "Where you go I will go, and where you stay I will stay. Your people will be my people and your God my God. Where you die I will die, and there I will be buried." Ruth is giving up her freedom— and a potential Moabite husband— to stay and serve her mother-in-law, to follow the otherwise abandoned Naomi to Bethlehem. With that pledge, she makes herself a Jew.

When Ruth and Naomi return to Bethlehem, the local women are shocked. They are stunned. Naomi, in one commentator's words, "looks . . . like the husk that has been left over after the core of life has been removed."

When they arrived in Bethlehem, the whole town was stirred because of them, and the women exclaimed, "Can this be Naomi?" "Don't call me Naomi," she told them. "Call me Mara, because the Almighty has made my life very bitter. I went away full, but the Lord has brought me back empty. Why call me Naomi? The Lord has afflicted me; the Almighty has brought misfortune upon me."

Like the names of Naomi's sons, Naomi's names are important. In English, *Naomi* means "pleasant," and *Mara* means "bitter." The women of Bethlehem, who serve as something of a Greek chorus in this book, ask her, "Is this Pleasant?" and she says, "Don't call me Pleasant; call me Bitter, for the Lord has dealt bitterly with me." Rashi tells one additional detail, the fullness and emptiness that Naomi speaks about is children. Once she was full with them, now she is empty. But Naomi's name change doesn't stick. No one ever calls her Mara. It is as if everyone else in the story understands that her fortunes are about to turn, that she will be returned to joyfulness, that the bitter dealings of the Lord are no more permanent than puppy love.

CHAPTER TWO OPENS with a small statement of fact: "Now Naomi had a relative on her husband's side." This was Boaz, a kinsman, someone who might be obligated to care for his destitute kin. Ruth asks Naomi to allow her to go to Boaz's fields and glean—pick through the crops left over after harvest.

When Boaz sees Ruth in his field, he is kind to her.

He orders the men loitering around not to bother her, he insists that she drink from his vessels when she is thirsty. He feeds her lunch. He is nothing but generous to Ruth, and Ruth and Naomi both praise him for it.

But Naomi knows this beggar's gleaning is not the foundation of a secure life. She tells Ruth to wash and anoint herself, and to dress up, and to go to the threshing floor where Boaz has been winnowing barley. "When he lies down," says Naomi, "note the place where he is lying. Then go and uncover his feet and lie down. He will tell you what to do." In other words, seduce the man.

Ruth does as she is instructed. "At midnight the man was startled," the Torah tells us. Boaz "turned over, and there, lying at his feet, was a woman!" He asks her to identify herself, and when Ruth does, Boaz treats her to a discourse about law, and how they will subvert the law so that they can marry. It is true, Boaz says, that he is her kinsman, but there is another man who is "more closely related than I," that is, who has primary legal responsibility for Ruth, and first dibs on her to boot. "Remain this night, and in the morning, if he will act as next-of-kin for you, good; let him do it. If he is not willing to act as next-of-kin for you, then, as the Lord lives, I will act as next-of-kin for you. Lie down until the morning." In the morning, Boaz tells the next-of-kin that Naomi is planning to sell her husband's land. The land is the next-of-kin's if he wants it, but when he learns that the burdens of Ruth come along with the acreage, he declines. "Take my right of redemption yourself," he tells Boaz. Boaz does just that, promising a happy ending to the tale that began in despair.

But instead of a simple happily ever after, the Book of Ruth ends with an elaborate and confusing statement of parentage.

Ruth and Boaz marry, and "the Lord made her conceive, and she bore a son." The son was Obed, who begat Jesse, who begat David. But who are Obed's parents? Ruth gave birth, but Naomi becomes Obed's nursemaid and "The women of the neighborhood gave him a name saying 'A son has been born to Naomi.'" To Naomi, to pleasantness. She thought she was too old to have another son, but due to God's making Ruth conceive and the women of Bethlehem's verbal tricks, Naomi has the son of her old age after all. Her earlier lament has been reversed. Naomi has a son, and Obed has two mothers, Naomi and Ruth.

Obed also has two fathers. First, Boaz declares that he is marrying Ruth not in his own name, but in the name of her dead husband. He says, "I have also acquired Ruth the Moabitess, Mahlon's widow, as my wife, in order to maintain the name of the dead with his property, so that his name will not disappear from among his family or from the town records." But, although Boaz has declared that Ruth is to "perpetuate the dead man's name," the final verses of the Book of Ruth are a genealogy that names Boaz, not Mahlon, as Obed's father:

This, then, is the family line of Perez: Perez was the father of Hezron, Hezron the father of Ram, Ram the father of Amminadab, Amminadab the father of Nahshon, Nahshon the father of Salmon, Salmon the father of Boaz, Boaz the father of Obed, Obed the father of Jesse, and Jesse the father of David.

Two mothers, two fathers. The Book of Ruth ends by suggesting that biological parentage is not the only kind of parentage that counts.

The Gospel of Matthew opens with a genealogy intended to remind the readers of the Book of Ruth:

A record of the genealogy of Jesus Christ the son of David, the son of Abraham: Abraham was the father of Isaac, Isaac the father of Jacob, Jacob the father of Judah and his brothers, Judah the father of Perez and Zerah, whose mother was Tamar, Perez the father of Hezron, Hezron the father of Ram, Ram the father of Amminadab, Amminadab the father of Nahshon, Nahshon the father of Salmon, Salmon the father of Boaz, whose mother was Rahab, Boaz the father of Obed, whose mother was Ruth, Obed the father of Jesse, and Jesse the father of King David.

And on and on Matthew's genealogy goes, through another twenty-four generations, until, finally, Matthew brings us to:

Matthan the father of Jacob, and Jacob the father of Joseph, the husband of Mary, of whom was born Jesus, who is called Christ. Thus there were fourteen generations in all from Abraham to David, fourteen from David to the exile to Babylon, and fourteen from the exile to the Christ.

Matthew wrote his gospel for a primarily Jewish audience, and he was at pains, throughout, to prove that Jesus fulfilled all the prophecies of Hebrew Scriptures, including the prophecy that the Messiah would come from the line of David. That is why he begins his Gospel with a long, tedious list, one that has lulled generations of Sunday schoolers into classtime naps, or sent them flipping through their Bibles for racier bits about adultery or war, or even dietary laws; anything's more interesting than a genealogy.

But the genealogy Matthew gives us is a crucial one. For Isaiah, in one of the clearest, most specific prophecies about the coming Savior, makes clear that the Messiah will be descended from Jesse, Jesse, who is Obed's son and King David's father. It was the very first thing Matthew had to establish before he went on to preach the Gospel to a Jewish audience. He had to show that this Jesus was in the line of Jesse. And that is what his genealogy lays out—from Ruth, to Obed, to Jesse, to David, on through the generations to Joseph, and then to Jesus.

The Christian me always stumbles a bit over that genealogy: the linchpin, after all, is Joseph. And Joseph, we Christians know, was not Jesus' father. God was Jesus' father. Something of a genealogical conundrum, but one whose solution is found in the Book of Ruth.

The Book of Ruth makes way for Jesus in two ways. It makes Jesus' birth biologically possible: Obed is Jesus' ancestor, his grandfather some thirty generations back. Had Ruth not slipped onto the threshing-room floor, we would have no Obed, no Jesse, no David, no Joseph, and no Messiah.

But the genealogy of Ruth, with all its confusions, its complications, its deviations from clear-cut biological parentage, makes way for Jesus literally, too, for Jesus isn't in the line of David in a blood-cell-and-amino-acid kind of way; he's in the line of David through Joseph, who wasn't after all, really his father. He's in the line of David through legal fiction, through subversion of the genetic lines of fatherhood. Jesus is not, biologically, Joseph's son; he is, rather, Joseph's son the way Obed is Mahlon's son or Naomi's son. Because Obed can have four parents—Mahlon and Boaz, Ruth and Naomi—Jesus can have two fathers, God and Joseph. In getting Ruth to the threshing-room floor and then making her conceive, God is making Jesus' birth biologically possible. In naming Mahlon Obed's father and Naomi Obed's mother, the Book of Ruth sets up a precedent of parenthood that makes Jesus' birth, and his complicated two-fathered-ness, literarily possible, too.

It makes sense, upon reflection, that Jesus' connection to the genealogy of the Israelites would be bigger than mere biology, because one of Jesus' tasks is extending God's grace beyond the bounds of Abraham's biological descendants. When God made His covenant with Abraham, He promised that He would "make your descendants as numerous as the stars in the sky." Jesus is the needle who sews the children of God who are not direct descendants of Abraham into that nighttime sky.

JEWISH PAPERCUTS LOOK something like Amish scherenschnitte. They are made by fastening a piece of paper to a wooden board and cutting out designs—usually symbolic representations of scriptural themes—with a sharp knife. Papercuts became popular among European Jews in the seventeenth and eighteenth centuries, when artists began to decorate scrolls of the Book of Esther and Jewish wedding contracts with papercuts. Women often hung amulets crafted from papercuts in nurseries and kitchens to protect their children and homes. Papercutting didn't take off in America, however, until the 1970s, when hippiefied Jews in New England turned to the old art form.

I have always loved these papercuts. They seem both fragile and strong. And when I look at papercuts, I remember the idiom *hidur mitzvah,* the idea that you don't merely follow the commandments, you beautify them. It is because of *hidur mitzvah* that Jews have lovely silk challah covers and elaborate ceramic kiddush cups and silver jewelry to decorate Torah scrolls. But these papercuts seem the most perfect fulfillment of *hidur mitzvah*. They usually illustrate verses of Scripture, so the commandment they beautify is the most important one of all: the commandment to read, to study, the Torah.

In a used bookstore on my corner, I buy another book about Ruth, and this one is illustrated with papercuts, six of them, pictures of different verses of Ruth. Roses intertwining with one another illustrate Ruth's cleaving to Naomi, and there is a lion and a lamb, and the words *"v'Rut ha'moaveah ha'oleed et-David."* "And Ruth the Moabite begot David." And there, on page 107, is a picture of Naomi's lament, Ruth 1:21: *"Ani melea halakhti v'raykam heshivani hashem."* "I went away full, but the Lord has brought me back empty." In this papercut, Naomi's words ark across the sky, Hebrew letters making a band around the moon. Below the moon and the words are three barren trees, and amid the trees' roots sit other Hebrew letters: Elimelech, Mahlon, and Chilion, the names of Naomi's dead husband and sons.

I track down the artist. Her name is Diane and she lives in New Mexico. I email her and ask if the papercut of Ruth 1:21 is available for sale. She writes back: She will sell me the picture for $900. It is a Friday afternoon that we exchange these emails, and she wishes me a Shabbat shalom, and I think, *Of course she thinks I'm Jewish*. I half-feel I am deceiving her by not spilling my entire religious autobiography to her over email. *(Are you sure you want to sell your art to a traitor?)*

When the papercut comes in the mail, I unwrap it with some ceremony, and hold it in my hands for a long time and then I hang the papercut on a wall with crosses—a sturdy, orange clay cross that I bought at that Episcopal church in Oxford, Mississippi, and a trio of iron crosses, Jesus' and the two thieves', that I found at a small craft shop in North Carolina. It hangs underneath those, and it looks delicate and just slightly out of place, like a bit of lace peeking out of a heavy woolen winter coat.

"It is a difficult verse," Diane writes to me in an her email. "The challenge for me was to capture the loneliness of the verse, and still imbue it with a sense of beauty. I suspect it reflects difficult losses for you."

⸺⸸⸺

MATTHEW IS NOT the only Gospel that echoes the Book of Ruth. In a passage of Luke that the church calls the Magnificat, Mary echoes Naomi's lament. The Magnificat is Mary's response to the angel Gabriel's news that she will have a baby; it's a speech that has been canonized not only in the Gospel, but has also made its way to the center of Christian liturgy. "My soul doth magnify the Lord," she says, "and my spirit hath rejoiced in God my Savior." In the middle of that speech, Mary reverses Naomi's words to the women of Bethlehem. "He hath filled the hungry with good things; and the rich he hath sent empty away," says Mary, recalling Mara's desolate, "I went away full, but the Lord has brought me back empty."

That we can hear echoes between Naomi and Mary, that biblical declarations can stretch back thirty generations, delights me. It makes me think that there are few ways I could better spend my time than reading the Bible.

But reading is not straightforward, and the resonance between the two women's speeches presses a question for Christian readers. How does one read Hebrew scripture as a Christian? How does one read the entire Bible, Old Testament and New Testament, as a coherent, God-made literary work, believing that the tents and speeches and promises and camels of the earlier books foreshadow events and proclamations in the Gospels—how does one read the Hebrew Scriptures Christianly, without turning the Hebrew Scriptures into nothing but a prelude to Jesus?

Naomi's and Mary's speeches are not the only passages of Scripture that raise those questions. It would be, it seems to me, almost impossible for a Christian to read the binding of Isaac and not understand that story as foreshadowing the sacrifice of Christ on the Cross. It would be impossible for a Christian to read the story of the Passover in Exodus and not think ahead to Calvary. But it is a question that comes up clearest, that comes up sharpest, in Naomi's and Mary's speeches, because in those speeches the question is not just about how Christians read Hebrew Scripture; the question asked in Naomi's and Mary's speeches is about the very covenant God made with the Jews. It would be easy for Christians to look at Naomi's speech, and then look at Mary's speech, to look at their trope of emptiness and fullness, and say, *Well, Naomi and all the Jews are in fact empty; no one is filled up unless she is in Christ.* It would be easy for Christians to grab hold of the language of *empty* and *full* and spin a story where not only is the Jewish text empty but the covenant God made with the Jews is empty, too. But if you are a Christian who believes, as Paul said in Romans, "The gifts and call of God are unrevokable," then you can't read Naomi and Mary that way, you can't believe that they are handing you, in a neat little bundle, instructions about the triumph of God's covenant through Christ and the irrelevance of His covenant at Sinai.

To read Mary's inversion of Naomi's words as a statement that what's empty and incomplete in the Hebrew Scriptures is fulfilled only in the coming of Christ is to miss the meaning of the Book of Ruth. Mary reverses Naomi's lament, but she is not the first to do so. The women of Bethlehem reverse it first. The whole point of the Book of Ruth is, in fact, reversing Naomi's lament. So Mary's proclamation doesn't so much fulfill an unfulfilled emptiness; rather, it reiterates the fulfillment that the Book of Ruth already offers. When Mary utters her famous lines, when she reverses Naomi's speech, she is repeating a reversal that is already there in the text. The Hebrew

Scriptures open up the possibility of a Christian reading, but they can also be read, complete, by themselves.

I AM JUST BARELY grammar-school age in Christian years, and what you learn in grammar school is how to read. The Book of Ruth is not a bad primer.

Speaking in Tongues

The story of Pentecost, in the Book of Acts, is where we learn about speaking in tongues. The immediate manifestation of the Spirit in Acts is the apostles' sudden ability to speak in languages they don't know, and to understand one another. It is the inversion, and the restoration, of the Tower of Babel, way back in Genesis, when the people were idolatrous and fighting with each other, and God cursed them all with different languages, rendering them unintelligible to even their nearest neighbor. The denomination of Protestants most given over to glossolalia (literally, "tongue babbling") takes its name from the holiday. They are Pentecostals.

I have heard people speak in tongues; it is a lovely, lilting, creek-rushing sound, like the keys at the high end of the piano dancing very quickly. Some of my proper Episcopalian friends write off glossolalia as made-up. They can't find space in their picture of Christendom for tongue-speak.

Before the 1960s, you would have been hard pressed to find many Episcopalians who knew what glossolalia was, let alone spoke in tongues themselves. But in 1959, Dennis Bennett, a priest at an Episcopal church in Van Nuys, California, began to speak in tongues. His bishop and his congregants responded by removing Bennett from his post. He quickly found a new parish, in Seattle, and from his pulpit there he sparked what is called a charismatic revival within the church. *Charismatic* comes from the Greek *charism*, "gift"; as in, *Speaking in tongues is a gift of the Holy Spirit.*

Hannah, now a Baptist, grew up Pentecostal. I ask her, shortly after we first met, if she still speaks in tongues. "Oh, sure," she said. "I don't have the gift of prophesy, so I don't try to communicate with anyone else in tongues. But I talk to God in tongues all the time. Otherwise, I simply wouldn't know what to say to Him. I want to thank God for all the awesome things He has done in my life, but my words are inadequate. When I pray in tongues, the Spirit gives me the words."

That's what all my friends who speak in tongues say. They say speaking in tongues lets them relax into their prayers. They say that they might not know, in their heads, what words to use to thank God, that our vocabularies seem so feeble when it comes to thanking God for the wonderful gifts He has bestowed upon us. In their prayer language, the Holy Spirit takes over. He gives voice to their thanksgivings. They are no longer confined by the silly, small limits of English. They can praise God as He deserves to be praised.

I HAVE *THOUGHT GRATITUDE* or *been grateful* plenty of times. I have received a present and liked the present and have been known to write a thank-you note, one that, per my mother's instructions, didn't just gush about how much I appreciated the sweater or the book of essays or the leather belt, but actually said, in a specific sentence all of its own, when I had read the book in question, that it had been just the thing on the long car ride to Virginia, or how the sparkly evening bag came in so handy for the big party at school last week, how at least half a dozen people complimented it. I know what gratitude is, and I know how to talk about it convincingly, but I have only *felt* gratitude twice.

The first bout of feeling came the March after I was baptized. I was spending Cambridge's month-long spring break in Charlottesville, at my mother's house, a skinny four-story town house with a copper roof that the Board of Architectural Review has stamped suitably historic. For most of March, I sat on my bed in the top room of that skinny house, reading books and staring out the window into the treetops and getting over jet lag, writing long letters and learning the Book of Common Prayer. Then one night, I was crouched on the floor, on the scratchy new terra-cotta carpet, picking through all the books I couldn't afford to ship to England, and it hit. I couldn't believe what God had done for me, and I was grateful to my toenails. In evangelicals' argot, you might say that there on the carpet I was *convicted of my sinfulness.* I was struck by the gaping gulch between perfect God and fallen me, and I was stunned with thankfulness that, though I was small and sinful, God, in His graciousness, saw fit to draw me near to Him anyway. It lasted for months, on and off, that feeling. I was on my knees, all the time, giving praise, thinking I had some taste of what it meant to be an angel and do nothing but sing hosannas all day.

The second bout was more recent. I was lying on my couch one night, reading a book about friendship by Beth Kephart. She writes about how friends are hard to make and hard to lose and how the only vocabulary we have for those losses is break-ups, romantic ones, but often the splitting apart of friends is harder, rarer, more long-lasting, grievous and generally devastating than any run-of-the-mill lovers' spat. My body lay on the couch like a valley, my head propped up on four fluffy pillows and my legs folded in, sit-up style, my back flat against the sofa's blue-and-white stripes. There I lay, listing all the friendships I had lost, all the people I'd betrayed or misled or just not kept up with, and then I felt gratitude again, felt it this time no less physically than hunger, felt the weight of it like a fog settling in over my stomach, felt it filling me heavy the way fruit fills a basket. Lying on the couch, I could not believe God had given me all these people to love. Even if I never had another friend ever, even if I spent the next seventy-five years rattling around lonely as a ghost of Christmas past, it would be too much ever to repay, all that love. I slept on the couch, then, blanketed by the weight of my gratitude, Beth Kephart's book under my pillow.

When I woke up, around four in the morning, the residue of gratefulness was still on me. I reached for my prayer book. I said the morning office. I dwelled over the Jubilate, Psalm 100: "O go your way into his gates with thanksgiving and into his courts with praise; Be thankful unto Him and speak good of His name; for the Lord is gracious." The prayer book can usually say what I'm feeling better than I can, but, this morning, it wasn't enough. I wanted something to do, something to give God, I wanted a Temple where I could deliver my first fruits or bread I had baked with my own hands.

I tried just talking to God about how grateful I felt, but that didn't get me much closer. "I feel really grateful," I said. "I want to thank you for all the amazing things you've given me, all the friendships, all my relatives. And I want to thank you for the gift of feeling grateful." It fell flat. I may as well have been reciting my grocery list.

This is what Hannah meant, I thought. This is what she meant when she said that she couldn't always come up with the words to say to God. This is what she meant when she said she wanted to express things to Him that she could not express on her own, that she needed the Spirit to give her the words.

I turned to a bookcase and found Dennis Bennett's book *How to Pray for the Release of the Holy Spirit,* which I had read about two years before. I began to read it again. I read it through four times that morning (it's a short book). Bennett distinguishes between two types of speaking in tongues. He calls the first "the gift of tongues"—that is, "a special kind of speaking in tongues in which someone brings words from God to a group of people." Not all Christians, writes Bennett, are given that gift, just as not all are given the gift of teaching or healing or leadership. Bennett calls the second type of speaking in tongues a "prayer language," with which one "simply . . . speak[s] to God, but instead of using the words you know in your own language, you trust the Holy Spirit to give the words He chooses in whatever language He selects—perhaps in a brand-new tongue that's never been spoken before." We just had to ask God to give the gift to us, and He would. It was a birthright.

I sat on my couch and I began to pray for a prayer language. I wanted to make the creek-rushing sounds. I wanted to thank God with words bigger than any words I had. I wanted to praise Him effortlessly, to not have to think of sentences all the time, to not be constrained by my own small vocabulary.

Okay, God, I thought. *Go for it. Any time now.*

Dennis Bennett, had he been in the room with me, would have reminded me that then I was supposed to open my mouth and start talking. And if the Spirit was going to gift me with this language, the language would come out. It certainly wasn't going to come out if my mouth was shut.

But I didn't open my mouth. It was as glued together as if I'd just eaten the world's stickiest peanut-butter-and-jelly sandwich.

Still, I kept entreating God. *Bring it on,* I thought. *Tongues tongues tongues.* And I kept keeping my mouth closed.

Then, I began to doubt.

This was a test—not of me, but of God. If He was who He said He was, if He was omnipotent and threefold, I would get my language. And if not, not.

I sat on the couch and every second that ticked by took on great meaning. Never mind that the books I had read told me that some-times people prayed for months before getting their prayer language. It all came down to this tongued litmus test. If God was real, if the New Testament was true, I would start to babble. *Tongues, tongues, tongues,* I thought. *Tongues, tongues, tongues.*

I looked at the clock and tapped my toes and thought the whole Jesus story, not to mention Pentecost and the Holy Spirit, must be bunk.

Then, grace swooped in. No, I didn't start to speak in tongues, but I did get up and walk around in a circle and open the curtains and look out the window. I had what Betty Friedan would have called a "click moment." I understood that the whole exercise had gone awry. I understood how backward and crazy and false it was for me to make this a test of God—I had started out to pray about gratitude and I had quickly turned into an ingrate. And I understood that I ought not ask for a prayer language until I could ask without making it the test of my entire faith.

Paring Knife

I find it hard to describe God in terms that are other than abstract, even a God who took on hands and toes and feet. It is still hard to describe Him with words I can hold in my hands or carry around in my pocket. Most of the God-words I reach for fly away before they land, like *ineffable* and *powerful* and *good*. The best words I have found so far are those words that God Himself spoke, ostensibly speaking not about God but His beloved; when God speaks about His people, He is usually telling us less about us and more about Him. In morning prayer, this first Friday of Pentecost, we read a verse from Luke 12: "For unto whomsoever much is given, of him shall be much required." It is one of the best verses in the Bible, and one of the hardest things about God. *For unto whomsoever much is given, of him shall be much required.* The passive voice is deceptive. It appears to obscure who's doing the action, who's doing the giving and who's doing the requiring. But it doesn't take too long in God's company to realize that it is He who does both.

Sometimes it is hard to explain what is being required. One week, I came to church late, over an hour late, after the Gospel reading, smack in the middle of the prayers for the people. I slipped into the back and started crying. I thought I was managing quiet, dignified tears, but I must have telegraphed my misery across the room, for a short black woman with a broad smile and a blue dress came up and hugged me and told me tears were the work of the Holy Spirit. You might have thought something terrible had happened—that I had just learned my mother had Alzheimer's, that I had suffered through a terrible weekend, that my house had burned down or I had just lost my dearest friend to a car crash; none of those things had happened, but you would have suspected them all given how hard I cried in that Holy Spirit woman's arms.

I cried, I think, because I was coming to understand in a new way just how much was required of me, how much God was going to strip away all my everything, like silver polish taking the tarnish off old forks. I cried because I know more and more how Chekov was right, how we are all running around desperate to make connections with one another, but mostly we are all just estranged. Because I know more and more that this glass here is so very dark, that this really is a long loneliness, that it is both lonely and long.

Sometimes I feel God has taken a paring knife to me. I know the way an apple feels.

Albemarle Pilgrimage

According to a national poll, Charlottesville, Virginia, boasts more households per capita engaged in "avid book reading" than any other town in the country. Considering the town's bookish history, this may not be surprising. Thomas Jefferson was early America's most devoted bibliophile; and over the years, Charlottesville has been home to illustrious writers like Edgar Allan Poe (who lived at 13 West Range during his ten months of study at UVA), and Faulkner (who spent his retirement years drinking and riding horses in Albemarle County). Today, not only is Charlottesville home to more readers than anywhere else in the country, but, as far as I can tell, it is also home to more writers. Novelist John Casey lives in town and teaches at the university, as does former poet laureate Rita Dove. Rita Mae Brown and her feline sleuth Sneaky Pie Brown live in Albemarle County, and Ann Beattie splits her time between Virginia and Maine. A few years ago, John Grisham moved to Charlottesville from Mississippi. The latest coup was, in my humble opinion, an even bigger deal; recently Jan Karon, author of the Mitford series, moved to Charlottesville.

I HAVE ALWAYS FELT faintly embarrassed about the role Jan Karon's Mitford novels played in my conversion. I'm sure God, who could have thrown a little Dostoyevsky or Barth in my path, was playing some sort of divine joke, figuring he would both get me to the baptismal font and erode some of my cherished intellectual snobbery in one fell swoop. Still, I often reflect on the books God has used in other people's conversions—Richard Gilman turned to Catholicism after reading Graham Greene and Georges Bernanos, for example, and Augustine famously became a Christian after reading the Book of Romans—and I feel annoyed that in His wisdom, He chose to reel me in with middle-brow Christian fiction. It could be worse, I suppose. I could have come to faith while reading *Left Behind*.

Embarrassment and all, I have something of a schoolgirl crush on Jan Karon, and when, over breakfast one morning while I am visiting Virginia, my mother tells me Karon has moved to the Charlottesville area, I begin daydreaming about running into her at the grocery store and becoming best friends over the Little Debbies or Wheat Thins. "I wouldn't get your hopes up," says my mother. "She's apparently keeping a very tight lip about where, exactly, she's living." Rumor has it that Jan Karon moved from her home in Blowing Rock, North Carolina, because she was constantly besieged by tourists pulling into her driveway, strutting about her yard, even knocking on her front door and expecting an invitation to come in and sit for a spell. Charlottesvillians all say she moved to Virginia to get away from her assertive fans, and the three or four locals who know her whereabouts are loyally keeping her secret to themselves. A recent article in *Southern Living* was especially vague; a profile of Karon's new digs, it allowed only that her farm was somewhere in the Commonwealth, not even daring to name a county.

My mother is explaining all this to me when I begin to jump up and down. "I know! I know!" I scream, still jumping (I tend to regress a little when I'm at my mother's). "We can go on a drive and find her farm! It'll be like a pilgrimage!"

My mother, once she realizes I am serious, thinks this is a little weird. "Lauren," she says, putting down her coffee and doing what I think they call fixing me with her eyes, "you live in *New York City*. Is this how you spend your weekends there? First a bagel and the *Times*, then a little field trip to see if you can locate Susan Cheever's apartment?"

But it's not often I suggest mother-daughter activities (at least, mother-daughter activities that don't require my mother to max out her credit cards at the mall), so she agrees.

MOM AND I TRY to imagine where, if we were millionaire novelists, we would buy farms. Having heard that Jan Karon eschewed the Episcopal churches of Charlottesville proper for a small country church, I say that maybe she visited Virginia, found a church she liked, and then picked a farm based on its proximity to her parish of choice. "That is how the people in her novels would do it," I say, "so maybe that is how she did it, too."

One possibility is Grace Episcopal Church, best known for adopting the English tradition of the Blessing of Hounds. The church began this practice in the 1920s, and members of the Keswick Hunt still perform it every Thanksgiving. "Jan Karon seems too down-to-earth to go in for that horsey stuff," I say to mom. "She probably doesn't attend Grace Episcopal." If Jan Karon wanted a very historic church, she might have chosen Christ Church Glendower, toward Scottsville; Thomas Jefferson served on the vestry, and Robert Rose, who was the minister there in the mid–eighteenth century, left the most extensive diary of any Anglican cleric in Virginia. But Mom eventually says we should try the Barboursville area, because maybe Jan Karon lives near All Saints' Episcopal, a tiny white chapel on Stony Point Road. "So we should just go driving around out by that church and see if we see her getting her mail or going jogging?" I ask.

"Seems as likely a plan as any," says my mother. There is, of course, nothing to suggest Jan Karon actually lives near Barboursville or attends All Saints' Episcopal Chapel, and the real reason Mom wants to head in that direction is that if you keep going another ten or fifteen miles past All Saints', you come to Gordonsville, home to Toliver House, one of her favorite restaurants in all of Virginia. "If we have to go on this crazy search," she mutters when she thinks I'm out of earshot, "may as well get a good meal out of it."

Our day does not get off to an auspicious start. First, we leave late, because I oversleep, having actually yanked the cord out of the socket in order to silence my alarm clock when it went off at nine. (In New York, I am used to waking up to NPR's *Morning Edition*. The alarm clock in Charlottesville, however, doesn't have a radio, or even a normal beep, just a choice of two different bell noises: cathedral or sleigh.)

After a stop at Spudnuts, the locally famed establishment that makes doughnuts from potato flour, and after about fifteen minutes on 20 North, we come to All Saints' Episcopal. Though the church is locked, we look in the windows. A sign announces services on the second and fourth Sunday of every month, and I wonder who attends. "This chapel looks sweet," says my mother. Local lore has it that shortly before the church was built, a three-year-old girl was killed by a rock that rolled down from a nearby mountain. The church engraved that rock with Matthew 18:3—"Except ye be converted, and become as little children, ye shall not enter into the kingdom of heaven"—and it became the cornerstone of the chapel. "I bet," says my mother, "that the death of that girl was the cornerstone of this church in more ways than one."

Mom—who, when we first moved to Charlottesville, purchased about ninety-seven books with titles like *Picturesque Perambulations through Postcard Virginia*—has brought along three guidebooks, figuring that, while we're looking for Jan Karon, we should also do a little historic sightseeing. According to one guidebook, this stretch of 20 North is one of the more historic patches of a very historic state: we see a former slave cabin, the estate from which Benjamin Franklin's grandson executed his short-lived Virginia medical career, several wineries, the ruins of a plantation that burned in the 1880s, and the farm on which part of *Giant,* starring Elizabeth Taylor and James Dean, was filmed.

"Hey," I exclaim, flipping through the guidebook, "did you know that Lottie Moon was from Albemarle County?" Our book says that Viewmont, an eighteenth-century plantation south of Charlottesville, was Lottie Moon's birthplace. "You're kidding," says my mother. Lottie Moon was a Baptist missionary to China in the nineteenth century, and she is one of the reasons my mother stopped being a Baptist. For the evangelism my mother's church undertook in Lottie Moon's name was not sharing the Gospel with those who'd never heard of Jesus, but sharing the Baptist Faith and Message with other Protestants.

"I remember saving my pennies for the Lottie Moon Christmas Offering," she says. "But even at age eight, I thought there was something screwy about our church sending a missionary to North Dakota to convert the Lutherans."

"Maybe that's her," my mom says, pointing to a blondish figure walking across a grassy hill near a barn.

"Lottie?" I ask.

"No—Jan," says my mother. "You know, there was an article about her in the paper, and I think in the photograph she was leaning up against a cross-hatch fence like that."

"Mom," I say, "every farm in this county has a cross-hatch fence." I squint at the figure moving toward the barn. "Anyway," I say, "that's definitely not Jan Karon. That's a man."

. . .

OVER OUR BARBEQUE sandwiches at the Toliver House, my mother asks, "Didn't you bring your copy of *At Home in Mitford?*"

"Hmmm?" I ask, munching a hush puppy.

"What are you going to do if we actually do spot her? Maybe she lives in Gordonsville and eats here at the Toliver House every Saturday. Don't you at least have books for her to sign if she walks in?"

"Mother," I say in that same sing-song voice I used when I was in seventh-grade and she said something outlandishly ridiculous, "if we saw her I couldn't actually *go up* to her. She'd probably think I was stalking her or something. That would be an invasion of her privacy."

I have been invited to a party later this evening, and since the dressiest item I brought to Charlottesville is a hooded sweatshirt, I ask my mother if she knows of any dress shops that are having a sale. My mother clears her throat and seizes the opportunity. "Razors," she says, "are always on sale." This, she thinks, is her great failing as a parent: that I don't shave my legs. She hopes that if I spend enough time in Virginia I will discover make-up, trade in my glasses for contacts, and start wearing what she calls "outfits," instead of just clothes. Whenever I visit her, she scatters a few bottles of shaving cream around the tub in the guest bathroom, just in case, you know, the mood should strike. I contemplate telling her that since the mood hasn't struck in the last decade, it probably never will, but this would make her wince and weep, so I refrain.

"WHY DO YOU LIKE Jan Karon's books so well, anyway?" asks my mother as we drive back from Gordonsville.

"Oh," I say, "Jan Karon really captures western North Carolina. Like there's this one character named Dooley." After the old mountain folk song about Tom Dooley, who will have to hang for Laurie Foster's death. "Also, the Mitford novels taught me about Jesus."

We drive by a clump of black and white cows standing in a meadow. They look like they are staring at us.

"Also," I say, "I like Father Tim. I think he is droll."

I hit the replay button on the CD player. We are listening to Schubert's thirteenth string quartet, and I like the andante. We didn't find Jan Karon, but sitting here with my mother, listening to all these minor chords, this is pilgrimage enough.

Credo

I am, by temperament, an annotator. I write in my books. I scribble things in the back. I underline.

My prayer book is no exception. I have decorated the margins, like the medieval Books of Hours I always visit at The Cloisters, only with words, not pictures. On page 66, where the Apostles' Creed appears, I have written this, from Diana Eck's *Encountering God*:

> The Latin *credo* means literally "I give my heart." The word *believe* is a problematic one today, in part because it has gradually changed its meaning from being the language of certainty so deep that I could give my heart to it, to the language of uncertainty so shallow that only the "credulous" would rely on it. Faith . . . is not about propositions, but about commitment. It does not mean that I intellectually subscribe to the following list of statements, but that I give my heart to this reality. *Believe*, indeed, comes to us from the Old English *belove*, making clear that this too is meant to be heart language. To say, "I believe in Jesus Christ" is not to subscribe to an uncertain proposition. It is a confession of commitment, of love.

And then on the first page of my prayer book, a quotation from the Gospel of Mark: "Lord, I believe; Help thou mine unbelief."

ONCE, WHEN WE WERE still dating, Steven read aloud to me from an obscure British novel (possibly, perhaps, by H. G. Wells, or possibly by Evelyn Waugh; I'm never able to remember); he read a scene in which a believer and a cynic are debating God. *Of course I know you believe in it,* the cynic says, *what I want to know is do you believe in it the way you believe in Australia?* Some days, I believe the Christian story even more than I believe in Australia. After all, I have never been to Australia, it is just a picture on a map. I don't know if I will ever go there, but I know that eventually I am going to Glory.

Living the Christian life, however, is not really about that Australia kind of believing. It is about a promise to believe even when you don't. After all, when I stand up in church to say the Creed, it may well be that that very morning I didn't really know for sure that some fifteen-year-old-virgin got pregnant with a baby who was really God. Saying the Creed is like vowing to love your bride forever and ever. That vow is not a promise to feel goopy and smitten every morning for the rest of your life. It is a promise to live love, even, especially, when you don't feel anything other than annoyance and disdain.

SOMETIMES, LATELY, I FEEL a sort of sinking staleness, and it feels familiar, and it scares me. I felt it the other day sitting in class. All of a sudden I felt, *This isn't working, I don't believe this Christian thing anymore, this is just some crazy fix I've been on, and now I've reached my toleration level, and it's not working.*

I thought about how Lamaze teachers tell you to breathe through your pain. I breathed. The feelings passed. But they'll come back. They are familiar. They are what I felt when I started to stop Judaism.

So I come home from the library, or I come home from class, or I come home from work, wherever I am when the staleness comes over me, and I think about what I've learned, and I think about how to do it differently, how to ride out the staleness this time, instead of switching religions when it all gets too stale.

I know, for starters, that the memory of that Daniel-Day-Lewis mermaid dream isn't going to do it. Dreams come and go. I might have another dream tomorrow, or I might forget I had the mermaid one.

My glue to Christianity will have to come from somewhere other than my dreams of salvation. It will have to come from God's place of faithfulness, not from some pot of faithfulness all my own. Fidelity to prayer books, never mind to the people who've taught me to pray with them, is not my strong suit.

Sometimes, some relative or friend asks me what religion I'll pick next; they ask when I'll convert to Buddhism. "You used to believe Orthodox Judaism was true," they say. "Now you believe Christianity is true. Maybe next week you'll believe something else is true." But I feel sure that there will be no conversions to Buddhism next week or next month or next year—for several reasons. First, Judaism and Christianity have something to do with each other. Judaism and Christianity make a path. They make a path through the Bible, and through history. Christianity and Buddhism don't make the same kind of path.

Second, I'm not seventeen anymore. I watch the Christian teenagers I know and I am awed at the way God fires up our faith when we are teens. I think about the impassioned letters I wrote my Orthodox cousin Jane, I think about the earnestness and fervor of my reaching for Orthodoxy, and I am transfixed by the fervor, and relieved, a little, that I'm no longer seventeen. I am not sure that I have the passion to fall in love with a religion again. How to fall in love is not, now, what I need to learn. What I need to learn, maybe what God wants me to learn, is the long grind after you've landed.

But the most important reason is this: I want to stay in Christ. I want to live in this Christian grammar as surely as I live in my apartment. I want God to give me the grace to stick with this, to stay here. And I believe He will.

My friend Meredith will be confirmed next week. She is terrified. She thinks she may run away. She says she would be less scared if she were getting married or being crowned the queen of England.

She says she is not having new doubts, just the same ones she has every Sunday, only magnified. "Every time I stand up to say the Creed, I wonder if I can say I believe these things," she says.

I tell her what I told her two years ago when she told me she wasn't enough of a Christian to go to church. I told her, "Go to church for a while and one day you may look down and discover you've become a Christian."

I tell her there is a Hasidic story. A student goes to his teacher and says, "Rabbi, how can I say 'I believe' when I pray, if I am not sure that I believe?"

His rabbi has an answer: "'I believe' is a prayer meaning, 'Oh, that I may believe!'"

THE SENIOR WARDEN at All Angels' writes poetry. He is just a beginner. He says he is forty-six writing poems college sophomores might write. "I feel encouraged about my potential," he tells me, "but painfully aware of my ignorance."

I tell him that is how I feel about being a Christian.

Oh, that I may believe!

Mary Johnson's Sampler

The breakfast nook in Hannah and Jim's kitchen is one of my favorite places in the world, both because of the blueberry pancakes Jim serves there, and because of an old framed sampler they have hanging on the wall. I have a fondness for early American samplers, which eighteenth- and nineteenth-century girls made to learn their stitches, and to display their handiwork to potential suitors.

Hannah and Jim's sampler, a wedding gift from Jim's sister, is larger than most I've seen, about the size of a proper bed pillow. The stitches are careful and precise. Like many samplers, the centerpiece is an alphabet, though Hannah and Jim's young seamstress, perhaps determined to show off her considerable skill, was not content to simply sew her ABCs. Instead, she stitched an elaborate acrostic, which girls in New England had been reciting since the seventeenth century:

In Adam's fall, we sinned all.
Heaven to find, the Bible mind.
Christ crucified for sinners died.

Thus the Puritans, and their Congregational descendants, taught both alphabet and worldview.

Below the alphabet is a picture of a house and a tree, and in the lower right corner, a bit of doggerel:

Mary Johnson is my name
America my nation
Greenwich is my dwelling place
And Christ is my salvation.

It's a common verse, which, with allowance for variation of name and town, marks many early American samplers. Other samplers sometimes conclude with less rhyme but more information: "made by Anne Cable, Aged Nine, 1812, Dedham"; "Phoebe Marshall, Age Eleven, 1782, Litchfield." Those lines give us our only clues about the girls who did the needlework.

I am struck by the elegance of Mary Johnson's sampler—the elegance of the fine, silken stitches, and the elegance of the theology. For there, in the first and last lines of her sampler, told in familiar rhythms that shaped the education of countless girls in early New England, is the essence of the Christian story: "In Adam's fall, we sinned all," and "Christ is my salvation."

JUDAISM, TOO, SPEAKS of sin and atonement, although with different inflections. Judaism's and Christianity's different understandings of atonement derive from different understandings of sin. To oversimplify, for Jews, sins are acts. To violate a commandment is to commit a sin. Christians, too, understand wrong deeds—lying, stealing, fornicating—as sins, but for Christians, sinful acts are always undergirded (and overshadowed) by our sinful state, endowed at the Fall.

Because, for Jews, sin is foremost people's behavior and action, God grants atonement upon a person's doing *teshuva*, upon his repenting, his rectifying past wrongs, his pledge, in daily confession or on Yom

Kippur, to go forth and sin no more. The Christian God is certainly interested in individuals' repenting of their sinful ways, but because sin is a state, not simply a collection of misdeeds, there can be no atonement without Christ's bearing our sin for us on the Cross. Jews can perfect their behavior; Christians can never be good enough to be reconciled to God without His sacrifice at Golgotha.

No one is more eager to point out these differences than rabbis. In 1945, Joseph Solevetchik, the leader of modern Orthodoxy in America, wrote that, for Christians, "Only the supernatural, miraculous intercession of God on behalf of the sinner" may cleanse one's sin. The Christian "is a passive, pitiful creature who begs for and attains divine grace." Three years later, Leo Baeck described the Jewish notion of atonement, which stands in obvious contrast to Christian ideas about the Cross. Atonement, Baeck wrote, "is no mere act of grace, or miracle of salvation, which befalls the chosen; it demands the free, ethical choice of the human being. . . . The sinner himself is to turn to God. . . . No one can substitute for him in his return, no one can atone for him."

Baeck and Solevetchik caricature the truth a bit. For Christians, grace is hardly "mere," and Judaism, to be sure, is more than ethics. But there is, in Baeck and Solevetchik, real insight. They have described the difference between Good Friday and Yom Kippur.

ON YOM KIPPUR, while Rabbi M. and Beth and most of the rest of America's Jews are in shul, I go to Hannah and Jim's in Brooklyn. I spend much of the day sitting in their breakfast nook reading, under the watch of Mary Johnson, a monograph about gambling in nineteenth-century America.

Shortly after sunset, Hannah and I set out for a walk. Jews are streaming out of their synagogues, having fasted and repented and pleaded with God to seal them for another year in the Book of Life. They have broken their fast on bagels or sweet cake, and they are headed home, out of fasting and back into life.

We spy one group of boys, wearing shiny black shirtwaists and black *kippot*, out hammering plywood in their yard. I explain to Hannah that the holiday of Sukkot, the Feast of Tabernacles, begins in a few days, and some Jews have the tradition of beginning to construct their sukkah right after Yom Kippur. "It is a way of connecting the two holidays," I say, "and it is also a way to smooth the transition from the holiest day of the year into ordinary time."

We watch as one boy, who looks to be about nine, clumsily drives a nail into two flimsy pieces of wood. "Like Jesus being hammered to the cross," murmurs Hannah. "Atonement is everywhere."

Religious Revivals

My parents seem to have gotten religion. Or they seem to be getting it, anyway.

Here is how it started, with my father: when I was in high school, I visited my dad, some weekends, in North Carolina, and I would want to go to shul Friday nights, and he would come with me. And then they hired a new rabbi at his synagogue. The man who held that pulpit when I was small was dull and drippy, the type of man who gives all rabbis a bad name. But then, when I was a teenager, he moved away, and they called a new rabbi, a professor with lots of kids and a keen wit and a sense of things. My father liked him. This new rabbi began to revive Saturday morning services, which hadn't been held at the synagogue for years and years, and my father began to attend them. What my father liked best was that after the service, the congregants would crowd into the rabbi's study and there they would all discuss the weekly Torah portion. Then my father began donating interesting items to the synagogue, children's prayer books for the high holidays, for instance, and he started sending bookstore gift certificates to all the Bar and Bat Mitzvahs in the congregation.

The rabbi asked him to chant the blessing of the haftorah at Rosh Hashanah services. Suddenly, my father was an elder of the congregation.

While all that was happening, I went to college, became Orthodox, and then became a Christian and moved to England. One Christmas I came home from England and found that my mother had started attending an Episcopal church near her house. This from the woman who had said for years—years and years—that you didn't need organized religion to be spiritual, that she didn't really understand the whole need for a god, that she didn't want to give her hard-earned money to some institutional church with collection plates.

Then I came home again later that year to find she was taking a confirmation class and was going to be confirmed by the bishop sometime during Eastertide. Then I came home again, and was snooping around her bedside table and discovered a Book of Common Prayer and a Bible with a ribbon marking Paul's letter to the Galatians. She began to send me emails asking my thoughts about Dallas Willard and Dietrich Bonhoeffer and other Christian theologians. She went on a trip to Israel, and instead of talking about her trip to Israel, she talked about her pilgrimage to the Holy Land.

A while later my father came to New York and we went out to dinner at a new French restaurant in my neighborhood. One of the specials was this scrumptious-sounding pork chop with apricot glaze, and I knew that pork chops were a favorite of his and I said, "So I assume you're getting the pork chop." He looked surprised and told me he had stopped eating pork and shellfish, foods the Bible says aren't kosher, almost a year ago. He ordered the trout.

Sanctification School

After morning prayer, Hannah and I sit at a coffee shop, and she says she has something to tell me. "Guess!" she says. "It has to do with the reading." The last time she did this, she was announcing her affair, but there were no adulterous women in today's readings. Our Old Testament passage today was from Nehemiah 13, in which the prophet rebukes the people for desecrating the Sabbath. "You're planning to go hiking on Sunday, instead of going to church?" I ask. Then I remember the epistle reading. "Oh," I say. "You're having a baby." The epistle reading was Revelation 12, John's vision of the pregnant woman "clothed with the sun, with the moon under her feet and a crown of twelve stars on her head."

"Yep," says Hannah. "In seven months. A baby." She smiles. I count. This is the beginning of November. Seven months is the beginning of June.

"Well that's great!" I say. I toast her with my latté. "To the baby."

"To the baby!" she says.

THIS, I THINK, *is what happens next.* First all your friends get married, and then they all start having babies. Hannah and three friends from college, too. I will become a regular at Baby Gap.

Sometimes, when I am praying with Hannah, I look down and catch the glint of her wedding band, and get consumed by jealousy. When this happens, I take a shower or go for a walk and try to think, calmly, about what exactly I'm jealous of. The obvious things: sex, and waking up next to someone every morning and, on the days that I forget that sometimes married people are lonely too, I feel jealous of the companionship, of the togetherness, of the intimacy. And I am jealous because, in getting married, and then again in having kids, my friends become adults, while I am stuck living like a college student, going on occasional dates to random New York restaurants, and writing a dissertation that, eventually, three people might read.

But I look at Hannah and I am also jealous because I believe that marriage is a school of sanctification. Sanctification doesn't require an affair—there is plenty of sanctification in the faithful, ordinary daily grind of lots of marriages, of Randi's, and Jeff and Amy's. But I have seen clearly the holy work done in Hannah and Jim's home this year. Being stuck with each other, being forced to stumble through her treachery and his heartbreak, has made them better spouses and better Christians. I have watched their marriage and I have seen that God has been who He said He would be. "He will be like a refiner's fire or a launderer's soap. He will sit as a refiner and purifier of silver; He will purify the Levites and refine them like gold and silver." He has used their marriage as soap.

I praise God for His soapiness, and then I get so jealous that I think I might literally start to see green. It is the old question, the pathetic question: Why them, Lord? Why them and not me?

WHEN I GET HOME from coffee with Hannah, I sit on my bed and try to picture it. I try to picture watching her be pregnant, I try to picture the baby shower, I try to picture a newborn downy person in a pink blanket, and I try, while I picture these things, to picture myself being happy for Hannah, and I can't. I can't imagine feeling happy. I just feel jealous and pathetic and lame. I feel miserable. On top of feeling jealous and miserable, I feel like a bad, selfish person, so uncharitable that I can't summon even a shade of joy when my friends do great joyful things like have babies.

Sitting on my bed, I tell God bluntly that I don't have the resources to watch Hannah have this baby. "I really don't want to feel this way," I say. "I really want to do right by my friend. But I don't know how to be a friend here, God." I don't think I can stand even five minutes of her crib-buying glee. I don't think I can give her a sympathetic ear when she complains about morning sickness. I look at my icons. "I am so jealous I can't stand up straight," I say. "If You want me to somehow look on during this pregnancy, You are going to have to give me the eyes to do it with." If I am going to do something other than crumple up and collapse, it will only be because God does it for me. Because He will gently pry me apart and prop me upright after I have crumpled into a ball on the floor.

Somehow, I know He will uncrumple me. I will be jealous and miserable all through this pregnancy, but I have known God long enough now to know that He will give me enough respite from my jealousy to go to Baby Gap. He will give me enough respite to listen to Hannah talk about her ultrasounds. If I ask for that respite and open my hands to receive it, He will give it to me. He will give me enough peace to be her friend. And, knowing God, He might even surprise me. He might give me, amid the months of envy, a few moments of gratitude and joy. He might give me a little burst of affection and excitement when I first see that downy bundle of pink.

LATER, IN THE SHOWER, I get it. I get that Hannah's pregnancy is my own school of sanctification. God is sanctifying Jim and Hannah through marriage and parenthood, but He is not just blessing them and leaving me out in the unblessed cold. He is using my ridiculous jealousy and my endless self-pity to sanctify me.

I will forget that, of course, at Hannah's baby shower. Sitting through that baby shower, I will forget about the sanctification and only remember the pain. But then I will come home, and I will pray, and I will remember. I will remember that God does not cause our suffering, but He uses it. I will remember that He is using that baby shower to somehow grow me into the person He wants me to be.

On Rebuilding a Jewish Library

When my mother and I moved to Charlottesville, I wanted to paint my new bedroom black (largely because Jessica Wakefield, in the Sweet Valley High series, had a Hershey brown bedroom, and black seemed the only way to top Jessica Wakefield). My mom, who usually let me follow my own whims, was not excited by the prospect of a black bedroom. "No black walls," she said. "But you can have black furniture if you want."

We went to a store called La Différence, and I picked out two black twin beds, a black dresser, a black reading chair with a black lamp, a black desk and a black stool, and four bookcases, two of them white, two of them black. Four bookcases, twenty shelves in all. The bookcases took up a whole wall in my bedroom, and one of my favorite activities, all through middle school and high school, was arranging and rearranging my books.

My goal was to fill up one entire shelf with Judaism books. The shelf in question was the middle shelf of the bookcase closest to my bed, and, gradually, it began to get full. *The Jewish Catalogue*. Adin Stiensaltz. *I and Thou* by Martin Buber. Slender books from university presses about secular Jewish women who had become Orthodox.

To Pray As a Jew by Hayim Halevy Donin. Collections of Hasidic tales and sayings.

I remember the day I finally filled that shelf. I was in eighth grade, and it was a Wednesday, Hebrew school night. My mother had dropped me off at the synagogue twenty minutes before class started with a five-dollar bill and instructions to walk to the downtown mall and buy a slice of pizza for dinner. I had the dilemma I always had on Wednesday nights: buy the pizza, or go hungry and buy a book? I wandered into the Book Cellar and found, for $4.50, a copy of Gershom Scholem's *Major Trends in Jewish Mysticism.* At home that night I wedged Scholem into the last crack of space on my Judaism shelf.

IN THE MIDDLE OF COLLEGE, when my relationship with Judaism began to fall apart, I rearranged my books. I put all my Judaism books in the corner by the desk. American history books were piled up alongside my bed.

I have learned by now that the first sign of my waning passion for something is my losing interest in the books. It's like being about to break up with someone. The first thing that happens when I lose interest in some man is that my libido lapses into a coma, and kissing him becomes as appealing as eating pepper jelly. I'd rather have him stuck over in the corner by the desk than anywhere near my bed.

When I finally came to understand that I was becoming a Christian, I got rid of all the Jewish books, keeping just the Bible Benjamin had given me, and a copy of *Seasons of Our Joy*, a book about holidays by Arthur Waskow, which Simone, a member of Congregation Beth Israel, had given me at my Bat Mitzvah. Inside she had written, "May all your seasons be joyful. You have brought much joy to my life, and I'm sure you will continue to do so for me and others."

And I set about collecting books on Anglicanism—a passel of

introductory texts, purchased at the Cathedral bookshop in New York: *The Anglican Vision* by James Griffiss and *What Is Anglicanism?* by Urban Holmes. I ordered about a third of the backlist from Cowley Publications, a press run by the Society for St. John the Evangelist, an Episcopal monastery out of Boston. A block from Clare College was the bookshop of the Society for the Promotion of Christian Knowledge, and I spent whole afternoons learning their stock.

And then, two years into England, I found myself forgetting the rabbis' words, and needing them. I piled in all those commentaries on Ruth. I stood in the Judaica sections of used bookstores, fingering underlined copies of Abraham Joshua Heschel and *Back to the Sources* by Barry Holtz. I was starting to think about rebuilding a Jewish library.

TODAY, AFTER LUNCH, I head to Labyrinth and buy books: Franz Rosenzweig's *Star of Redemption*; a commentary on the Book of Hosea; a collection of essays on Judaism and gender, which I choose mostly because it has an essay by my friend Susan in it (though when I get it home I discover there are lots of other good reasons to have this book, foremost Daniel Boyarin's declaration that "I became Orthodox for love of the Talmud"; you know that already if you have ever read anything else Boyarin has written, but it is good to see it laid out just so). I also buy a copy of Lamentations Rabbah, and *Nine Talmudic Readings* by Emmanuel Levinas. The clerk who rings up my purchases says, "I have never read any Levinas, but my friend who is a philosophy major says that when we look back on the twentieth century, he will be one of the outstanding philosophical minds."

"Yes, I think so," I say, not having the heart to correct his pronunciation—he had made "Levinas" rhyme with "penis." I should have corrected him. I went around mispronouncing *Walter Benjamin* for several years before Randi finally set me right. I am glad that she did.

In the spring of my second year at Cambridge, I got a phone call out of the blue from Benjamin, whose family's Pesach seders in Washington had been my first step toward Orthodoxy. We hadn't talked in almost two years. Our last conversation had been just before college commencement. I told him, in that conversation, that I was off to England and that I had been dreaming about Jesus and I thought I would start attending church, and I thought that maybe I would be baptized, that maybe I was becoming a Christian.

When he called me in Cambridge, it was just a few hours before Shavuot. He was living in Jerusalem, studying at a yeshiva. He said he wanted to wish me a *chag sameach*, a happy holiday, and then he asked if I had converted to Christianity and I said yes.

He called back as soon as Shavuot was over, saying he had spent the whole day anxious about my soul. He said he had talked to his rabbi about my conversion, and that his rabbi said I was *chayav mita*.

When he said those words, when he said *chayav mita*, I knew that I knew them. They were familiar, rattling around my brain, in the corner marked "Hebrew." But I couldn't latch on. I couldn't remember what they meant. I couldn't remember how to translate them. I reached for my Hebrew dictionary and, of course, it wasn't there. I had long since given it away.

Benjamin sounded almost like a Christian. He can't have said, "There is a burden on my heart for you," for that is a phrase only evangelical Christians use, but his point was the same. He was worried about my soul; there was a burden on his heart for me. He said it was fitting that he had called me just before Shavuot. Shavuot is the day that God elected the Jews to be His special people, a people I had cut myself off from. Benjamin wanted to help me return to that people.

"There is a story about Shavuot," Benjamin was saying, "from the Gemora." He pronounced it with Yiddish inflections, and wide, round vowels. *Gemora,* not the crisp, proper Hebrew *Gemara.* "It was told in the name of Reish Lakish, who was explaining a verse in the first chapter of Genesis. Why does the Torah speak of *the* sixth day of Creation, when it speaks of the other days as *a* second day, *a* third day? Why the definite article? The definite article comes to teach us that there was a caveat when God created the world. If the Jewish people accept the Torah when God gives it to them on the sixth day of the month of Sivan, the world would remain intact, but if they reject it, the world would revert back to nothingness."

As he spoke about Reish Lakish and the mystery of the definite article, I suddenly remembered: *Chayav mita* meant "obligated to death." If the Temple still stood, if we could still convene the Sanhedrin, someone could call me before a *bet din* for my apostasy, and they could order me stoned.

—◦∞∞◦—

MY APARTMENT IN New York is filled with bookshelves. In my bedroom is colonial American history, and Christian theology and ethics. In the kitchen is fiction and poetry, and cookbooks, the Moosewood and Martha Stewart and other recipes for dinners I will never cook. In the den is European history and Chinese history and ancient history. By the couch is segregation and the Civil Rights movement. Then there is a shelf with feminist theory and literary theory and a little Marx. There is a row of reference books, guides to American Supreme Court decisions and an encyclopedia about American presidents. Then come the books about religion in contemporary America — ethnographies of evangelical churches and Conservative synagogues, books about Buddhist communities in California, books in which sociologists opine about the future of the Protestant main line. Memoir, and essay, and nineteenth-century American history are all in the hall, and there is a bookcase, closest to my bedroom, of books about Judaism. Books about the holidays, and the Torah, and the law.

Benjamin has recently moved to New York. He is applying to law school and playing guitar in a band that takes its name—Orchard—from a midrashic tale about four rabbis, Ben Azzai, Ben Zoma, Elisha ben Avuya, and Rabbi Akiva. The four rabbis, the midrash tells us, ventured into *pardes,* the "grove" or "orchard"; that is, they plumbed Jewish mysticism for a taste of paradise. Ben Azzai glimpsed paradise and dropped dead. Ben Zoma glimpsed paradise and went crazy. Elisha ben Avuya became a heretic (the story calls him Aher, which means "other"). Only Rabbi Akiva (the same Akivah who would be killed by the Romans) survived his trip into the grove.

Pardes means something else, too. It is an acronym for the words *Pshat, Remez, Drash,* and *Sod,* the four levels of reading a text—the simple meaning; the hint or allusion; the midrashic interpretation; and the secret, hidden meaning. So the name of Benjamin's band is also an instruction manual for reading.

Benjamin came by my apartment last night. He wears a long beard, and *tzitzit,* the knotted fringes Orthodox men wear under their shirts to fulfill Deuteronomy 22:12, "Make tassels on the four corners of the cloak you wear," and a snug brown *kippah.* He looked around my apartment at all the Jesuses and asked if I really believed this stuff, and then he stopped mid-sentence and I pressed him and he said, "I was just noticing all your beautiful *sefarim.*" *Sefer* is Hebrew for "book."

"I was just noticing all your beautiful *sefarim,*" he said, and he gestured to the rows of Jewish books on my bookcase. Rashi's commentary on the Torah, bound in fat maroon volumes; shiny turquoise Torah commentaries by Nechama Liebowitz; Umberto Cassuto's books about Genesis. Benjamin looked at the books and reached for the Bible he had given me almost a decade ago and then looked up at me. "You've spent all these hours studying Torah," he said. "How could you be taken in by that carpenter?"

We argued until the middle of the night, about who Jesus was and what it meant to say "the word made flesh" and whether or not He fulfilled the prophecies in Isaiah, and finally I said, "Enough, we aren't getting anywhere, this is just painful and pointless." We gave up and sat on my sofa holding hands and smoking and listening to an Emmylou Harris CD.

MY FIRST TRIP BACK to West Side Judaica after I became a Christian was like my first day of school: I didn't want to go. I was sure Yaakov or one of the other redheaded, nebbishy salesmen would see me for who I was, cry, *Apikoros*, "heretic," and refuse to sell me even a pencil. I thought about donning a long denim skirt, so I could look the part of a young Orthodox woman, but decided against it. I did, however, take the cross off my necklace.

Some of the books I am buying are just replacements, second copies of books I used to have: *The Book of Our Heritage*, Eliyahu Ki-Tov's magisterial work on the holidays; and Rashi; and Hebrew prayer books.

I haven't replaced my Talmud yet, or anything by the Ramban, the thirteenth-century rabbi sometimes called by his Latin name, Nachmanides. I haven't bought another copy of *Shemirat Shabbat*, the compendium of Sabbath law that Beth and I sometimes studied in the mornings before shul. My copy was two volumes, navy blue, and opened, like all Hebrew books, right-to-left. The cover was always cool to touch, like jade.

Some of the books I am buying are new. I have never owned them before, or read them before. The Jewish philosophy is new—the Levinas is new and the Moses Mendelssohn and the Herman Cohen are new, and the books about Judaism after the Holocaust, Arthur

Cohen's *Tremendum* and Emil Fackenheim's *To Mend the World*, all these are new.

Mostly, though, I am reading rabbinic commentaries on the Bible, some of which I read when I was Orthodox, and some of which I should have read then, but didn't. In morning prayer, the lectionary always directs us to a reading from the Old Testament, and sometimes, after I pray, I sit on my bed with the lectionary and a Bible and a spoonful of Hebrew, trying to learn and relearn what the rabbis had to say about the golden calf and the tabernacle and Ezekiel's chariots of fire and other biblical things.

On Sunday, I go to West Side Judaica after church. I make a prize purchase, *A Hebrew and English Lexicon of the Old Testament*, a book I've been hemming and hawing over all year. It's a heavy book, over a thousand pages, the reference book you start with if you're trying to read Hebrew Scripture in the original. It was edited by Francis Brown, S. R. Driver, and Charles A. Briggs, and those in the know lovingly call this lexicon the BDB.

The BDB was originally published in 1906, and it was created by Christians — the editors taught at Union Theological Seminary and at Christ Church, Oxford — for Christians, but I discovered it as a Jew, the woman I studied Talmud with on Wednesday nights introduced me to it, and it remains for me a Jewish book. I will shelve it next to Rashi, in a different room altogether from my Christian dictionaries and lexicons.

I have looked at this dictionary, at West Side Judaica and at Labyrinth, for months and months. I have picked it up and balanced its weight on my hand and smoothed my fingers over the pages, and I have always put it back on the shelf. Too much money for a piece of nostalgia, I've told myself, for a book I barely used the first time I owned it, a book I will surely never open now.

This Sunday, I buy the book. I am lured, finally, by the dust jacket, a deep periwinkle blue. My first copy had just a plain white cover. This blue will stand out on my bookshelf. Maybe the blue will beckon me, and I will open the book, and read with it; maybe I will use it this time more than I did before.

WHEN I LEAVE THE STORE, turning north on Broadway to walk back home, I spy a short man with a funny grin and a trim gray beard. For a second, I think it is Rabbi M. I am mistaken, of course; it isn't he. I do that every once in a while, think I am seeing him or some other past person, and my heart begins to race a little and I try to figure out what to do, hide or approach him, and then I realize I'm wrong, it isn't Rabbi M. at all.

Walking up Broadway, I look at the books in my arm and think that I probably should be a librarian. I think that if I had lived in an earlier age, before all the superstores, I might have opened a quaint little bookshop, complete with rocking chairs and teacups and a cat. I think, *I can't remake all those relationships, but I can rebuild my library.*

Advent

Shabbat Morning

On Saturday, I wake up, and I am given to understand that I will go to shul this morning. I wake up and shul seems as necessary as breakfast, as obvious as making my bed. And that is what I do. I get up, I make my bed, I eat breakfast, I pull on a plaid winter dress, and I leave the apartment. I don't know why I am going, only that I am going.

On 117th Street, I stop. *Am I really supposed to be going to shul?* I ask God.

Go, He says.

On 115th Street, I stop again. *You're not going to do something dramatic and big that's going to screw up my life, are you?*

Just go, He says.

I PICK AN OUT-OF-THE-WAY shul, where I'm not likely to see anyone I know. I climb the stairs to the balcony, and I sit in a corner and reach for a prayer book. I wonder if I will remember what to do. I wonder if I will remember when to stand. I wonder if I will remember how to pray as a Jew.

I am late, we are already halfway through the morning prayers, but women will be straggling in for another half an hour, all through *shacharit*, making it just in time for the Torah reading. I flip through the siddur and realize I shouldn't have worried about remembering these prayers. I will always remember these prayers.

After the long thanksgivings and petitions, the Torah service begins. This week's Torah reading is *parshat Vayishlach*, the middle of the story of Jacob and Esau. Somewhere in the middle of the Torah reading my mind wanders and I think through the rest of the service and I remember what the haftorah for this week is. The haftorah that always follows *parshat Vayishlach* is the Book of Obadiah.

Obadiah is the shortest book in Hebrew scripture, only twenty-one verses long. It is a prophecy about the Edomites, the descendants of the treacherous Esau, age-old enemies of the Jews. The prophet Obadiah was not the only Edomite convert to Judaism. The Malbim (a nineteenth-century rabbi from Volhynia) tells us that all the Edomites converted during the reign of Herod, but their conversions were insincere. When the time came to destroy the Second Temple, they pitched in, lining up shoulder by shoulder with the Romans. As Obadiah says in his message to the Edomites, "On the day the nations took the Jewish people captive, and entered the Jewish gates casting lots over Jerusalem, you were also amongst them."

According to Obadiah, things don't look good for the Edomites: "The house of Jacob will be a fire and the house of Joseph a flame; the house of Esau will be stubble, and they will set it on fire and consume it. There will be no survivors from the house of Esau."

Okay God, I think, as we turn from the Torah to the haftorah, *could you clarify, please? You sent me to shul to hear the book of Obadiah? To read about the punishment that comes to folks who convert to Judaism and then betray the Jews?* I think about all the Orthodox Jews I knew in college. I wonder if I have become to them an Edomite.

The cantor begins to chant the haftorah. In my lap I hold a Bible open to Obadiah and I follow along. It is not until the fifth verse that I begin to cry: "If thieves came to you, if robbers in the night— Oh, what a disaster awaits you—would they not steal only as much as they wanted? If grape pickers came to you, would they not leave a few grapes? But how Esau will be ransacked, his hidden treasures pillaged!"

I cry and cry, for the loss of it all and for how good God is.

———∞∞∞———

TOMORROW MORNING, I will wake up and do this all again. I will make my bed and eat breakfast and find a dress and I will walk the blocks to church. When I get there, I will look for God and I will pray. It is Advent, and we are waiting for Jesus. We will read the Gospel of Luke, and we will say a special collect that reminds Jesus to come.

As I pray that collect, I will think about a story from the Talmud, from *masechet Sanhedrin*, the tractate that deals with the high rabbinic court. In the story, Rabbi Yehoshua ben Levi met the prophet Elijah and asked him when the Messiah would come. Elijah answered, "Go and ask the Messiah yourself."

"But where is he?" asked Rabbi Yehoshua.

"At the gate of Rome," replied Elijah.

"How will I recognize him?" asked the rabbi.

"He sits among the wretched ones with sores and wounds," said Elijah. "All the others uncover their wounds all at once and bind them up again all at once, but he uncovers and binds each one separately, for he thinks, 'Maybe I will be summoned today; I don't want to be detained.'"

So Rabbi Yehoshua went and found the Messiah, and said to him, "Peace be with you, Master and Teacher."

The Messiah replied, "Peace be with you."

"When is the Master coming?" Rabbi Yehoshua asked.

The Messiah replied, "Today."

Rabbi Yehoshua returned to Elijah, who asked him, "What did he say to you?"

The rabbi was annoyed and disappointed. "He lied to me. He said he would come today, and he has not come."

Then Elijah said, "He meant, today, if you would only listen to His voice."

Notes

Sukkot

7   *his heart "was strangely warmed"* John Wesley, *The Heart of John Wesley's Journal,* ed. Percy Livingstone Parker (New York: Fleming H. Revell Co., 1903), 43.

13   *Rabbi Akiva . . . says that the original sukkot were flimsy . . . and sometimes even sleep there* Michael Strassfeld, *The Jewish Holidays: A Guide and Commentary* (New York: Harper and Row, 1985), 140–45.

Advent

34   *"Return with us, return to us"* Ursula K. Le Guin, *Always Coming Home* (New York: Harper & Row, 1985), 404.

36   *"Hard as it is to swallow"* Barbara Cawthorne Crafton, *Let Every Heart Prepare: Meditations for Advent and Christmas* (Harrisburg, PA: Morehouse Publishing, 1998), 2.

49   *"Of course you should pray"* Numerous translations of this passage are available, including Philip Birnbaum, *A Book of Jewish Concepts* (New York: Hebrew Publishing Co., 1964), 133. My translation is drawn from http://www.vbs.org/rabbi/hshulw/kervshbt_bot.htm.

Christmas

74   "*The whole concept of God taking on human shape*" Jane Von-
     negut Yarmolinsky in *O Holy Night: Timeless Meditations on
     Christmas*, ed. A. Jean Lesher (Winona: St. Mary's Press,
     1998), 125.

Epiphany

83   "*may have been a more practical and pleasant time for celebration
     than the barely glimmering new moon . . . full moon of Av*"
     Arthur Waskow, *Seasons of Our Joy: A Handbook of Jewish Fes-
     tivals* (New York: Summit Books, 1982), 105–6.

90   "*A wife who refuses to perform any kind of work*" Maimonides,
     Mishnah Torah, Hilchot Ishut 21:10.

95   "*When the community is suffering, one may not say*" Taanit 11a.

95   "*Do not separate from the community*" Pirkei Avot 2:5.

102 "*what happens in megachurches . . . between a fundamentalist
     and an evangelical*" David Brooks, "One Nation, Slightly Di-
     visible," *The Atlantic Monthly*, December 2001, 53.

103 "*the fighting, feuding . . . God has people in all his churches . . . the
     one badge of Christian discipleship*" Graham quoted in William
     Martin, *A Prophet With Honor: The Billy Graham Story* (New
     York: William Morrow and Company, 1991), 220–22.

106 *38 percent of Democrats in America are born-again Christians* A
     2001 poll conducted by the Barna Research Group, Ltd., http://
     www.barna.org/cgi-bin/PageCategory.asp?CategoryID=8.

Lent

128 "*To read, when one does so of one's own free will*" Sven Birkerts,
     The Gutenberg Elegies: The Fate of Reading in an Electronic Age
     (New York: Fawcett Columbine, 1995), 80.

135   *"Prayer is profitable because it makes us the familiars of God"* St. Thomas Aquinas, *The Three Greatest Prayers: Commentaries on the Lord's Prayer, the Hail Mary, and the Apostles' Creed,* trans. Laurence Shapcote, rev. ed., (Manchester, N.H.: Sophia Institute Press, 1990), 105.

137   *separate meat and milk completely* This list is inspired by Elizabeth Ehrlich, *Miriam's Kitchen: A Memoir* (New York: Viking, 1997), 14–17.

139   *"talk about their prayer lives"* Jennifer Egan "Why A Priest," *New York Times Magazine,* April 4, 1999, 28–33, 38, 49, 54, 59.

142   *"support the spirit and prescribe it to a fixed path"* Edith Stein, *The Hidden Life: Hagiographic Essays, Meditations, Spiritual Texts,* trans. Waltraut Stein (Washington: ICS Publications, 1992), 39.

145   *the story of Lienhart Sietz . . . "he was supposed to forgive his enemies"* David Waren Sabean, *Power in the Blood: Popular Culture and Village Discourse in Early Modern Germany* (Cambridge University Press, 1984), 38.

148   *"Of his bounty, the Lord often grants not what we seek"* St. Augustine quoted in St. Thomas Aquinas, 105.

153   *Procopius of Gaza . . . the sign of the Cross* Mark Gustafson, "The Tattoo in the Later Roman Empire and Beyond," in *Written on the Body: The Tattoo in European and American History,* ed. Jane Caplan (Princeton: Princeton University Press, 2000), 29.

154   *pilgrims to the shrine of Loreto* Jane Caplan, "Introduction," in Caplan, xvii.

154   *European visitors to Palestine* Jane Caplan, "Introduction," xvii; Juliet Fleming, "The Renaissance Tattoo," in Caplan, 79.

154   *"They . . . mark the Arms of Pilgrims"* George Sandys quoted in Fleming, 79.

154 *two verses in the New Testament* Gustafson, 29; Fleming, 80; Charles W. MacQuarrie, "Insular Celtic Tattooing: History, Myth and Metaphor," in Caplan, 35–36; C. P. Jones, "Stigma and Tattoo," in Caplan, 10.

155 *"Her figure was elegant"* Jane Austen, *Pride and Prejudice,* (London: Oxford University Press, 1970), 48.

Holy Week

173 *"The welding of people into a people"* Franz Rosenzweig, *The Star of Redemption,* trans. William W. Hallo (Notre Dame: University of Notre Dame Press, 1985), 317.

181 *"Express the juice of the grapes . . . from one communion to another."* Letter to the editor, *The Union Signal: A Journal of Social Welfare,* January 31, 1884, 4.

188 *Viaticum was a Roman term . . . "the journey will be too great for you"* William Latane Lumpkin, *Meditations for Communion Services* (Nashville: Abingdon Press, 1968), 28.

190 *"Perhaps some man . . . don't try to escape"* Cyril of Jerusalem, "Procatechesis," in Edward Yarnold, *Cyril of Jerusalem* (New York: Routledge, 2000), 81.

192 *35 percent of born-again Christians say that Jesus never had a bodily resurrection* A 1995 poll conducted by the Barna Research Group, Ltd., http://www.barna.org/cgi-bin/PageCategory.asp?CategoryID=6.

194 *"the things that began to happen . . . is better than the one before"* C. S. Lewis, *The Last Battle* (New York: Macmillan, 1956), 173–74.

194 *"created to praise, revere, and serve"* St. Ignatius of Loyola, *The Spiritual Exercises of Saint Ignatius,* trans. George E. Ganss (Chicago: Loyola University Press, 1992), p. 32.

195   *"prompts"* St. Augustine, *Confessions,* trans. Albert C. Outler, MCMLV (Library of Congress Card Catalog Number: 55-5021), bk. 1, chap. 1. (http://216.239.51.100/search?q=cache: nsiKd6NyVvgC:ccat.sas.upenn.edu/jod/augustine/conf.pdf+ oulter+augustine+confessions&hl=en&ie=UTF8).

195   *"Jesus is fishing for you"* Cyril of Jerusalem in Yarnold, 81.

Eastertide

200   *"I pray You, noble Jesu, that as You have graciously granted"* The Venerable Bede, *A History of the English Church and People,* trans. Leo Sherley-Price, rev. R. E. Latham (New York: Penguin Books, 1968), 338.

212   *"The lot of penitents . . . was not a happy one"* Joseph Martos, quoted in John Macquarrie, *A Guide to the Sacraments* (London: SCM Press, 1997), 93.

214   *"Post-baptismal sins . . . the end of sin as far as that person is concerned"* Macquarrie, 89.

215   *"Christ became our Brother in the flesh . . . am going to God"* Dietrich Bonhoeffer, *Life Together,* trans. John W. Doberstein (San Francisco: Harper San Francisco, 1993), 111–112.

Pentecost

233   *KiTov, in his commentary, asks after the nature of revelation* Eliyahu KiTov, *Sefer HaParshiyot* (Jerusalem: Aleph Publishers, 1965); Parshat Terumah, 128; Avot 6:2; Lawrence Kushner, *God Was in This Place and I, I Did Not Know: Finding Self, Spirituality, and Ultimate Meaning* (Woodstock, VT: Jewish Lights Publishing, 1991), 30.

234   *Moses ascended to Mount Sinai and found God sitting* Menahot 29b.

236   *Moses says, "Lord of the universe, you have shown me Akiva's Torah"* Menahot 29b.

241   *Vayhee, the Talmud explains* Megillah 10b.

242   *Mahlon and Chilion mean "sickness" and "ending"* Rachel Adler, *Engendering Judaism: An Inclusive Theology and Ethics* (Boston: Beacon Press, 1999), 148.

242   *"The man who spoke for her"* Adler, 149.

243   *"looks . . . like the husk that has been left over after the core of life has been removed"* Avivah Zornberg, "The Concealed Alternative," in *Reading Ruth: Contemporary Women Reclaim a Sacred Story*, ed. Judith A. Kates and Gail Twersky Reimer (New York: Ballantine Books, 1994), 66.

248   *the idiom hidur mitzvah* My appreciation for and discussion of both *hidur mitzvah* and papercutting is influenced by Roselyn Farren, especially her "Values of Torah, Values of Art," *Perspectives: The Jewish Magazine of Columbia University* 17, no. 3 (April 1997).

257   *"the gift of tongues . . . never been spoken before"* Dennis Bennett, *How to Pray for the Release of the Holy Spirit: What the Baptism of the Holy Spirit Is and How to Pray for It* (reprint, Gainsville: Bridge-Logos Publishers, 2001), 19–21.

261   *"avid book reading"* Kara Carden, "Charlottesville, Va., Jefferson's Literary Legacy," *American Profile* Southeast Edition, August 19–August 25, 2001.

263–64 *Blessing of Hounds . . . Thomas Jefferson served on the vestry . . . a three-year-old girl* Susan De Alba, *Country Roads: Albemarle County, Virginia* (Natural Bridge Station, VA: Rockbridge Publishing Company, 1993), 27, 39, 124.

268   *"The Latin credo . . . a confession of commitment, of love"* Diana L. Eck, *Encountering God: A Spiritual Journey from Bozeman to Banaras* (Boston: Beacon Press, 1993), 95–96.

271   *a Hasidic story* Michael Neff, *One Small Hand: Hasidic Meditations* (Ardmore, PA: Seth Press, 1985), n.p.

274   *"Only the supernatural, miraculous intercession of God"* Joseph Solevetchik, "Sacred and Profane," *Hazedek* 2, no. 213 (May–June 1945), 4–20, excerpted in Philip Goodman, *The Yom Kippur Anthology* (Philadelphia: Jewish Publication Society of America, 1971), 142–46.

274   *"no mere act of grace"* Leo Baeck, *The Essence of Judaism* (New York: Schocken Books, 1948), 166–67, excerpted in Goodman, 139–41.

284   *"for love of the Talmud"* Daniel Boyarin, "Justify My Love," in *Judaism Since Gender*, ed. Miriam Peskowitz and Laura Levitt (New York: Routledge, 1997), 131.

Advent

295   *a story from the Talmud* Sanhedrin 98a. Thanks to Dana Charry for calling this Midrash to my attention.

Acknowledgments

First-time author jitters pushed me to push drafts of this manuscript into the hands of an embarrassingly large number of people, and I am grateful to all of them for their suggestions and smiles. Frederica Mathewes-Green, Mary E. Lyons, John Wilson, Helen Lee, Jonathon Kahn, Susan Shapiro, Randi Rashkover, Rodney Clapp, Rebecca Marshall, and Debbie Caldwell read chapters. Lil Copan, Jana Riess, Phyllis Tickle, Kim Phillips-Fein, Vanessa Ochs, Nora Gallagher, Mark Oppenheimer, Jenny Blair, and Beth Samuels generously worked through the entire manuscript. For last-minute research help, thanks to Terry Todd and Mary Kay Cavazos.

Extra special thanks to two who went above and beyond the call of duty. Bobby Gross improved virtually every page of this book and prayed with me through the final stages of revision. Charles Marsh has been trenchant critic, enthusiastic cheerleader, and steadfast friend.

Last but not least. Thanks to Carol Mann, agent extraordinaire, for finding a good home for this book, and thanks to Amy Gash and other folks at Algonquin for being that home.

GIRL MEETS GOD

LAUREN F. WINNER

A READER'S GUIDE

1. A major theme in *Girl Meets God* is friendship. Who are some of Lauren's friends, and what role do they play in her spiritual journey? Do friends play a similarly important role in your own life?

2. Fidelity is a motif in *Girl Meets God*. How does Lauren respond to her friend Hannah's infidelity? Why is infidelity such a poignant and pointed topic for her?

3. Two different chapters in this book have the title "Conversion Stories." Why do they have the same title? Do they tell similar or different stories about religious conversion?

4. Lauren's book is structured according to the Jewish and Christian calendars—it is organized around liturgical seasons and holidays like Sukkot and Advent. Why is the book structured this way? What effect does it have on you, the reader?

5. Lauren suggests that "ruptures are the most interesting part of any text, that in the ruptures we learn something new." (p. 8) How is Lauren's story marked by ruptures, and what do we learn from them?

6. Upon converting to Christianity, Lauren gives up all things Jewish—she even says that "trading my Hebrew prayer book for an Episcopal Book of Common Prayer felt exactly like filing for divorce." (p. 9) Is divorce an apt metaphor for Lauren's relationship with Judaism? Does she eventually recover some of her Jewish practice?

7. What is the plot of *Girl Meets God*? Is it a coming-of-age story? A story of a quest? Does it present clear questions at the outset, and, if so, does it offer tidy answers to those questions at the end? When Lauren is a teenager, a woman from her synagogue gives her a poem

that instructs "Return with us, return to us, / be always coming home." (p. 34) Is *Girl Meets God* a story of homecoming?

8. Lauren says that the "very first thing I liked about Christianity, long before it ever occurred to me to go to church or say the creed or call myself a Christian, was the Incarnation." (p. 51) What is appealing to Lauren about the Christian story of the Incarnation?

9. Lauren's story is one of spiritual change and conversion, or making and remaking her spiritual self. In what ways is the story of reinvention a distinctively American story? Have you experienced an analogous remaking or reinvention of self?

10. Geography and place play a central role in Lauren's narrative. To what extent do the landscapes of the American South and New York City shape her experiences?

11. Lauren readily admits to being a bookworm. What role do books and reading play in her spiritual development? How have books been important in your own life?

12. Memoir, as a genre, involves the author presenting a particular self to her audience. To what extent does Lauren suggest she has "arrived" as a Christian? Does she readily admit to spiritual failings, or is she eager to present herself as someone with all the answers?

PHOTO: JEN FARIELLO

LAUREN F. WINNER is the author of three books, *Girl Meets God*, *Mudhouse Sabbath*, and *Real Sex: The Naked Truth about Chastity*. She has appeared on PBS's *Religion & Ethics Newsweekly* and has written for *The New York Times Book Review*, *The Washington Post Book World*, *Publishers Weekly*, *Books and Culture*, and *Christianity Today*. Winner has degrees from Duke, Columbia, and Cambridge universities, and holds a Ph.D. in history. The former book editor for Beliefnet, Lauren teaches at Duke Divinity School. She travels extensively to lecture and teach, and lives in Durham, North Carolina.